DATE DUE

at. 9 2013	
april 8, 2014	

POLICE CULTURE IN A
CHANGING WORLD

CLARENDON STUDIES IN CRIMINOLOGY

Published under the auspices of the Institute of Criminology, University of Cambridge; the Mannheim Centre, London School of Economics; and the Centre for Criminological Research, University of Oxford.

GENERAL EDITOR: IAN LOADER
(*University of Oxford*)

EDITORS: MANUEL EISNER, ALISON LIEBLING, AND PER-OLOF WIKSTRÖM
(*University of Cambridge*)

JILL PEAY AND TIM NEWBURN
(*London School of Economics*)

LUCIA ZEDNER AND JULIAN ROBERTS
(*University of Oxford*)

Recent titles in this series:

Social Order and the Fear of Crime in Contemporary Times
Farrall, Jackson, and Gray

Black Police Associations: An Analysis of Race and Ethnicity within Constabularies
Holdaway

The Prisoner Society: Power, Adaptation, and Social Life in an English Prison
Crewe

Making Sense of Penal Change
Daems

Punishing Persistent Offenders: Exploring Community and Offender Perspectives
Roberts

Police Culture in a Changing World

BETHAN LOFTUS

OXFORD
UNIVERSITY PRESS

Great Clarendon Street, Oxford OX2 6DP

Oxford University Press is a department of the University of Oxford.
It furthers the University's objective of excellence in research, scholarship,
and education by publishing worldwide in

Oxford New York

Auckland Cape Town Dar es Salaam Hong Kong Karachi
Kuala Lumpur Madrid Melbourne Mexico City Nairobi
New Delhi Shanghai Taipei Toronto

With offices in

Argentina Austria Brazil Chile Czech Republic France Greece
Guatemala Hungary Italy Japan Poland Portugal Singapore
South Korea Switzerland Thailand Turkey Ukraine Vietnam

Oxford is a registered trade mark of Oxford University Press
in the UK and in certain other countries

Published in the United States
by Oxford University Press Inc., New York

British Library Cataloguing in Publication Data

Data available

Library of Congress Cataloging-in-Publication Data

Loftus, Bethan.
    Police culture in a changing world / Bethan Loftus.
        p. cm. — (Clarendon studies in criminology)
    Includes bibliographical references and index.
    ISBN 978-0-19-956090-5 (hbk. : alk. paper) 1. Police—Social aspects. I. Title
    HV7921.L645 2009
    363.2—dc22

                                                                    2009034085

Typeset by Macmillan Publishing Solutions
Printed in Great Britain by the MPG Books Group, Bodmin and King's Lynn

ISBN 978-0-19-956090-5

1 3 5 7 9 10 8 6 4 2

This book is dedicated to my grandmothers,
Blodwen and Cordelia

General Editor's Introduction

Clarendon Studies in Criminology aims to provide a forum for outstanding empirical and theoretical work in all aspects of criminology and criminal justice, broadly understood. The Editors welcome submissions from established scholars, as well as excellent PhD work. The Series was inaugurated in 1994, with Roger Hood as its first General Editor, following discussions between Oxford University Press and three criminology centres. It is edited under the auspices of these three criminological centres: the Cambridge Institute of Criminology, the Mannheim Centre for Criminology at the London School of Economics, and the Centre for Criminology at the University of Oxford. Each supplies members of the Editorial Board and, in turn, the Series Editor.

In this book, Bethan Loftus revisits some apparently well-trodden criminological ground and reappraises what has become a familiar idea—that of police culture. Her starting point—and reason for a return visit—is that today our received understanding of police culture is largely derived from a series of pioneering observational studies conducted over three decades ago, for the most part in metropolitan cities. Much in the world has changed in the intervening years. The wider climate of economic, social, and cultural relations within which police work is performed has altered significantly. But so too have police organizations themselves, as they have come to be staffed by more civilians, graduates, women, members of minority ethnic groups, and gay and lesbian officers. Policing, in other words, is today conducted in a world, and by police forces, that have been re-shaped by the demands for recognition of diverse social and ethnic groups. How though have police officers—and their sense of the job they do and the settings in which they do it—themselves shaped and responded to these changes? What, in this altered context, remains of value in the 'classic' texts from which we have come to know what police culture is? These are the questions that Bethan Loftus set out to answer.

Police Culture in a Changing World is based on extended observational research, and a series of individual and group interviews, with officers working in two divisions of an English police force—one in a multi-ethnic and multiply-deprived city, the other in a rural location in the surrounding county. It was a force undergoing a process of internal reform driven by senior officers and organized largely around the agenda of 'policing diversity', one in which, as Loftus points out, police culture was conceptualized within the organization as one of the problems to be tackled. What her research finds is a force in which many of what have become clichéd characteristics of police culture—the sense of mission, the defensive solidarity, the masculine ethos—persist, finding expression today within a defensive, resentful posture of officers who more than ever consider themselves as challenged, beleaguered and unrecognized. This co-exists with new ways of thinking about and doing police work and with forms of practice—in respect of, say, domestic violence—which have changed. These police accommodations with identity politics nonetheless mask what Loftus thinks of as the most crucial finding of her work—namely, the stubborn and powerful significance of class as a determinant of police practice and object of officers' unchallenged scorn. In the midst of partially successful national and local reform efforts aimed at improving the policing of a 'diverse society', the police's unreformed relation to, and routine contempt towards, the 'white residuum' stands as a telling exception. On the basis of this, and many other findings of this rich ethnographic study, Loftus cautions against sanguine accounts of how greatly police culture has itself, in a changing world, changed and reminds us of the difficulties of achieving such change in societies marked by enduring inequality.

It will quickly become apparent to the reader that Loftus is a careful and modest young scholar who is properly cognizant of, and fully acknowledges, the debt she owes to the 'classic' police ethnographies on which she draws. It is not unreasonable to suppose that this book will, in time, come to be counted among their number.

The Editors welcome this important edition to the Series.

Ian Loader
University of Oxford,
February 2009

Preface

Research and reflection on the police has long acknowledged the important role that the informal occupational norms, values, and assumptions associated with the rank and file play in shaping their everyday decisions and practices. Ethnographic accounts of what has become known as police culture have spanned several decades, and continue to be widely debated in contemporary discussions of policing and police work (Banton 1964; Skolnick 1966; Westley 1970; Cain 1973; Rubinstein 1973; Reiner 1978; Punch 1979; Ericson 1982; Holdaway 1983; Smith and Gray 1985; Young 1991). Much of these works have identified recurring themes within police dispositions and practices over time and space. It is now cliché to refer to what Reiner (2000*a*: Chapter 3) describes as the 'core characteristics' of police culture. Police, it is said, have an exaggerated sense of mission towards their role and crave work that promises excitement. They celebrate masculine exploits, show willingness to use force and engage in informal working practices. Officers are also continually suspicious, lead isolated social lives, and display defensive solidarity with colleagues. Police are mainly conservative in politics and morality and their culture is marked by cynicism and pessimism. Their worldview includes a simplistic, decontextualized understanding of criminality, and they are intolerant towards people who challenge the status quo. Finally, racism has been identified as one of the most central and problematic features of police culture. These features are believed to arise as officers adapt to the demands of the police role, but two propositions have nevertheless remained central to understandings in this area. Firstly, police culture exerts considerable influence over the way officers think about and interact with different strata of the public and colleagues—often for the worse. Secondly, the informal ideologies which comprise the police identity can also undermine endeavours to reform the police.

Notwithstanding the wealth of literature in this area, recent understandings of police culture rely almost exclusively on the aforementioned bodies of work and accordingly reflect culture of a much earlier and different social, economic and political milieu.

Most of the studies were conducted over thirty years ago, while others were carried out in diverse urban settings. Our understanding of police culture is also shaped by pioneering work in the USA, while more recent contributions have examined police culture only in circumstances of social and political turmoil (Glaeser 2000; Altbeker 2005; Marks 2005). We are left, as a result, with an account of police culture which largely predates the transformations which have since taken place inside police organizations and in newly identified social fields of policing.

Since the classic ethnographies there have been many developments within policing contexts, many of which could be expected to impact upon the cultural expressions of the police. There has been a notable increase in the number of minority ethnic, female, and gay and lesbian police officers. An allied development is the changing face of police personnel under what is referred to as the workforce modernization agenda (HMIC 2004). Processes of civilianization carry considerable implications for cultural, ethnic, and gender diversification and may serve to dilute the traditional white, heterosexual, male composition of police organizations (Loveday 2007). Similarly, the archetypal young working class, high school educated workforce may become altered by the growing recruitment of more mature and better educated officers (Punch 2007). Reconfigurations in the external policing environment have also transformed the character of the differing 'publics' the police come into contact with. Post-war immigration and the recent expansion of the European Union has granted free movement to workers from former commonwealth countries and new member states into the United Kingdom. The upshot is that British society is more ethnically, linguistically, religiously, and culturally diverse. Added to this, political sensitivity around policing has changed remarkably since the early police ethnographies. A pivotal development is the emergence of respect for diversity and recognition of cultural and gendered identities in policing discourse and practice. Not least in the aftermath of the Macpherson Report (1999), police organizations are under pressure to understand themselves as sites of diversity and as providers of a fair and equitable policing service. Yet this repositioning has also been encouraged by a broader shift in the political climate of society where minority groups are seeking recognition for their social differences (Parekh 2000; see also Fraser 1997; Taylor 1992). Recent years have also witnessed an unprecedented rethinking of what public policing should comprise. Community policing has become adopted across nearly all police forces throughout the Western world, and requires officers to become better embedded in the communities they are charged with serving (Fielding 1995; Brogden and Nijhar 2005). The recasting of the public within policing discourse has likewise been accompanied by a shift in public sentiment towards the police. As Loader and Mulcahy (2003) observe, police organizations now deal with a less compliant and more demanding public.

It is also noteworthy that officers work in a markedly different environment where greater adherence to legal rules is required. This has been supplemented with enhanced demands and mechanisms for their accountability. Added to this, new public management, or NPM, has also had a significant impact on policing and refers to a variety of practices derived from the private sector and applied to the public sector, including performance management techniques and the creation of customers (McLaughlin *et al* 2001). At the same time, officers inhabit a moment where political discourse about 'law and order' has become intensely salient and increasingly punitive (Downes and Morgan 2002; Loader 2006; Reiner 2007). Alongside these changes in the political sphere, late modern societies are also characterized by widespread economic division (Dahrendorf 1985; Taylor 1999; Young 1999). Growing numbers of people are excluded from secure employment and experience burgeoning hardship and insecurity. We could add that the desire to integrate the new residuum into society has also waned. As Reiner (2000*a*) notes, the changes that have occurred in the political economy of Western capitalism have profound implications for a larger and increasingly alienated 'police property'.

The classic police culture paradigm which has been much invoked to describe and explain a range of police perspectives and behaviour appears today somewhat exhausted. New lines of research and reflection are needed to track how, exactly, these events are shaping the cultural manifestations of the police. It is, in other words, crucial to *revisit* the idea of police culture in this changed, and changing, world. What aspects of the occupational culture are enduring, and what have become discontinued? What do police officers think about greater social diversity in the external and internal policing environment? How do they experience the new policing realities? Have the reorganizations in policing posed any significant threat to established police dispositions and practices? Answering these questions is vital if we are to develop sociological understanding of what policing culture in Britain currently looks like.

My purpose in this book is to document and make sense of how the occupational value systems and practices of officers have been shaped by two transitions in policing: firstly, the national context of social, economic and political change and, secondly, the local context of changes made to reform the culture of what I shall call Northshire Police Force. In recent years, senior officers have embarked on a top-down reform programme aimed primarily at improving the working conditions of personnel inside the organization and the delivery of an effective and equitable service to the various publics they are charged to serve. The case of Northshire Police provides an invaluable context for examining the relevance of previous studies of police culture for the altered landscape.

The empirical research underpinning the ensuing chapters derives from extensive fieldwork with front line officers and, in this sense, remains true to the tradition of the classic ethnographies. It draws upon of over 600 hours of direct observation of operational policing across two contrasting terrains, and thereby takes up Reiner's (2000b) recent appeal for police research to return to its ethnographic past in order to expose the low visibility practices of routine policing. In this book I foreground various features of police culture which have hitherto gone unnoticed, including an examination of how increasing diversification within and beyond policing organizations are shaping traditional relations, the impact of prevailing management practices on the way officers think about and perform their job, and the forms police culture takes under conditions of late modernity. By observing, documenting, and making sense of the values, beliefs, and outlooks police officers bring to bear on their work; *Police Culture in a Changing World* endeavours to produce a revised and fully contemporary account of police culture and accordingly extend our understanding of the inner-world of policing.

The book begins in Chapter 1 with a theoretical discussion of the concept of police culture. It addresses received understandings of the term, and explores the main properties of this phenomenon as identified by a long line of police scholars. I then examine recent thinking which challenges the conceptualization and existence of a monolithic police culture. In presenting the principal themes derived from research and reflection on police culture, this chapter provides a platform on which to pose the following question: does this orthodox account of police culture still hold relevance today?

Chapter 2 traces the wider 'field' of contemporary British policing. In addition to outlining developments in the legal context, I am concerned primarily to locate the emergence of respect for diversity and political recognition of cultural and gendered identities in policing discourse, and the widespread economic exclusion of late modern societies. I argue that the new societal configuration raises seminal questions for police culture and the policing of social groups. Before presenting the findings from the empirical investigation, I bring into focus the research context and explain the methodology I employed in revisiting the occupational value systems and practices of the police.

Chapter 3 tracks the way in which Northshire Police has developed policies aimed at managing the current demands of greater diversity. Drawing on comments made by officers from different social backgrounds, I explore how the extension of recognition for hitherto marginalized groups has shaped the interior culture. In defence of threats to their increasingly beleaguered identity I show that white, heterosexual, male officers have emerged as prime propagators of resentful discourse that operates to devalue the revised accent on diversity and preserve the traditional culture.

Chapter 4 leaves aside seminal questions of ethnicity, gender, and sexuality and tests the contemporary relevance of other classic themes of police culture for the altered context of policing. The narrative captures interesting sources of variation between the cultures of those working within the two policing areas, but finds that officers mainly shared a related set of assumptions, beliefs, and practices which transcended the contrasting terrains. In exploring the endurance of these proverbial characteristics, I point to broader questions about the very essence of the police role.

Chapter 5 examines how the new policing realities have shaped relations between the police and those groups emphasized in 'policing diversity' policy agendas. I show that responses to the policing context are contradictory and uneven. In the wake of the diversity emphasis, aspects of the culture are being revised and unlearned. However, other features remain remarkably unchallenged by the reorganizations that have occurred in policing.

Chapter 6 questions the current dominance of diversity within policing agendas by demonstrating that issues of class remain crucial in understanding policing discourses and practices. Taking class contempt as a relatively unexamined feature of police culture, I argue that sections of the white 'underclass' operate as uncontentiously legitimate terrain for the unchallenged exercise of police discretion and authority. This was also the group that occupied an overridingly prominent position in the police mind as socially defiling.

The book concludes in Chapters 7 and 8 with an identification of the main findings and implications of the research. My argument locates a tension between the changes that have clearly occurred in the policing landscape and the persistence of police cultural characteristics as observed by earlier scholars. In contradistinction with current scholarship I question the extent to which police culture has changed in light of developments in policing. Police culture endures, I argue, because the basic pressures associated with the police role have not been removed and because social transformations have exacerbated, rather than reduced, the basic definitions of inequality. These wider dilemmas underline the contradictions of achieving any meaningful reconfiguration of police culture.

Acknowledgements

This book is based on my doctoral thesis, which was completed at the Centre for Criminological Research at Keele University. During this time I benefited enormously from the support granted to me by supervisors. I would like to thank Ian Loader for his valuable supervision in the early days of the research. Philip Stenning was a welcome addition to the supervision team and was a wonderful source of inspiration and moral support throughout. Many thanks for your insightful comments and for helping to me to keep going when I was overwhelmed by the research process. I need to extend enormous gratitude to Bill Dixon who, since the first day, was a constant stream of support. Thanks for your unwavering interest in the research and for reassuring me that I could deliver the goods. Your meticulous reading of my work and ability to get the best out of me has, I hope, been worth it. I am enormously grateful to my PhD examiner, Robert Reiner, for his enthusiasm of the research and recommendations for publication.

This is also my opportunity to express my deepest gratitude to all the police officers who allowed me into their working world. Your openness and tolerance in allowing me to observe your work and answer my questions made the fieldwork not only possible, but enjoyable. I am indebted to the former Chief Constable of what I have called Northshire Police for his permission to conduct the research in two Local Policing Units. Special thanks are extended to the LPU Commanders for their support of the research and for making me feel welcome. I owe particular thanks to Deb for facilitating access, providing me with relevant sources of information and for your general support and friendship.

Preparing this book was made significantly easier by a Postdoctoral Fellowship at the Centre for Criminology, University of Oxford. This afforded me the space to develop the thesis for publication and also provided a stimulating intellectual environment. I owe special thanks once again to Ian Loader for taking the time to read and provide valuable comments on chapters. I could not have wished for better counsel throughout the process.

I would also like to express gratitude to friends and colleagues who have cheered me on from the sidelines and made me laugh along the way. Particular thanks must go to Charlie Wilson, Marie Jones, Conor O'Reilly, Helen Beckett, Helen Wells, Else Lyon, Maria-Christina Dorado, and Matthew Millings. My greatest debt of gratitude must go, however, to my family for their boundless support and encouragement throughout my academic career so far. Mum, dad, and Brendan, your belief in my ability to complete the work dampened any thoughts of giving up. I am also grateful to Val and Will for their encouragement, and for the much needed holidays in Pembrokeshire—diolch o'r galon. The final thought is reserved for Robin, without whose love and patience would have made completing this work considerably more difficult.

*

The author and Oxford University Press would like to thank the following publishers for permission to reproduce material for which they hold copyright: the *British Journal of Criminology* for an initial version of Chapter 3 which initially appeared as 'Dominant culture interrupted: recognition, resentment and the politics of change in an English police force' 48/6 (2008) 756–777; and Emerald Group Publishers Ltd for sections of Chapter 6 that first appeared as 'Policing the irrelevant: class, diversity and contemporary police culture', in: O'Neill, M., Marks, M., and Singh, A. (eds) *Police Occupational Culture: New Debates and Directions* (2007).

Contents

List of Abbreviations   xix

Part I Situating Police Culture

1   Replaying the Classics   3
     Origins and Significance   3
     The Orthodox Account   8
     Challenging Accepted Wisdoms   15
     Changing Police Culture   19

2   The New Social Field of Policing   21
     Law and the Politics of Order   22
     Policing a Diverse Society   28
     Exclusionary Times   35
     The Retreat of Class in the Age of Recognition   42
     Revisiting Police Culture   46

Part II Police Culture in Motion

3   Dominant Culture Interrupted   51
     The 'Old Regime'   52
     Changing Culture   56
     Disseminating the New Organizational Ethos   62
     Narratives of Decline and Discontent   63
     Durable Discrimination: Minority Perspectives   73
     New Contestations and the Preservation of Dominance   80
     Concluding Remarks   83

4   Classic Themes, Altered Times   85
     From 'Beirut' to the 'Mary Celeste'   86
     Imagining Policing   89
     A Masculine Ethos   96
     Organizational Realities   99

	Managing Policing Realities	105
	Maintaining Dominance	112
	Isolation and Loyalty	117
	On Patrol	122
	Enduring Themes of Police Culture	125
5	Policing Diverse Publics	127
	Policing *for* Women?	128
	'Deviant' Sexualities	139
	Policing the Multi-ethnic Society	141
	Responding to the New Realities	157
6	The Continuing Significance of Class	159
	Rethinking Police Culture	160
	A Contradiction Emerges	162
	The Classed Nature of Police Culture	183

Part III   Conclusions

7	Police Culture in Transition?	187
	Classic Characteristics in an Altered Landscape	189
	Police Culture in a Diverse Society	192
	Beyond Diversity	196
	Police Culture and its Tenacity	198
8	Ethnography with the Police	201
	Gaining Access and Becoming 'Accepted'	202
	Reflexive Ethnography	206
	Recording and Interpreting the Field	208
Bibliography		**211**
Index		**227**

List of Abbreviations

ACR	Area Control Room
BAWP	British Association for Women in Policing
CAT	Community Action Team
CBO	Community Beat Officer
DVIR	Domestic Violence Investigation Record/Domestic Violence Intelligence Record
FSA	Female Support Association
HMIC	Her Majesty's Inspectorate of Constabulary
IMU	Incident Management Unit
IP	Injured Party
IR	Immediate Response
LAGPA	Lesbian and Gay Police Association
LGPG	Lesbian and Gay Police Group
LPU	Local Policing Unit
MPN	Multicultural Police Network
NBPA	National Black Police Association
NPM	New Public Management
PCSO	Police Community Support Officer
PDP	Performance Development Portfolio
PDR	Performance Development Review
PNC	Police National Computer
RTC	Road Traffic Collision
NPIN	Northshire Police Intelligent Network

PART I
Situating Police Culture

1

Replaying the Classics

In this chapter I provide an account of the principal theoretical perspectives on police culture. I begin by explaining why it is important to examine police culture before reviewing a number of the classic ethnographies that continue to exert considerable influence over this area of study. I then discuss the works which have subsequently followed and provide a thematic discussion of the central characteristics of police culture. Towards the end of the chapter I explore recent challenges to its conceptualization, before going on to discuss the issues associated with police change. In setting out what has become the orthodox conception of police culture, this chapter provides a platform on which to consider the relevance of these renowned features for the altered context of policing—the empirical exploration of which is attended to in ensuing chapters.

Origins and Significance

Most occupations share some cultural attributes among their members which become expressed through various forms, including codes of manners and dress; a shared language, humour and sentiments; rituals and norms of behaviour; and transmissions of myths and stories (Billington *et al* 1991). However, it is the occupational culture of the police—especially the lower ranks of the organization—which has received considerable attention within the social sciences because of the pervasiveness and longevity of its more problematic elements. The idea of police culture has been variously defined. Reiner (1992*b*: 109) describes it as 'the values, norms, perspectives and craft rules which inform police conduct'. Chan (1996: 110) proposes a definition of police culture as the 'informal occupational norms and values operating under the apparently rigid hierarchical structure of police organisations', while Manning (1989: 360) defines it as 'accepted practices, rules, and principles of conduct that are situationally applied, and generalised rationales and beliefs'. Central to these understandings is the idea that the police hold a distinctive set of norms, beliefs, and values which determines their behaviour, both amongst themselves and operationally out on the streets.

Understanding police culture, and its social impact, is an important task for several reasons. First and foremost, the police play a fundamental role in society. They are the visible symbol of the law (Van Maanen 1978*b*) and are granted vast discretionary powers to stop, search, detain, and arrest individual members of the public—and can do so with a legitimate use of coercive force (Bittner 1970; Klockars 1985). The police are typically the first agency the suspect comes into contact with and, in this sense, can have a key influence on *who* enters the criminal justice system (McConville *et al* 1991). Police use of discretionary power means that officers can likewise influence what becomes defined as crime (Ericson 1993). Finally, because the police represent the most visible aspects of the body politic, the practice of policing provides people with one of their most tangible experiences of the state (Van Maanen 1978*b*; see also Manning 1978*a*).

Academic interest in police culture was stimulated by two factors. First, depictions of police brutality and corruption during social unrest in the 1960s and 1970s led to an increased concern with citizens' rights and a critical focus on state agencies such as the police (Prenzler 1997). This shift coincided, secondly, with theoretical and methodological changes that were taking place in the social sciences at this time. As Reiner (1997) reminds us, the inception of labelling theory shifted attention away from those who broke the law to those who enforced it. This was likewise accompanied by a methodological turn towards qualitative approaches, namely ethnography and participant observation. By observing the police in naturally occurring situations police researchers were, for the first time, able to document the everyday norms and values which guided their routine decision making. What emerged was an apparent disparity between the way police organizations presented themselves to their public constituents, and the lived realities of everyday policing (Manning and Van Maanen 1978; Holdaway 1980).

One of the central debates surrounding the informal dimensions of police work was the empirical discovery that officers could essentially choose which crimes to pay attention to (Reiner 2000*b*). The realization that officers had extensive discretionary powers, and that the use of such powers were influenced by their *cultural* norms, meant that the role of the police in identifying and labelling people as deviant became a central focus for deviancy theorists. The discovery that the police-crime relationship was in practice malleable generated studies of how the cultural predispositions of the police produced, or amplified, deviance (see especially Young 1971). These studies were concerned to bring the social world of the police into much sharper focus, and since the 1960s, a plethora of literature on the working environment of the police has come to the fore. Police ethnographies and monographs have appeared over several decades, and their contents continue to be widely debated in contemporary discussions of policing (Banton 1964; Skolnick 1966; Bittner 1967; Westley 1970; Cain 1973; Rubinstein 1973; Reiner 1978; Punch 1979; Holdaway 1983; Smith and Gray 1985; Young 1991; 1993). Such studies have highlighted the usefulness of police culture in understanding how officers learn the craft of policing; the day to day functioning of police work; police deviance; differential law enforcement; and the impact of reform initiatives (Paoline 2003). Research has, moreover, identified recurring characteristics within police culture over time and space. Before exploring these in more detail it is valuable to revisit, briefly, the origins of a sociological policing scholarship which first brought to light the inner world of the police.

Early understandings of the internal culture of police organizations were the result of pioneering work conducted by scholars in America and Britain. One of the first studies was American researcher Jerome Skolnick's (1966: 42) depiction of the police's 'working personality', in which he sought to investigate the 'effects of a man's work on his outlook of the world'. Skolnick argued that a collective culture, shared primarily by the rank and file, arises from the common dilemmas and tensions inherently associated with the job of being a police officer. Chief among these tensions is the potential danger which officers face in their day-to-day encounters with the public. The police role is unique in that its defining task requires officers to confront situations in which there is an unpredictable element of risk of physical danger. Secondly, the fact that the police are the visible symbol of authority (backed by the potential to use legitimate coercive force) places them in a potentially alienated position from those they police. Finally, he argued that these distinctive elements of danger and authority in the police role are joined by a 'constant pressure to appear efficient' or, more simply, a pressure to get results.

For Skolnick (1966: 42) these basic features of the police environment converge to produce 'distinctive cognitive and behavioural responses in police: a working personality'. In defence of the inherent danger in police work, a primary feature of the working personality is suspiciousness towards people, places, and events. Skolnick identifies the 'symbolic assailant' as a person whose 'gesture, language, and attire the policeman has come to recognise as a prelude to violence' (ibid: 45). Because of their authority he also suggested that officers became socially isolated from the outside world and exhibited a high degree of internal solidarity with their colleagues. Skolnick further identified moral conservatism as a behavioural response in the police; as he explains, 'the fact that a man is engaged in enforcing a set of rules implies that he also becomes implicated in *affirming* them' (ibid: 59; emphasis in original).

Another pioneering study of the police is that by William Westley (1970). He set out to explain police violence in an American town and, like Skolnick, also isolated the strained relationship between the police and the public as pivotal in generating distinctive group customs among the police. As he observes:

> The duties of the policeman bring him into contact with greatly varied proportions of the public . . . Sooner or later he meets them all and finds them in a range of human sentiments and human problems. Mostly he meets them in their evil, their sorrow, and their degradation and defeat . . . He sees the public as a threat. He seldom meets it at its best and it seldom welcomes him. In spite of his ostensible function as protector he usually meets only those who he is protecting them from, and for him they have no love (ibid: 49).

Because officers invariably come into contact with the policed, the public come to be seen as the enemy. The response is that the police hold the public at a distance and display cynicism and aggression towards them. Westley found that violence was a central part of routine police work, and this was cemented by the cultural traits of silence, secrecy, and solidarity. These informal features, he argued, are 'an occupational directive, a rule of thumb, the sustenance and the core of meanings' (ibid: 49).

The British work of Banton (1964) further underlined features of the police world which had previously gone unexplored. Banton's (1964: vii) study arose from the notion that it may be 'instructive to analyse institutions that are working well in order to see if anything can be learned from their success', but his examination of the social dimensions of the police role meant that his work can be seen as a seminal account of police culture (McLaughlin 2007: Chapter 2). Like the American works, Banton (1964) recognized the unique position the police occupied in society. He found that in order to identify with the British public the police were drawn primarily from the working class, a group with whom they frequently came into contact. This common background, he suggested, was integral for maintaining the relationship between the police and the policed. However, the authority officers employed over their community also made them a socially isolated group. One of his most insightful findings was that officers engaged mainly in an array of services to the public and are better described as peace keepers—a proposition that undermined the popular conception of the police as quintessentially law enforcers. It is these previously uncharted aspects of the police role which provided an innovative insight into police work, and subsequently paved the way for a new kind of British policing scholarship which extended beyond mere descriptions of police organizations (McLaughlin 2007). In broader terms, however, his research neglected problems of police corruption and the adverse treatment of certain members of the community and thereby assumed a 'primarily harmonious view of British society' (Reiner 2000*b*: 213).

It was Cain's (1973) description of the occupational ideologies and behaviour of the police in Britain that offered a more critical analysis of the relationship between the police and the community. She observed police work in rural and urban locations and found that urban officers were oriented principally towards a crime fighting image of their role—a task which in practice formed only a small part of their daily workload. In order to achieve an authentic policing experience as crime fighters, she found that officers would focus on relatively petty crimes. 'Real' police work became associated with the act of arresting an individual and police defined the time between action-oriented incidents as boring. Officers filled the time between exhilarating incidents by engaging in an array of 'easing behaviour' (ibid: 72), such as drinking cups of tea or visiting the local public house. Another way of relieving the boredom of a shift was to make marginally legitimate arrests. This provided officers with an opportunity for excitement and also gave them some kudos. Urban officers viewed themselves separate to the public and Cain noted rank and file prejudice and suspicion towards minority ethnic populations. Although crime fighting was central to urban officers' definition of their role, rural constables were more integrated into the community they policed. She found that relations between the police and the public were friendly and rural patrols tended to be a 'quiet and leisurely affair' (ibid: 75). By exploring rural policing culture, Cain offered a unique insight into how police culture varied according to location.

These early American and British studies provided a rich, socio-logical interpretation of the working lives of the police. My aim here has been to review of some of the pioneering police culture studies, but I duly note that other scholars made equally substantial contributions to the field (Bittner 1967; Rubinstein 1973; Van Maanen 1974; Manning 1977; Muir 1977; Reiner 1978; Punch 1979; Holdaway 1983). Collectively, these works provided a deeper understanding of how officers made sense of their so-cial world, used their time, and interacted with people in differ-ent settings. Above all, the classic ethnographies prompted the beginnings of research into one of the most powerful institutions in society and accordingly provided a central reference point for other researchers.

The Orthodox Account

The themes first identified by the classic ethnographers appear to be evident in the occupational thinking and practices of sub-sequent generations of police officers. Indeed, the features of policing culture appear to be so timeless that they have today assumed the status of something approaching sociological ortho-doxy. It is now cliché to refer to what Reiner (2000a: Chapter 3) describes as the 'core characteristics' of police culture. A new wave of writers has begun to challenge received understandings of police culture. Yet if the aim of this book is to revisit police cul-ture, then it is crucial to consider this orthodox conception.

In pursuit of crime

A central characteristic of police culture is what Reiner (2000a: 89) identifies as an exaggerated 'sense of mission'. Police ascribe great pride to the job of policing and acclaim its uniqueness and potential to make a difference. The result is that officers invariably interpret their role as one that, first and foremost, involves fighting crime (Smith and Gray 1985; Young 1991). Although this trad-itional representation can be undermined once the real nature of public police work is considered, the image to which the police—and the public—firmly subscribe is that of crime fighters. In his earlier study, Reiner (1978: 230) found that the 'new centurion' approximates to this type of idealized policing; as he puts it, 'the new centurion is a man with a mission. He is dedicated to a crusade against crime and disorder'. A problem here is that the logic of mission in the police outlook can encourage officers to engage in 'noble cause corruption' to get results (Box 1983; see also Skolnick and Fyfe 1993). The moral imperative to fight crime also makes police resistant to efforts to redefine their role as one which encompasses a less confrontational dimension (Marks 2005). Added to this is that officers hold a pragmatic view of their work, conceiving their occupation as one in which a healthy dose of common sense is required (Crank 2004). More often than not police just want to get the job done with a minimum of hassle (Reiner 2000a).

The preoccupation with crime means that officers seek out work which is considered to be thrilling and action packed. In their observational study of the police in London, Smith and Gray (1985) found that officers would drive at high speed to incidents that did not require a rapid response. They took every opportunity to participate in anything offering the promise of excitement, and routinely told stories which glorified violent and confrontational encounters with the public (Punch 1979; Holdaway 1983; Young 1991). But these war stories are more important than just canteen talk; they serve as an influential source of information for the socialization of new recruits and provide cues for police behaviour (Shearing and Ericson 1991).

The obsession with excitement and action means that some aspects of routine policing are considered less important. In the police mind, incidents which fail to conform to the values of 'real' police work epitomize 'bullshit' (Van Maanen 1978b) and 'rubbish' (Holdaway 1983). As I explore below, there has been no shortage of evidence that officers regard being called to domestic violence incidents as rubbish work. Although officers tend to celebrate the exhilarating aspects of their role, police work is mainly uneventful and tedious (Manning 1977). Nevertheless, the craving for action and excitement is pervasive and undermines change initiatives. As Marks (2005) points out, officers who delight in the thrills of action and chase are disinclined to undertake less adventurous forms of police work.

Intolerance and prejudice

Policing has traditionally been an overwhelmingly white, heterosexual, male-dominated occupation and this poses considerable challenges for those who do not correspond with this norm because of their gender, ethnicity, or sexuality (Foster 2003). A renowned feature of police organizations is the taken for granted masculine ethos where police are 'expected to be physically and emotionally tough, aggressive and engage in traditionally masculine activities' (Waddington 1999b: 99). Lending support to this, several pieces of research have captured the heavy drinking habits and somewhat predatory heterosexuality of male officers (Martin 1980; Smith and Gray 1985; Young 1991).

These exaggerated heterosexual orientations tend to reflect misogynistic and patriarchal ideologies. Women have encountered significant difficulty in gaining legitimate acceptance within police organizations. In particular, a 'cult of masculinity' (Smith and Gray 1985: 363) has encouraged various forms of sexual harassment and discrimination (Martin 1980; Heidensohn 1992; Sapp 1994; Brown 1998). Women are underrepresented in police work generally, and find it peculiarly hard to climb the 'greasy pole' of promotion (Halford 1993). Stereotypical assumptions regarding their gender have also underpinned the *type* of work women perform (Heidensohn 1992; Westmarland 2001b). In a highly gendered environment, they are under pressure to either perform the roles which reinforce gender stereotypes or reject part of their femininity by adopting aspects of the masculine culture. Such a choice has been pertinently summed up by Martin (1980), who argues that as officers, women are forced to choose between becoming *police*women or police*women*. But, even when policewomen attain a senior position within the organization, they then have to work in an environment where a 'smart macho' culture dominates (Silvestri 2003; see also Brown 2007).

The masculine culture of the police also influences attitudes and behaviours towards female victims of crime. Edwards (1989) argues that it is the patriarchal sentiments of police culture which constructs domestic violence incidents as the inconclusive, low status work which distracts officers from their pursuit of 'real' police work.[1] In dealing with 'domestics', officers frequently avoid

---

[1] However, Edwards (1989) also blames the wider role of the law for sustaining this bias.

arresting the (usually) male perpetrator and thereby undermine the legal implications of what has taken place. The formal response has been to merely provide 'advice' to the parties—an action which essentially redefines this criminal matter into a civil dispute (Grimshaw and Jefferson 1987). Recent policing agendas have, however, attempted to improve the way officers respond to domestic violence incidents—a matter I discuss in subsequent chapters.

The accepted ethos of robust heterosexual masculinity can also exclude people whose sexuality is at odds with the dominant norm. In addition to experiencing a complex process of marginalization and discrimination, homosexual officers have found themselves adopting the values and qualities associated with the prevailing heterosexual culture (Burke 1993; Miller *et al* 2003). These studies found that gay men are held at a distance until they can 'prove' their masculine traits, through backing up colleagues in violent encounters for instance.

Racism has been identified as one of the most central and problematic features of police culture. Black and minority ethnic officers working within white-dominated organizations have articulated their experiences of isolation and discrimination within policing organizations (Holdaway and Barron 1997; Martin 1994) and there is a long history of persistent police harassment and intolerance towards members of minority ethnic groups outside the organization. As far back as 1966, Skolnick suggested that within the police mind the African American constituted the symbolic assailant (see also Lambert 1970). More recent scholars have similarly noted police suspiciousness and hostility towards minority ethnic communities, and have drawn much attention to the over-policing of such groups (Smith and Gray 1985; Holdaway 1996; Chan 1997; Bowling and Phillips 2003). Ethnographic accounts have likewise captured the ubiquitous use of overt racist language among the police. Smith and Gray encountered one white officer in London who stated the following:

How does an experienced officer decide who to stop? Well, the one that you stop is often wearing a woolly hat . . . is dark in complexion . . . has thick lips, and usually has dark fuzzy hair (1985: 129).

Racial bias can also occur in more subtle ways within police forces. Smith and Gray found reluctance on the part of the police to investigate adequately offences involving minority ethnic people as victims of crime. This practice resonates strongly with the recent assertion made in the Macpherson Report (1999) that failure to properly investigate the racist murder of black teenager Stephen Lawrence in London owed much to 'institutional racism'. Yet in examining the racist element of police culture, a number of additional points have been made. Smith and Gray noted a marked disparity between what the police say about minority ethnic people, and their actual behaviour when interacting with such groups (see also Foster 1989). Others have questioned whether the racism displayed by officers is merely a reflection of the racist tendencies of the broader society from which they are drawn; as Reiner (2000*a*: 100) puts it:

> The crucial source of police prejudice is societal racism, which places ethnic minorities disproportionately in those strata and situations from which the police derive their property. This structural feature of police-ethnic minority relations bolsters any prior prejudice police officers have.

According to this reasoning, then, hostility towards members of minority ethnic groups becomes inexorably reinforced in the localized experiences the police have with such groups (see also Jefferson 1991).

A suspicious and cynical disposition

The pervading sense of danger and unpredictability experienced by officers means they are alert to anything suspicious. Following Skolnick (1966), an abundance of other research has identified suspicion as a widely shared attribute of the police worldview (Rubinstein 1973; Brown 1981; Swanton 1981; Holdaway 1983; Young 1991). These works point to incongruence as the primary basis for stimulating suspicion. Police develop an extensive repertoire of indicators which, for them, signal a person's possible involvement in crime. Invariably, these indicators are driven by aesthetic and behavioural cues in the working environment (ibid: see also Rubinstein 1973; Brown 1981). Suspicion is related to the stereotyping of people and it is widely accepted that police attention falls disproportionately on those marginal and excluded groups at the bottom of the social strata. As Reiner (2000*a*) confirms, the stereotypes found within the occupational culture both reflect and reinforce the patterns of disadvantage within the broader social structure. A more detailed analysis of the people who find prominence within the police's occupational consciousnesses is presented later on. Although suspicion is a cultural response to the police role, it is also encouraged by formal organizational training and is built into the law itself (Skolnick 1966; Brown 1981).[2]

Police also possess a uniquely cynical and pessimistic view of their social world. They have an intimate relationship with people who are profoundly disadvantaged and are routinely called to deal with a range of difficult and challenging incidents. This makes policing a leading 'dirty work' occupation (Hughes 1962; see also Waddington 1999*b*). Added to this, officers routinely encounter people who lie to them and who try to pass the blame onto others (Van Maanen 1978*b*). As a result, the police have a jaundiced view of the public *per se*. As Manning (1977: 26) puts it:

. . .people in general are viewed as stupid, fallible, greedy, lustful, immoral and hypocritical. Man is seen as a translucent Machiavelli, easily uncovered by insightful probing or public action.

Police also tend to discount what ordinary members of the public tell them. Police scepticism is liable to manifest itself in an outwardly detached and unsympathetic manner during interactions. But another cultural response underpins exchanges with the public. Because police believe that moral standards and respect for authority are rapidly disintegrating (Reiner 1978), officers like to maintain control over and extract deference from people who are seemingly disrespectful or defiant towards the symbolic dimensions of their authority (Sykes and Clarke 1975; Smith and Gray 1985; Young 1991). If people fail to succumb to their authority, officers are prone to inflict a range of formal and informal penalties, ranging from invading the personal space of their adversaries to arrest.

The cynical element of the police outlook also extends to senior officers within the organization (Neiderhoffer 1967; Reiner 1978; Graef 1989). The most common complaint of the rank and file is that their superiors are detached from the 'sharp end' of operational policing. This is captured by Waddington (1999*b*: 231), who explains, 'from the perspective of the rank and file, senior ranks are divorced from reality, living in a comfortable and trouble-free existence on the upper floors of police headquarters'. This sense of betrayal by management reinforces a marked sense of solidarity among the

---

[2] In Britain, the police need 'reasonable suspicion' to exercise their stop, search, and arrest powers. This term has been the subject of criticism because it is loosely defined and largely subjective (see Dixon 1997).

rank and file and can subsequently thwart top-down reform initiatives. Equally, because 'management cops' (Reuss-Ianni and Ianni 1983) are concerned to perpetuate an image of professionalism and efficiency, ordinary constables experience pressure to conform to organizational directives. A predisposition to 'cover your arse' consequently ensues and is a deeply ingrained feature of policing culture (Van Maanen 1978b; Chan et al 2003). Police cynicism also becomes directed towards the law and criminal justice system. Officers complain that soft touch laws, imprudent judges and corrupt lawyers all undermine the hard work done to keep 'the streets' safe (Reiner 1978; Graef 1989). A dark sense of humour is another offshoot of the cynical perspective. Humour is a useful resource for releasing the tensions associated with their dirty work environment (Waddington 1999b), but it nevertheless serves to undermine the imposition of external rules and reinforce solidarity among the rank and file (Powell 1996).

Isolation, mutual solidarity, and conservatism

As Waddington (1999b) observes, the police are an extremely insular group and make a clear-cut distinction between 'Us' (the police) and 'Them' (the rest of the population). This sense of togetherness is reinforced by defining features of the police role, including working the arduous hours of the shift system together; difficulties in separating work from home life; needing to rely on colleagues in times of danger; and the isolating nature of their position as the impersonal face of coercive authority (Reiner 2000a). But this solidarity has a dark side; it protects and covers up colleague infringements of procedure (Westley 1970; Skolnick and Fyfe 1993; Mollen Report 1994).

The police make a sharp distinction between the 'respectable' and 'rough' citizenry (Shearing 1981), and this determines whether or not a person is considered to be deserving of policing services. Those falling into the latter category have been classified by the police as 'slags' (Smith and Gray 1985) 'pukes' (Ericson 1982) and 'prigs' (Young 1991). Several other groups challenge the police milieu. First, there are those people which Lee (1981: 53–4) calls 'police property'.[3] The term is used to describe those socially, economically, and politically powerless people whom the majority

---

[3] This concept was initially coined by Cray (1972) but has been subsequently developed by Lee (1981).

see as problematic and offensive. They are the people society leaves for the police to deal with and typically include the homeless and unemployed; disenfranchised youth subcultures; drug addicts and prostitutes; and minority ethnic groups. Holdaway (1983: 77–81) identifies other categories. 'Rubbish' denotes those people who are seen to make trivial calls to the police, while 'challengers' refers to professionals from various disciplines that are in a position to scrutinize the work of the police. Along with civil libertarians and lawyers, academics are seen as core challengers to the police milieu. A final group are what Holdaway calls 'disarmers'. These are socially fragile groups, such as children and the elderly, who the police find it difficult to deal with because of their potential to invoke public sympathy. A morally and politically conservative outlook perpetuates these views (Baker 1985).

Challenging Accepted Wisdoms

According to the orthodox account of police culture, officers possess a range of predominantly negative behavioural tendencies which arise in defence of the police vocation. This shared mindset underpins and informs how officers relate to people within and beyond the organization, and works in opposition to public service ideals and reform endeavours. The characteristics which comprise police culture are, moreover, culturally transmitted and reinforced through the immediate peer group. Traditional recruitment patterns have overwhelmingly enlisted white, heterosexual males from a working class background and have produced an apparently homogenous grouping. This orthodox account has exerted considerable influence over understandings in this area, but recent reflection has called into question the existence and conceptualization of a monolithic police culture.[4]

In conventional accounts police culture is presented as homogenous, static, and unchanging. However, the occupational culture can vary according to rank, department, and force. While some scholars have found differences between rural and urban officers (Cain 1973; Young 1993), others have noted variations at the local (Foster 1989) and international level (Bayley 1976). In their study, Reuss-Ianni and Ianni (1983) identified a prominent distinction

---

[4] For an influential critique of the way police culture has been conceptualized see Chan (1997: Chapter 4).

within the police organization between 'street cops' and 'management cops'. In a similar vein, Manning (2007) proposes that police organizations are characterized by three subcultures of policing according to rank: command, middle management, and lower participants. Divisions also exist between detectives and constables (Hobbs 1989 Young 1991) and there is evidence of variability in styles of policing between individual officers (Reiner 1978) and departments (Wilson 1972). These works support the contention that there are possible subcultures contained within what is usually presented as 'mainstream' police culture. Yet Fielding (1989) suggests that even these characterizations are too narrow because they overlook the varied conflicts and rivalries between officers themselves. Notwithstanding these clear divergences, representations of police culture have tended to generalize police culture as a singular and homogenous entity (Chan 1997; see also Hobbs 1991). In order to reflect the nuances in what has traditionally been seen as the dominant culture, scholars increasingly argue that discussions of police culture are better referred to in the plural—that is, as police *cultures* (Foster 2003; Cockcroft 2007).[5]

The issue of homogeneity draws attention to the manner in which officers become socialized into the occupational culture. As Chan (1997: 66) notes, most accounts imply that the 'acculturation process' is one-way and thereby portray officers as manipulated and docile learners. This approach is too deterministic and fails to appreciate the agency of officers in making up their own mind as to whether or not to accept the features of the culture—and, furthermore, to what extent they accept them (see also Fielding 1988). Whether, if at all, new recruits accept the cultural values will depend on many factors including their own individual biography and personality. Police culture is also presented in profoundly depressing terms; as Waddington (1999: 287) argues the notion of police culture is 'frequently invoked by academic researchers and commentators to explain and condemn a broad spectrum of

[5] In this book, I intend to retain its singular use. In part, I do so in order to capture the commonalities between the cultural tendencies of officers that I observed. As McConville and Shepherd (1992) have argued, all police organization share something of a common police culture (see also Holdaway 1989). This does not mean, however, that the variations in police culture will be ignored or overlooked. Where relevant, such differences will be duly highlighted and explored. Nevertheless, my own conceptualization of police culture is understood as capable of incorporating both differences and similarities.

policing practice'. By focusing only on the negative characteristics of police culture researchers fail to take account its episodic nature in so far as positive police behaviours are equally identifiable. Police culture is a valuable device for supporting officers as they deal with their environment and, in this sense, is a rational response to the unique role of policing. Even when aspects of police culture are internalized they do not necessarily determine police behaviour; as Reiner (2000a: 85) makes clear, 'an important distinction can indeed be made between "cop culture"—the orientations implied and expressed by officers in the course of their work—and "canteen culture", the values and beliefs exhibited in off-duty socialising'. Along with a disparity between police talk and conduct, there may also be something of a divergence between language forms and deeply situated values and beliefs. What officers say does not necessarily reflect what they in fact think.

Another critique of the way police culture has been conceptualized is its assumed insularity from the broader social, economic, legal, and political landscape in which it operates. Culturalist interpretations of police culture emphasize the immediate peer group of officers and posit that the police behave in the way they do because a strong cultural force influences them (Dixon 1997). A focus on culture has the advantage of steering understandings away from psychological accounts, but it nevertheless overlooks the wider contextual influences that shape police thinking and practice. For instance, most studies acknowledge that police attention falls heavily on the marginal and powerless groups in society—with young, black, working class males habitually forming the core targets of policing. Some writers have questioned the extent to which such patterning is solely the product of rank and file culture, and in so doing, have exposed the influence of formal policies and management directives and the law in shaping police behaviour (Grimshaw and Jefferson 1987; McBarnet 1981; Herbert 1998).[6] As Reiner (1997) reminds us, moreover, police work is also structured by the core mandate. This emphasizes the control of public spaces which, in turn, is socially patterned

---

[6] These critiques also highlight the limitations of an ethnographic approach for understanding police culture. Preoccupation with the day to day work of the rank and file has led some to comment that 'studies of police culture have been coterminous with patrol culture' (Reiner 2000a: 86; see also Dixon 1997).

by class, age, gender, and ethnicity.[7] Police contact with young men from economically and ethnically marginal groupings can be explained by the fact that this group are more likely to inhabit public—and therefore *police*—street space and are also more likely to depend on the police for assistance.

However, other writers have revived the occupational culture as a determinant of policing and argue that by placing police culture in a subordinate position these accounts underestimate the importance it plays in shaping, and being shaped by, the formal dimensions of policing. As Holdaway (1989) points out, the law and formal policies can certainly influence policing, but the point is that they become reworked to resonate with the preferences of the occupational culture (see also Ericson 1993). In a similar vein McConville *et al* (1991) underline the influence of police 'working rules' in determining behaviour, but they also recognize that policing takes place within a political context which is sufficiently permissive to allow the police to work within police-defined objectives. Thus the key for understanding the patterning of policing is to appreciate the influence of police culture *and* the wider context in which it takes place. As I explore in a moment, the work of Chan (1997) suggests that social and political sensitivities in the wider policing landscape have the potential to shape the culture of police organizations.

These critiques imply that police culture may be losing its expediency as a concept. To be sure understandings of police culture have been overstated in some accounts, but others remind us that successive generations of researchers have observed prominently similar characteristics in the sentiments and practices of officers across different times and jurisdictions (Waddington 1999a; Reiner 2000a; Crank 2004). In this book I have chosen to retain the term police culture because, in my view, it appears to be germane for explaining the way officers think about and interact within their social world. Equally though, my forthcoming analysis does not seek to overlook the challenges made to the concept.

---

[7] Although I should emphasize that routine police work also involves widespread interaction with people in private spaces, including their homes.

Changing Police Culture

One of the central assumptions of the orthodox account is that changes are needed to police culture. However, changing police culture has been understood as an extremely difficult task (Goldsmith 1990; Brogden and Shearing 1993; Savage 2003). Not only are reform endeavours resisted by the rank and file, but they are also compounded by other features of policing. The police are afforded wide discretionary powers and because of this much of their work takes place in conditions of low visibility and beyond the effective scrutiny of supervisors (Goldstein 1960). Changing the confrontational element of police culture may likewise prove difficult when dealing with crime, criminals, and social unrest are defining features of the police role (Prenzler 1997; Waddington 1999*b*).

Endeavours to reform police organizations have many dimensions, including changes in policy, recruitment, and training; an emphasis on progressive leadership; amendments in the composition of the workforce; the introduction of measures to mainstream equality; and shifts in the organization's guiding principles. Yet, as Marks (2005) observes, meaningful police change encompasses not only structural shifts but, also, behavioural and attitudinal changes. The latter is a peculiarly challenging task given that it involves altering the entrenched values, beliefs, and assumptions of officers. It is such ingrained dispositions which inform police rationales, ways of viewing those they interact with, and use of policing styles. Evaluating the nature and extent of 'change' is similarly problematic. Although shifts in behaviour are relatively observable, changes in values and beliefs are much more difficult to determine. A concerted top-down reform programme aimed at rule tightening may induce conformity in police behaviour, but it runs the risk of leaving existing dispositions intact (ibid; Brogden and Shearing 1993). What is needed, therefore, is a more holistic approach to police cultural change.

The work of Chan (1997) has rebooted debate about the possibilities for changing police culture. In her view, approaches to police culture are limited because they use an outdated conceptual model. Relaying much of the criticism previously outlined, Chan provides a rethinking of police culture that allows for the prospect of change. Drawing on Bourdieu's (1990) theory of culture and practice, and organizational theorists such as Sackmann (1991) and Schein (1985), she identifies the importance of examining the interaction between the 'field' (the wider organizational, historical, legal, socio-economic, and political conditions of police work) and the 'habitus' (the dispositions and informal norms and values of officers). For Chan (1997) police culture arises from the intrinsic relationship between the field and the habitus to the extent that attempts to reform police culture remain limited when changes in the habitus are not supported by transformations in the field of policing. In other words, the wider social, political, and legislative context must also be ripe for police organizational change to occur. Her study of attempts by New South Wales Police in Australia to reform endemic corruption and racism does indicate that external pressures can have some success in changing police culture.

According to Chan, social and political sensitivities in the broader policing environment have the potential to shape the character of police organizations and their working culture. The British policing landscape has been fundamentally transformed within recent years and arguably presents fresh challenges for the cultural ethos that has long underpinned the police identity. One of the greatest developments, I suggest, is the emergence of respect for diversity and recognition of cultural and gendered identities in policing discourse and practice. At the organizational level, the gradual rise in the number of people from minority backgrounds within police forces could be expected to weaken the racist, sexist, and homophobic elements of the traditional police culture. Likewise, the archetypal young, working class, high school educated workforce may become altered by the growing recruitment of more mature and better educated officers (see Punch 2007). Related to this, the wholesale adoption of community policing philosophies may have modified the way officers now think about and interact with the public. Policing is, then, an occupation that has experienced, and is experiencing, a great deal of change. Is it reasonable to propose that the stability of police culture can no longer remain dominant?

My aim in this chapter has been to set out the principal themes in thinking and research on police culture. In laying down the orthodox conceptualization, my primary concern has been to provide a platform on which to pose the following question; does this description of police culture still hold relevance today? In the next chapter I trace the altered landscape of policing in late modern Britain. Drawing on data from the empirical investigation, the remaining chapters then explore how much of the classic characteristics have survived the period of transition.

2

The New Social Field of Policing

... it has never been more important to forge a critical police studies that is capable of conceptualising policing developments against
socio-cultural, economic and political transformations. It remains the
case that studying the police in the broadest contextual manner is of vital
importance. (McLaughlin 2007a: ix).

The collective evidence of ethnographic studies has identified
various features within the occupational ideologies and practices
of rank and file officers. However, it is increasingly recognized
that the finely grained characteristics of police culture cannot be
divorced from the broader context in which it is situated. The
policing landscape has transformed significantly since the early
police culture studies. While the legal and accountability mechanisms for policing have changed, so too have political and public
ambiance towards 'law and order'. By far the greatest development is the dominance of respect for diversity and recognition of
cultural and gendered identities in current policing discourse and
practice. The sentiments which comprise police culture have been
challenged by the sharp ascendance of identity politics, where
minority groups are seeking equality for their social differences.
The extension of recognition for hitherto marginalized groups is
a crucial development in policing, but police culture needs also
to be considered in relation to other key transformations in the
economic and cultural landscape of late modern Britain.

In this chapter I identify what I consider to be the defining
developments to have occurred in the British policing landscape.
What is of pivotal importance here is that these developments
have transformed the nature of society in which police culture
is currently located. I draw upon three broad axes of change to
delineate the new social field of British policing: the legal context
of policing; the greater political recognition of minority groups;
and the burgeoning economic exclusion of late modernity. I show
that the new societal configuration raises seminal questions

for the cultural expressions of the police and the policing of social groups.

Law and the Politics of Order

Police officers today work in a markedly different legal environment than their predecessors. This is true both in relation to the settlement of legislation to govern police practices and the ascendance of punitive public and political approaches towards crime and crime control.

Challenges to police culture

Police conduct has come under considerable scrutiny in recent years. Concerns have principally centred on police involvement in miscarriages of justice; abuses of power and corruption; lack of accountability; and erosion of civil liberties. As Choongh (1997) reminds us, police interests are driven predominantly by a crime control as opposed to due process model of policing.[1] Their main aspiration is to bring to justice those they 'know' to be guilty of crime, rather than to ensure that suspects' rights are fully considered. Police involvement in perpetuating miscarriages of justice has been well documented (Dixon 1999; Maguire 2003; Naughton 2004) and police interrogation practices have come under particular scrutiny. Outside the police station, controversial aspects of patrolling have likewise been criticized. During the 1980s, these concerns about the way the police conduct their work resulted in a momentous legislative response.

The Police and Criminal Evidence Act (PACE) 1984 is a comprehensive set of rules aimed at governing police powers and procedures in England and Wales. The act was initially contested by differing groups, but upon its inception introduced a new set of procedural requirements designed to regulate the conduct of officers and enhance the rights of suspects.[2] The system is heavily codified, with detailed rules covering each stage of the process. It is not my intention to consider all of these in detail but, rather, to identify significant elements of the act.

---

[1] See also Packer (1969).

[2] As Reiner (2000a) notes, the act was opposed by the Labour Party and interest groups, who saw it as an expansion of police powers.

A defining characteristic of the police is their general right to stop, search and detain individual members of the public. As Newburn (2007: 607) summarizes, the basic powers of stop and search under PACE encompass the following requirements: s.1 (2) allows a police officer to 'detain a person or vehicle for the purposes of a search', and s.1 (3) allows an officer to 'stop and search an individual if he has reasonable grounds for suspecting that he will find stolen or prohibited articles'. The act provides safeguards for suspects. Most notably, stop and search can only take place if the officer has 'reasonable grounds' for suspecting that stolen or prohibited articles will be found. The code also states that reasonable suspicion can never be influenced by the appearance (ethnicity, age, clothing, and so on) of the suspected person, or the fact that he or she is known to have previous convictions for offences. The suspect cannot be detained for any longer than is necessary during the encounter, and the officer must provide their name, police station, grounds and object of the search prior to conducting the search (Choongh 2002). Suspects must also be told that a written copy of the search will be made available if so requested.

PACE created other requirements for police practices, most notably investigative procedure inside police stations. Among the most important innovations is the formal appointment of a custody officer, independent of the investigation, and with specified duties in relation to the welfare of the detained person. Custody officers are intended to act as the 'guardian' of the rights of those held in police custody. Alongside ensuring the legality of the detention and welfare of the suspect, PACE also places strict limits on how long a person can be detained (see Maguire 2002). Suspects have access to free legal advice, and are accorded the right to have someone known to them notified of their arrest (ibid; see also Dixon 1997). The Code of Practice also places restrictions on the manner in which suspects can be questioned by officers, and these provisions are bolstered by the 'right to silence' (Maguire 1988; Dixon 1997; Moston and Stephenson 2006). The Act stipulates that police interviewing of suspects must be audio-recorded in order to validate the accuracy of the record and PACE places vigorous obligation on officers to ensure that contemporaneous records are kept throughout their interactions with suspects.

The impact PACE has had over the last twenty years on police attitudes and practice has been heavily debated (Maguire 1988; Bottomley *et al* 1991; Leng 1995; Brown 1997). In particular, the assertion that it amounted to a u-turn for the preservation of suspects' rights has been called into question. A key principle underpinning PACE was that of achieving balance between competing rights and interests of the suspect and the police. This became translated into legislation only to the extent that suspects' rights were *matched* by enhanced police powers; as Maguire (2002: 80) puts it, 'while detained persons gained the rights to notify friends or relatives of their arrest and to receive legal advice, the police gained greater powers to enter and search their homes'.

Studies of the practical operation of PACE have focused on the extent to which officers have conformed to the letter of the law (Brown 1997). Despite the apparently critical changes in the area of stop and search, studies found that the police can circumvent the requirements (Bottomley *et al* 1991). Officers may fail to make a formal record of the encounter and given the vagueness of 'reasonable suspicion' can merely invent grounds for the search on the spot (Smith 2002). Another way officers get round the formal requirements is to initiate consensual encounters with people. Significant numbers of interactions between the police and the focus of their attention go unrecorded, and consequently unchecked, because most people simply 'consent' to being stopped, questioned and searched (Dixon 1997). There is evidence of stop and search being used to gather intelligence on certain populations (Choongh 1997) and observational studies demonstrate that such encounters are driven by police stereotypes of people as more likely to be involved in crime (Young 1991). Finally, far from encouraging a decline in arrests, PACE has actually led to an increase in officers using the power of arrest (McConville *et al* 1991).

The subtle exploitation of procedures inside police stations has also been a focal point of empirical research. One tactic, as noted by a study conducted under the auspices of the Royal Commission in 1995, was to thwart the mandatory recording of investigative interviewing by conducting 'informal' interviews (cited in Wilson *et al* 2001). Officers conducted interviews in private spaces (such as in the back of police cars) and made informal prison visits to clear up crimes which were unaccounted for. Custody officers have also been found to collaborate with detectives by failing to record custody visits—a pattern which led Reiner (1992*b*: 89) to conclude that 'the idea of the custody officer as an independent check has proved chimerical'. During formal interviews police tend to exaggerate their specialist knowledge of the legal system to infer what the outcome will be if cooperation is forthcoming and, by the same token, the likely outcome if cooperation is unforthcoming (Sanders and Young 2000). Other informal strategies used by officers include delaying legal representation and inflating the amount of evidence they actually possess (McConville *et al* 1991). It would appear, then, that PACE has not had a momentous effect on police sentiments or conduct. For some, the regulatory framework can be better described as 'presentational rules'; they create the appearance that the police are subjected to more legal constraint than they actually are (Dixon 1997).[3] It is of enormous relevance for the current work that the informal tactics adopted by officers to circumvent formal procedure demonstrates the influence of their *cultural* resources in reworking the disparity between law in books and law in action.

But it would not be accurate to say that PACE has failed to transform some aspects of the working culture of policing. As Morgan (1995) argues, the act has dramatically reduced the risk of mistreatment and oppressive interviewing by the police. In support of this, a review of the research ten years after its implementation found clear evidence of revised police professionalism in the areas of stop and search, entry and arrest and detention (Brown 1997). Suspects also had a heightened awareness of their rights and there was 'little evidence that rights are systematically denied' (ibid: xii). The widespread recording of critical events and decisions also signals that the police are acting, for the most part, in accordance with clearly formulated rules. As Waddington (1999: 138) argues, the adoption of extensive codes of practice represents a marked 'extension of citizenship' to those who are suspected of having committed a criminal offence. By ensuring suspects are made aware of their rights, PACE maximizes the accountability of officers and increases the visibility and reviewability of their decisions and actions. It is also worth noting that successive generations of officers are formally socialized into the requirements of PACE as a matter of course. Official training can certainly be challenged by the informal culture, but the act has undoubtedly become embedded within the police mind as the regulatory framework governing their decisions and actions. The impact of PACE remains disputed, but it is unequivocally

[3]   An expression first coined by Smith and Gray (1985: 441).

the case that contemporary police officers work in a substantially different legal context than previous generations. There is now a regime of safeguards to protect suspects' rights and, as a result, much improved mechanisms for police accountability.

In recent years, however, it would seem that these favourable features of PACE have become steadily undermined. Police powers are being dramatically enhanced, but without the accompanying safeguards for suspects. For some, this symbolizes just one manifestation of a new paradigm where concern with crime and crime control has become increasingly dominant and punitive.

A punitive turn

The paradigmatic shift which has occurred in the politics and culture of law and order has been cogently analysed by David Garland (2001) in *The Culture of Control*. His basic premise is that the social insecurity of late modernity finds its expression in an increased preoccupation with risk and fear of crime, and consequently results in more punitive sentiments of the public. Seeking political advantage, politicians seize upon these insecurities and introduce even tougher law and order policies. The ascendance of this new terrain has likewise been debated by others, and requires no detailed attention here (Bauman 2000; Garland 2001; Morgan 2000; Downes and Morgan 2002; Loader 2006; Jones and Newburn 2006; Reiner 2007).

The overtly political stance towards law and order came into prominence during the height of Thatcherism in the late 1970s and early 1980s. Eager to exploit public anxieties about burgeoning crime and disorder, the Conservative party campaign was directed towards the hardening of penal policy and enhanced modes for punishment. But it was also geared towards the creation of a new crime control package—and it was the police who stood at the forefront of this (Loader 2006; see also Green 1990). The law and order posture adopted by the Conservatives capitalized on what was declared to be Labour's propensity to be 'soft' on crime (Reiner 2007). Although the former located crime firmly with individual pathology, Labour understood crime to be the product of structural determinants, particularly economic inequality and lack of opportunity. However, the transition from 'Old' Labour to New Labour has involved a conscious effort to distance itself from the law and order 'skeletons in the cupboard' (Downes and Morgan 2002). New Labour has since reversed its traditional pose and declared itself as the real and pre-eminent party of law and order.

This ideological repositioning has found broad currency with growing anxieties about crime and declining moral standards, and has only cemented the flurry of punitive activities and legislative developments. The extent of these have been discussed by Loader (2006), who suggests that no less than 49 Acts of Parliament were passed between 1997 and 2005. He also estimates that the Labour government has created a minimum of 1,018 new criminal offences. Added to this is that 'crime' is becoming increasingly defined in narrow terms. The Crime and Disorder Act 1998 has been pivotal to the criminalization of behaviour not previously considered to be criminal. As Burney (2005) demonstrates, political discourses around antisocial behaviour have criminalized whole populations, including children and those with mental and social problems. Harsher sentences and expansion in the prison system characterize the new climate, but policing remains critical to the punitive agenda. Without even taking into account the unabashed extension of the 'police family', the number of sworn officers in England and Wales has reached an unparalleled high of over 143,000 (Reiner 2007: 134).[4] Expenditure on the police by New Labour has also surpassed that of previous governments and police resources and powers have expanded dramatically:

> There has been a remorseless growth of police powers . . . New powers to intercept communications, conduct covert operations, stop and search and arrest, and the creation of new public order offences by the Police Act 1997, Crime and Disorder Act 1998, Regulation of Investigatory Powers Act 2000, Terrorism Act 2000, and the Criminal Justice and Public Order Act 2001 . . . The pressures on the police to achieve results have intensified in the new crime control climate, and they are increasingly armed with new powers unfettered by safeguards (ibid: 137).

These legislative developments have been further bolstered by sporadic initiatives such as police 'crackdowns' and 'zero tolerance', focused predominantly on minor incivilities (Downes and Morgan 2003; see also Johnston 2000; Dixon 2003). Notwithstanding the safeguards initially introduced under PACE, civil liberties and procedural safeguards are becoming eclipsed by crime control

---

[4] We could also add that these numbers are supported by the enormous resurgence in the expansion of other people and institutions engaged in 'policing' activities (Johnston 1992; Crawford 2003).

demands. There has been a wearing down of the requirement for the reasonable suspicion in some proactive policing situations and the right to silence is becoming severely challenged (O'Reilly 1994; Newburn 2003). This harsher politics of law and order is unequivocally the 'dominant discourse of the age' (Reiner 2007: 122). As the visible symbol of law and authority, the police are equipped with greater powers and resources to implement the new crime control agenda. This punitive turn looks set to continue and is exacerbated by a series of social, economic, and cultural upheavals—a matter I return to later. For now, it is necessary to examine another development in the field of policing.

The current social world is marked by the emergence of identity politics where there has been an extraordinary shift in the 'grammar of political claims making' (Fraser 1997: 2). Culturally defined groups, along the axes of ethnicity, gender, and sexuality, have emerged to protect their identities and seek recognition of their cultural and gendered differences (see also Taylor 1992; Parekh 2000; Sayer 2005; Zurn 2005). The ascendance of a politics based on culture and difference has been transposed onto the contemporary policing landscape. British police forces are under increasing pressure to understand themselves as sites of 'diversity'. In particular, the equitable policing of ethnic minorities have become intensely salient in policing discourse and practice. In what follows, I trace the emergence of this new policing paradigm.

Policing a Diverse Society

Post-war immigration and the recent expansion of the European Union has granted free movement to workers from former commonwealth countries and new member states into Britain. The upshot is that British society is more ethnically, linguistically, religiously, and culturally diverse. The challenges of policing multicultural populations, especially in major urban centres, have resulted in growing tensions between the police and those diverse communities they are charged to serve. Invariably locked in deprived inner city neighbourhoods, ethnic minorities have long been subjected to adverse policing strategies (Lambert 1970; Bowling 1999; Bowling and Phillips 2003). But in recent years, problems of racist language, over-policing, and excessive use of force against such groups have led to official critiques of policing practices. A variety of initiatives have subsequently taken place—both at the formal policy and operational levels of police organizations—to alter the way officers respond to the task of policing multicultural societies.

The beginnings

The report of Lord Scarman in 1981 into the violent riots between the police and black youth in Brixton, South London, is often taken to be the principal text which placed on the political agenda the way the policing of multi-ethnic populations was carried out in Britain. The catalyst for the disturbances was the implementation of Operation Swamp 81, an aggressive policing strategy in which the police used their powers to conduct raids on houses and subject the predominantly minority ethnic residents to a stop, search, and arrest campaign.[5] Residents perceived their intimidation by the police as blatant discrimination and the event culminated in a spectacular and violent clash between the two groups.

Lord Scarman was appointed to chair an inquiry into the disturbances, and attempted to investigate the source and implications of the riots. From the viewpoint of the local black community the persistent stops; use of paramilitary policing tactics; racially abusive language; and violence displayed by the police amounted to racial harassment. There was also a broader perception that while black and minority ethnic groups were over-policed as suspects of crime, they were under-protected as victims of crime (McLaughlin 2007a). In contrast, the police perspective was that such tactics were necessary because multi-ethnic areas such as Brixton were responsible for a large part of the crime problem (ibid; see also Cashmore and McLaughlin 1991).[6] The ensuing report by Scarman identified various problems contributing to the violence in Brixton, some of which were attributed to the police themselves. In particular, the racial prejudices of individual

---

[5] I should note that disturbances between the police and people from minority ethnic backgrounds is not a new phenomenon, and my initial focus on the Scarman Report (1981) does not seek to overlook other important inquests such as Lord Justice Salmon's inquiry into the 1958 Notting Hill riots.

[6] The belief that young minority ethnic men were the core perpetrators of crime was no doubt encouraged by the wider social construction of black youth as core perpetrators of the 'mugging' phenomenon which characterized debates about crime and urban centres during the 1970s (see Hall *et al* 1978).

officers and the paramilitary tactics were identified as key con-
tributors in fuelling local resentment among the black community and thereby causing the collapse in relations between the two
parties.

Scarman's explanation of the riots has been subject to much
criticism. Although he highlighted broader matters including
unemployment, deteriorating social conditions, and the alienation
experienced by black youth, he nevertheless portrayed the riots
as 'essentially an outburst of anger and resentment by young
black people against the police' (cited in, Bowling and Phillips
2003: 531). His analysis accordingly separated the issues of the
police organization, police powers, and police conduct from the
question of racial discrimination (Bridges 1983). Moreover, by
focusing on the prejudices of individual officers, Lord Scarman
refuted the existence of an institutionalized form of racism.

The recommendations of the report were multifaceted. Central
to its requests was the acknowledgement that white and masculine
police organizations had to reconsider the way they policed ethnically and culturally diverse communities (McLaughlin 2007a).
Identifying and disciplining officers who displayed racist conduct
became elevated as a pressing concern. The report also suggested
that police organizations should recruit more minority ethnic
officers, and called for officers to be better educated on the cultural and racial backgrounds of minority ethnic communities.
Another recommendation was that 'public tranquillity' should
take precedence over law enforcement objectives. Officers would
be required to become better embedded into their communities
and demonstrate commitment to treat minority ethnic people
fairly and without discrimination.[7] Other measures included
increasing the transparency of the police. This was to be achieved
through establishing statutory police and community consultations (PACC) with the community and the introduction of lay visitors to police stations. In short, the recommendations outlined in
the report stressed the development of peaceful relations with minority ethnic communities based on fairness and tolerance.

However, wider debates which racialized crime as the problem
of black youth intensified and further riots between the police and

---

[7] Ideas about 'community policing' came into prominence in Britain as a response
to the decline in legitimacy of the police following the 1981 riots (Waddington
1999b; Reiner 2000a).

minority groups occurred in other major urban centres, including Toxteth, Moss Side, and Tottenham (Bowling and Phillips 2003). Wide levels of variation were noted in the way the new 'community policing' programmes were being implemented on the ground and the effectiveness of PACC meetings and introduction of lay visitors to police stations was likewise criticized (Brogden *et al* 1988).[8] More problematically, there was pervasive internal resistance towards minority ethnic officers by what remained to be a hegemonic white police culture. During the early nineties several officers brought high profile claims of racial discrimination against their employers—some of which revealed clear intolerance of female and gay officers (Holdaway 1996; McLaughlin 1996).

Despite these continuing problems in police culture, the legitimacy of the British police was deeply challenged by the 1981 disturbances and its resulting report. The report represented, for the first time, a formal condemnation on the character of racism and its influence on policing. More importantly, it generated a new way of thinking about and structuring policing provision in Britain (Reiner 2000*a*; Newburn 2003). But the report also represented, I contend, the early beginnings of a contemporary paradigm where policing and 'diversity' have become politicized. This paradigm has been augmented by another critical moment in policing.

Towards policing diversity

Political sensitivity around the policing of minority ethnic populations has further resonance in a second major report by Sir William Macpherson in 1999. The report followed a public inquiry examining the Metropolitan Police Service's investigation into the racist murder of black student, Stephen Lawrence, in South London during 1993. The Metropolitan Police Service was accused of conducting an investigation which was deeply flawed. Despite a private prosecution brought by the parents of the victim, all of the white perpetrators were acquitted of murder charges as a result of the botched police investigation.

The report on the police handling of the investigation and its wider implications for policing in Britain has been extensively debated and requires no detailed discussion here (McLaughlin and

---

[8] Most notably, that the meeting were atypical of local communities and that debate tended to centre only on trivial—as opposed to critical—policing issues.

Murji 1999; Marlow and Loveday 2000; Reiner 2000*a*; Bowling and Phillips 2003; Foster *et al* 2005; McLaughlin 2007*a*; Rowe 2007). Suffice to say the inquiry team found a multitude of failings at nearly every level of the organization. The problems were so severe that, for McLaughlin (2007*a*: 148), the report represented a 'public relations catastrophe' for the police. Yet unlike the earlier report by Scarman, the Macpherson Report (1999) found that the professional incompetence of the Metropolitan Police Service to properly investigate the murder of Stephen Lawrence owed much to 'institutional racism'—a concept defined in the following terms:

'Institutional racism' consists of the collective failure of an organisation to provide an appropriate professional service to people because of their colour, culture or ethnic origin. It can be seen or detected in processes, attitudes and behaviour which amount to discrimination through unwitting prejudice, ignorance, thoughtlessness, and racist stereotyping which disadvantage minority ethnic people (Macpherson 1999: 6.34).

Over seventy recommendations were made in the report, but the two that prompted the most immediate action held remarkable similarity to those proposed by Scarman; namely to recruit more minority ethnic officers and to improve community and race relations training (Cashmore 2002). There were, however, some important differences between the documents. The report placed vigorous pressure on police organizations to enhance the way information about racist crime becomes recorded and investigated, and it also created new disciplinary and complaints procedures. Racism was made a disciplinary offence, punishable by dismissal from the police. The rules surrounding stop and search were to be tightened and new accountability mechanisms introduced. Police forces were also brought within the ambit of the Race Relations (Amendment) Act 2000 and were required to adopt a multitude of anti-racist policies. The sheer number of recommendations emanating from the report rendered it the most comprehensive reform programme ever undertaken in British policing history (McLaughlin and Murji 1999).

  Since the publication of the report, police forces across Britain have introduced a wealth of documents and initiatives in the field of community and 'race' relations. As McLaughlin (2007*a*) observes, these have generally fallen into three broad areas. The first relates to the greater recruitment of personnel from minority backgrounds, but with a renewed emphasis on the retention and career progression of officers. The second area of police reform involves making diversity training a central aspect of police education, while the third focuses on a revision of operational policing policies and practices which could lead to discrimination against minority ethnic communities.

The report has been subjected to various criticisms, but it was the term institutional racism that generated the most debate—especially in the media—at the time of its publication (see McLaughlin and Murji 1999). Notwithstanding the extensive reform efforts, change within the police appears to be slow and uneven (see Foster *et al.* 2005) and other evidence suggests that the institutionalization of diversity is resented across police organizations. This was brought most forcefully into public consciousness in October 2003 when an undercover BBC investigation entitled *The Secret Policeman* exposed outrageous displays of racist behaviour amongst new recruits. As McLaughlin (2007*a*) points out, what is of significance here is that these were officers who had been recruited under the new context of concentrated reforms. In the immediate aftermath of the documentary, another flurry of activities to eradicate police racism and other forms of discrimination was initiated. Most notable was the establishment of an independent inquiry by the Commission for Racial Inquiry (Commission for Racial Equality 2005). The report made over 125 recommendations, including creating a new disciplinary offence of racial misconduct. However, it also expressed the concern that aspects of the diversity agenda could provoke 'a real potential for backlash, particularly among some white officers' (Commission for Racial Equality 2005: 95). Another programme called 'Undercover Copper' by *Dispatches* in 2006 further revealed the endurance of sexism and bigotry within the police.

Early indications suggest that expressions of discrimination have undergone transformation within the new terrain. As McLaughlin (2007*a*: 170) surmises, police organizations may be 'grappling with the problem of stealth racism'. The apparent resistance towards the institutionalization of diversity is clearly problematic, but there is no doubt that the Macpherson Report has had a major impact on the British policing landscape. It has brought the policing of minority ethnic communities to the national political forefront in a way previously unseen (Reiner 2000*a*; McLaughlin 2007*a*). It has been described as a 'landmark' and 'watershed' in policing, the consequences of which will 'reverberate for years to come' (McLaughlin and Murji 1999: 372). Finally, with its recognition of institutional racism the report carries enormous implications for all police forces across the Western world (Walklate 2000).

At least at the level of rhetoric, the police have since undergone momentous change in relation to the recognition of social and cultural diversity. Police organizations are under the scrutiny of the government—and media—and they have to be seen taking seriously questions of diversity. There is, now, an active pursuit of a Diversity Agenda by external official inspecting bodies and strict adherence to the new rules is important to career success. This is true not only for the rank and file but, also, for senior officers. The category of ethnic origin has been recast as a prime administrative indicator in documenting the composition and patterning of the workforce, and is also used for recording and monitoring the street level practices of officers (Long 2003). In other words, the police are under enormous pressure to manage 'race' and diversity in a new way (see also Holdaway 1997). We could add that this repositioning has been accompanied by an awakening amongst black and minority ethnic groups of their position as enduring targets of adversarial policing practices; where they now have a 'clear identity and consciousness of being discriminated against' (Reiner 2000a: 79).

The prominence placed on ethnicity has been extended to gender and sexuality. Of course the policing of women—principally as victims of physical and sexual crime—has its own troubled history (Dobash and Dobash 1980; Stanko 1985; Edwards 1989) but the political agenda towards women has experienced something of a resurgence in recent years (Walklate 2000; Hoyle 2000; Heidensohn 2003). By adopting a model of policing which directs constables to arrest the assaulting partner where there is evidence of an assault, police forces are taking a more proactive approach towards women as victims of domestic violence.[9] In similar vein specialist units to deal with homophobic and other 'hate' motivated crime have been established to improve the police response to crimes committed against gay, lesbian, and transsexual people.

---

[9] There has, however, been much debate about the success and appropriateness of mandatory arrest policies (see Hoyle and Sanders 2000).

The British policing terrain is, then, characterized by a new *politics of policing diversity* and this presents seminal challenges to the cultural ethos that has long underpinned the police identity. The repositioning of diversity is paramount for those who have previously found themselves inadequately served by policing by virtue of their cultural and gendered differences but, in my view, this paradigm overlooks another feature of the policing landscape which has equally important implications for police culture. Along with the greater political recognition of social and cultural diversity, the current field of policing is also characterized by widespread economic exclusion and division. This is a result of changes which have occurred in the political economy of Western capitalism and throws up new contingencies for crime and its control by the police. In particular, the changes have decisive consequences for the policing of a new 'police property' (Lee 1981).

Exclusionary Times

The image of the British police as an emblem of order and national pride has become eroded in recent decades (Reiner 1992*a*).[10] To be sure, the problematic relationship the police have with groups along distinctions of ethnicity, gender, and sexuality have added to this, but deeper social changes have provoked another major challenge:

While the majority participate, albeit very unevenly and insecurely, in unprecedented levels of consumption, a substantial and growing 'under-class' is permanently and hopelessly excluded. Certainly, with the political dominance of free-market economic policies there is no prospect at all of their incorporation into the general social order. In other words, the 'police property' group is far larger than ever before and more fundamentally alienated (Reiner 2000*a*: 216).

As I mentioned earlier, the punitive turn towards crime and crime control in public and political thinking has been exacerbated by a series of social, economic, and cultural upheavals. Prior to carving out the implications of these changes for police culture, it is necessary to explore this newly configured social field in more detail.

---

[10] See Loader and Mulcahy (2003) for an alternative perspective.

A new social configuration

Several commentators have discussed the radical changes which have occurred in the social, cultural, and economic order of society in recent decades. The differing accounts of the emergence of these changes have been accompanied with wide variation in the level of analysis—ranging from grand social theories (Dahrendorf 1985; Beck 1992; Giddens 1991; Taylor 1999; Young 1999; Bauman 2001) to empirical enquiries concerning the social and spatial consequences of such changes (Blackman 1997; Craine 1997; Williamson 1997; Wacquant 2000; Bourdieu *et al* 2002). These accounts differ to some extent, but they all agree that society is experiencing profound change. The social transformations are considered to be so intense that for Reiner (2000*a*: 199) they indicate 'a fundamental break in the trajectory of world development analogous in its scope to the rise of industrial capitalism some two centuries earlier'. Various concepts have been used to conceptualize this incisive reordering of society, and I do not wish to debate them here (for a discussion see, Crompton 2005: 218). Suffice to say in what follows I use the concepts of 'late modernity', 'postmodernity', and 'post-Fordism' interchangeably.

  The most common theme within debates about this new social order is the increasing economic exclusion experienced by large numbers of the population. That British society has become more fractured and unequal since the Second World War reveals something of a paradox. While the language of modernity emphasized equality of opportunity, economic prosperity, and democracy (Young 1999), the booming economic affluence characteristic of British society is not equally shared.[11] More people than ever live comfortably and participate in mass consumerism, but an increasing faction of the population experience chronic poverty and insecurity. Since 1979 the number of people living within the accepted definition of relative poverty has tripled, and currently stands at over 12 million (Toynbee 2003). Furthermore, as Taylor (1999) observes, the difference in income between the highest paid and the lowest paid is the largest it has been since records began in 1866. Drawing on research conducted by the Joseph Rowntree Foundation in 1995,

---

[11] I should note, however, that membership to the modernist project of 'inclusivity' (Young 1999) has not been equal for everyone (see Yar and Penna 2004).

Taylor also illustrates that globally there has been a complete shift in the distribution of wealth towards the richest populations of the world and away from the poorest sections. A number of phrases have been coined to reflect these new forms of social and economic division. Hutton (1995) has famously asserted that Britain is, now, a '30:30:40' society. While 40 per cent of the population are in stable employment, another 30 per cent are structurally insecure. Added to this, however, is another 30 per cent of the population who experience chronic unemployment or inadequate jobs and become marginalized through their poverty. This arrangement has also been termed the 'two-thirds society' (Dahrendorf 1985: 103) in which two thirds are *in* and one third is *out*—that is, excluded from citizenship and the prosperous economy.

For many, these qualitative and quantitative expressions of exclusion are a product of post-Fordism (Taylor 1999; Young 1999; Crowther 2000*a*: Wacquant 2000). While Fordist economic arrangements offered low male unemployment levels, job security, and a stable income, the post-Fordist culture of work is increasingly insecure. Characterized by technological advancement, globalization of capital and its resulting deindustrialization post-Fordist economies have resulted in a 'massive haemorrhaging of full time employment throughout the Western world' (Taylor 1999: 13).

High rates of unemployment, long periods of joblessness, and new insecure forms of work have emerged. As traditional sources of employment have disappeared, large sections of the workforce have become thrown on the scrapheap. There are distinct gendered dimensions to this. Young men have been badly affected by economic restructuring and are more likely to experience long term unemployment and its related social and material disadvantage (MacDonald 1997; McDowell 2003). Excluded from work and consumption Young (1999: 12) describes the following scenario:

Young men are bereft of social position and destiny . . . they are cast adrift; a discarded irrelevance locked in a situation of structural unemployment. They are barred from the racetrack of the meritocratic society yet remain glued to the television sets and media which alluringly portray the glittering prizes of a wealthy society.

Increasing never-employment (Reiner 1992*a*: 771) is the product of the transition towards the deregulated market place and has been exacerbated by privatization and the creation of 'flexible' labour markets. The themes of unemployment and poverty clearly find resonance across historical accounts of social stratification (Yar and Penna 2004), but the *new* aspects of inequality can be emphasized. For Dahrendorf (1985: 98), the inevitable joblessness characteristic of societies is termed the 'new unemployment'. Wacquant (2000: 107) similarly refers to the 'new regime of marginality' to describe the recent polarizations which have removed whole populations from the middle to bottom layers of the class structure, and the remaining inhabitants who occupy the lower strata have been termed the 'new lumpen' (Crowther 2000*b*: 136). The Marxist overtone of the latter draws our attention to the increasingly aggressive nature of capitalist economies.[12] It is important to note that these novel forms of unemployment and polarization are not a consequence of temporary economic trends, as Wacquant (2000: 107) warns:

> The advanced marginality . . . is not a residue from the past, as theories of deindustrialisation and skills or spatial mismatch have it but are, rather, a harbinger of the future.

These economic changes which characterize late modernity have been accompanied by key developments in the cultural domains of society. One of the most significant changes relates to what Young (1999: 4) identifies as the 'patterns of desire'. Consumption is at the centre of everyday life and increasingly represents the motivation for human action (see also Davis 1998; Taylor 1999; Bauman 2001). Contemporary inequalities are exacerbated by images of wealth, and living in poverty today is a very different experience than it was during the nineteenth century or the Great Depression of the 1930s. Dominated by unfettered free market economic policies and thinking, the prevailing 'market society' (Taylor 1999: 52) is a society in which '*everything* (from consumer goods to public goods, like health or education) is "for sale"'. A major consequence of this rampant consumerism is the elevation of self-interest, or individualism, over public interest (Hutton 1995; Young 1999; Reiner 2007).

The increasingly unstable nature of the social order has seminal ramifications for personal relationships. In addition to rising economic insecurity, the escalating cultural diversification of society has resulted in pervasive feelings of ontological insecurity (Giddens

---

[12] The concept of 'turbo-capitalism' (Reiner 2000*a*: 200) aptly describes the way in which capitalist thought and economy is infusing the everyday organization of society (see also Lawson 2006).

1991; Young 1999). As noted earlier, this sense of instability finds its expression in an increased risk consciousness and fear of crime and results in a more punitive outlook. But it also has a profound influence on perceptions of 'others' and 'otherness' and has adverse consequences for marginal groups, as Young (1999: vii) explains:

Social blame and recrimination ricochets throughout the social structure: single mothers, the underclass, blacks, new age travellers, junkies, crack-heads—the needle spins and points to some vulnerable section of the community to whom we can apportion blame and who can be demonised.

There has been a sharp rise in intolerance towards the poor and a decline in the motivation to integrate this group into society (see also Young 2003). Marginal groups invariably experience the brunt of formal control mechanisms, but they are also increasingly subjected to a range of informal control measures. In particular, the majority make attempts to declare the residuum as lacking in value (Young 1999; Sayer 2005). Of pivotal significance here is that the exclusion of the residuum becomes perpetuated through the institution of policing.

Policing the new residuum

The economic and cultural shifts which characterize late modern societies have resulted in a more unstable social world. As Reiner (2000b: 209) argues, the implications of this 'social earthquake' for crime and social control responses to it are profound. One principal manifestation of exclusion under late modern conditions is the extension of a structurally marginal 'underclass'. Although a great deal of debate surrounds the term, the notion of an underclass has value for understanding the policing of the new residuum (see also Crowther 2000b).[13]

The underclass refers to chronic unemployment and under employment; low educational attainment; dependency on welfare; intergenerational diffusion of poverty; a shared spatial location (including homelessness); and over involvement in patterns of victimization and the criminal justice system (ibid; Katz 1989;

[13] The concept essentially arose from the Right and came to the fore in Britain through the controversial writings of Charles Murray (see Murray 1996). However, the association of the term with the Right has arguably impeded research into the experiential realities of the 'underclass' and has likewise arrested a critical focus on processes of stigmatization (see also Bagguley and Mann 1992).

MacDonald 1997).[14] It is now academic orthodoxy that, in their work, the police deal overwhelmingly with the least powerful and marginal groups in society (Reiner 1997; Choongh 1998). These enduring targets of policing have been aptly identified as 'police property' which Lee (1981: 53) suggests are:

Any category of citizens who lack power in the major institutions of their society (institutions in the economy, polity, education, media, etc.) are liable to become police property . . . that is, categories of people over whom the police successfully exert superior power.

A defining characteristic of police property is that their control by the police is 'supported by an apparent social consensus to "let the police handle these people"' (ibid). What I want to emphasize is that the marginal underclass created in western societies are a new and extended guise of police property. Poor young men are prime inhabitants of this category and, because of their increasing unemployment, are propelled to live out more of their daily lives in public—and thus police—space. We could add that male unemployment has always been considered problematic following its perceived association with crime and disorder (Box 1994). Moreover, against the backdrop of their social and economic marginalization contemporary generations of young men struggle to assemble a masculine identity. Their arrested masculinity becomes evident in what Connell (1995: 77) calls 'protest masculinity'—that is, where populations of young men become implicated in certain types of street crime and experience adversarial contact with the police (see also Taylor and Jamieson 1997; Taylor 1999; McDowell 2003).

The proposition that the economically impoverished are the foremost targets of policing is not a novel one. As a visit to the historical literature would confirm, the poor have formed the enduring targets of police thinking and practices throughout the modern era. As Storch (1975) argues, the initial conception of the New Police was rooted in the changes in capitalist and economic relations. They were created to confront the 'undesirables' (prostitutes, homeless, unemployed, and illiterate) who occupied the streets and who threatened bourgeois order, bourgeois property, and bourgeois notions of respect and propriety (Cohen 1979; Brogden

---

[14] I should note that different individuals will experience differing levels of the above criterion depending on their age, ethnicity, gender, and so on.

1982; Brogden *et al* 1988; Jefferson 1993). This was made possible by changes in the economy which constructed a symbolic division between the 'rough' and 'respectable' classes. The police have always considered themselves as belonging to the latter and, in their work, differentiate between 'those they do things *for* and those they do things *to*' (Shearing 1981: 288; see also Ericson 1982). Routine patrol work was aimed to target areas associated with the poor, a pattern that was not pursued in the stable working class and affluent areas (Emsley 1996). It would not be entirely accurate to view the occupational preferences of the police as the only means though which the urban poor became controlled. Class bias in legislation—most notably the New Poor Law 1834, successive vagrancy acts, and the Contagious Diseases Act 1864—also structured police decision making. Public order law provided the primary enabling power to further control the 'roughs' who spent more time on the streets.

Police culture developed on the streets in nineteenth century Britain and was directly related to the broader structural changes that were taking place during this epoch. These changes ensured a practical focus on the poor, and have since carried forward into contemporary policing culture. As Choongh (1998) confirms, the control of the 'dross' remains pivotal to the police role. Policing is informed by a cognitive map of the population, which is distinguished across broad class lines:

A special conception of social class, mixed with an idea of conventional or proper behaviour . . . is just as important to the police officers as racial or ethnic groups. In this scale the 'respectable' working class and the suburban middle class stand highest while the 'underclass' of the poor and rootless . . . stand lowest (Smith and Gray 1985: 389).

But there are some new dynamics at work here. I think that the location of the residuum within police culture takes on *renewed* significance under conditions of late modernity. The police have become increasingly charged with the task of managing the symptoms of deeper social ruptures and are destined to control the human debris left by adverse social, cultural, and economic restructuring of society (Reiner 1992*a*). Moreover, the advent of private provision means that policing increasingly involves patrolling the residual areas of public space—a space to which the excluded 'underclass' are increasingly relegated. On the ground, officers find themselves guarding a social order which is divided between the dreadful enclosures of the poor and the defensible locales of the wealthy. The style of policing to which these two environments are subjected differs considerably:

Local policing of particular communities remain, but with sharp differences between service-style organisations in stable suburban areas, and 'watchman' bodies with the rump duties of the present police, keeping a lid on the underclass symbolic locations (ibid: 217).

External pressures to manage crime efficiently have only exacerbated this; as Reiner (2000*a*: xi) puts it, 'policing is under increasing pressure to have zero tolerance of the socially marginal and outsiders'. It is somewhat inevitable that the police's cultural knowledge (Chan 1997) will direct their practical attention towards those at the base of the social hierarchy.

The Retreat of Class in the Age of Recognition

The new market economy has aggravated distinctions of class and forms an integral feature of the policing landscape. Yet, despite the widening of economic inequality, matters of class are of declining interest in current social thought and political practice. Various reasons account for the current lack of interest in class. It may be due to its previous association with socialist discourse in which other axes of inequality were overlooked (Crompton 2005). Likewise, a complex blurring of boundaries between different classes means that 'class' has become both theoretically and empirically problematic in recent decades. The occlusion of class in prevailing political debates stems from New Labour's attempts to discard their 'Old' Labour image. Not wishing to alienate their middle England constituents, class has become something of a 'risky concept' (Sayer 2005: 12). Added to this is that the working class have been unable to construct an authentic political identity in recent years (Charlesworth 2000). As I have made clear, the industries on which class consciousness is built have become severely contested under post-Fordist economic arrangements. Moreover, the 'working class hero' of post-war Britain has been replaced by the stigmatized identities of young, unemployed men (McDowell 2003). Political rhetoric of Britain as a 'classless society' has undoubtedly contributed to the lack of debate about class inequality—but these discourses inevitably serve class interests because they undermine the reality of class disadvantage (Charlesworth 2000; see also Adonis and Pollard 1998).

However, one of the possible reasons for the decline of interest in class is the recent ascendance of identity politics. Greater political recognition of hitherto denounced identities is crucial because of their previous neglect, but a politics based on culture and difference has coincided with the depoliticization of class and poverty. Claims for recognition of group difference have diverted attention away from equally pressing issues of distributive inequality (Ray and Sayer 1999; Fraser 1997; Feldman 2002; Sayer 2005). The theoretical meeting point of this dilemma has concerned the relationship between the politics of recognition and the politics of distribution and, as Zurn (2005: 89) points out, the central question in this debate is 'can cultural misrecognition and economic maldistribution be fought simultaneously'?[15] In connecting the ostensibly separate dilemmas of recognition and redistribution, some authors have maintained that in addition to the problem of redistribution the economically impoverished are likewise bound up in the struggle for recognition. It is valuable, therefore, to explore how class and the inequality it generates in everyday lives has been conceptualized in recent thinking.

Normative dimensions of class

The turn away from class is peculiarly paradoxical given that it is happening at a time of accelerated economic division. Class is important not just because it affects material and economic security but, also, because it has the potential to thwart a person's life chances. Class position shapes how others value and respond to individuals and thereby affects feelings of self worth (Sayer 2005). In order to revitalize thinking in this area Sayer argues for an analysis of class that appreciates its 'moral significance'—that is, the usually unacknowledged, normative dimensions of class inequality. A limited number of other works have explored these moral aspects of class and, in so doing, have demonstrated that class is something that people live in

[15] While some have viewed economic inequality as the underlying problem, others have attempted to develop an integrative theoretical framework which is sensitive to the various issues concerning both economic and cultural justice—see, in particular, Fraser's (1997; 2000) 'bivalent' approach.

and experience through their bodies and minds. They show that in equal measure to ethnicity, gender and sexuality, class infuses daily experiences of the social world and has the potential to be a profound source of injury (Sennett and Cobb 1972; Charlesworth 2000; Bourdieu *et al* 2002).

Class is, then, a powerful exclusionary device that is played out in interactions across social fields. However, the widespread turn away from class is problematic because it allows 'class contempt' (Sayer 2005: 163) and other forms of symbolic domination to persist largely unobserved and unchallenged. For Sayer, class contempt 'like other kinds of "othering", ranges from visceral revulsion, disgust and sneering, through to the tendency not to see or hear others as people, to the subtlest form of aversion' (see also Skeggs 2004).

It is dislike for people and their behaviour by virtue of their class position. Class contempt can be 'felt up or down' (Sayer 2005: 164) but it refers mainly to the deep aversion felt towards the economically impoverished. Not necessarily expressed verbally, it can reveal itself through subtle and exaggerated facial expressions—'from the raising of the upper lip into a sneer' or 'from slightly grimaced smiles to aggressive sneers' (ibid). A potent force of 'othering', class contempt also works to maintain the ideological facade that the lower strata are lacking certain virtues the majority have, and as a result, reifies class relations. Class contempt also has a tangible dimension; it manifests itself through a person's response to visual and moral 'markers', including appearance and demeanour; accent and language; values; lifestyle and possessions; and actions. But what is paramount here is that these signifiers of class position serve as prompts for judgements of worth, and can colour the way people are perceived and treated. The injuries of class are to be found not only in economic disadvantage but, also, in experiences of class contempt and its ensuing symbolic domination. This latter point finds particular resonance in the study by Charlesworth (2000) which focuses on the personal testimony of people living in a milieu characterized by chronic poverty and processes of rapid deindustrialization. He argues that the poorest classes find themselves 'linguistically dispossessed' (ibid: 77) in describing their diminishing dignity, sense of alienation and domination. Lacking the resources necessary to represent and defend themselves against hegemony and symbolic domination, he warns that the poor are becoming the forgotten fatalities of late modernity.

It is important, finally, to explore another strand to the debate about class disadvantage in the context of identity politics. Class inequality is clearly experienced in gendered and racialized ways, but recent attention has been afforded to the exclusion of the white working class. As Haylett (2001) argues, while the move from political economy to culture has decentred class from discussions of social justice, it has also rendered the white poor as 'illegitimate subjects'.[16] Excluded from notions of multiculturalism and progress, this group are currently perceived as culturally burdensome and are uniformly subjected to a range of disparaging discourses. In such discourses, poor, young, white men stand forward as the embodiment of disorder and distaste.[17] A brief reflection on the whiteness of this group is important in understanding their denigration. Like any other skin 'colour' whiteness is a social construction (Frankenberg 1993). Frequently, it is assumed to be a category of privilege but such an assumption conceals the uneven socio-historical, economic, and political character of its ascription to particular groups of people. In nineteenth century Britain when racial purity was emphasized, the urban white poor were excluded from any such mark of privilege—they were, put simply, not white *enough* (Bonnett 1998). In the current project of multiculturalism when the accent is on cultural diversity and recognition, conversely, it would seem that the white poor are *too* white—they are 'offensively and embarrassingly white' (Haylett 2001: 355).

My purpose in this chapter has been to outline the revised context in which police culture is currently located. The themes of police culture are not divorced from the wider organizational and societal context; rather, they are generated and sustained by the nature of the world in which it operates (Reiner 2000*a*). Since the classic police culture studies the legal context of policing has changed as have political and public ambiance towards law and order. Police organizations are expected to manage the demands of greater diversity, but are simultaneously required to control the human debris left by the adverse reordering of society. In the remaining chapters of this book I draw upon ethnographic fieldwork to explore how, exactly, the

---

[16] See also *The Economist* (26.10.06).
[17] As McDowell (2003: 63) notes, there is a range of disparaging representations of this group in current popular discourses. She argues that such representations would 'cause outcry' if used to refer to members of minority ethnic group or women (see also Charlesworth 2000; Haywood and Yar 2006; Harris 2007).

inner life of policing has been disturbed by these broader currents of change. Before doing so, it is necessary to provide an outline of the research context and explain the methodology I employed in revisiting the occupational value systems and practices of the police.

Revisiting Police Culture

The research underpinning the ensuing chapters was conducted in Northshire Police Force, a somewhat provincial constabulary located in England. The Force is responsible for serving just over 1 million people. The county is relatively diverse in terms of race and ethnicity. According to official data, the number of people from minority ethnic backgrounds residing in the Northshire policing area is a little over 30,000. Concentrated predominantly in the densely populated towns of the north, this figure mainly comprises those of Pakistani, Indian, and Black Caribbean ethnic origin. In addition to employing nearly 1,500 police support personnel, the Force has over 2,000 sworn officers and covers a mixture of rural and urban geographical terrains.

In recent years, Northshire Police has embarked on a conscious enterprise to produce structural and cultural transformation. The impetus for change was generated primarily from within the organization when a new Chief Constable and almost entirely new group of senior officers arrived in the Force during the mid 1990s. Numerous changes were made to the organizational structure, but one of the most substantial was the reduction in the number of territorial divisions from ten to four. Commanded by an Inspector, each division became further divided into Local Policing Units (LPU). This was accompanied, in turn, by the creation of Community Action Teams (CAT) and Incident Management Units (IMU). The latter are designed to manage those incidents requiring an immediate response or ones within short timescales, while the former are involved in community work. Each LPU also houses a specialist unit which deals with particular forms of crime, such as prostitution for example.

Of greater significance is Northshire Police's involvement in a top-down drive to produce cultural change. The change programme was aimed primarily at improving the working conditions of personnel inside the organization, and the delivery of an effective and equitable service to the various publics outside the organization. The reform programme incorporated a range of policies and initiatives, but some of the more notable efforts included enhancing the recruitment and career progression of officers from minority backgrounds; improving the diversity training; establishing support associations organized around ethnicity, gender, and sexuality; and the official interdiction of discriminatory language and conduct. Externally, the endeavours to transform the organizational culture focused on improving the service delivery to minority ethnic communities and other cultural and gendered identities. The changes introduced to enhance the way officers relate to their publics were also supported by a broader move towards community policing.

The fieldwork began in March 2004 and ended over eighteen months later in October 2005. During this time I accompanied rank and file officers from a range of shifts and units as they went about their ordinary duties on and off the streets.[18] The fieldwork took place in two contrasting LPUs across the Northshire Police area, with nine months being spent in each site. The sites were chosen in order to access a range of policing environments with respect to local social, economic, and crime dynamics. The first of these was Northville LPU, which is situated in the Northern policing division. Its patch covers an urban geographical terrain which is densely populated, and home to various minority ethnic communities. Along with other urban centres, this landscape was characterized by a high level of social and economic deprivation. In some contrast, the second site was Southville LPU, which is situated in the South of the county. The LPU covers many of the affluent provinces of South Northshire, and is responsible for policing a large and predominantly rural geographical terrain. I would add that Southville provides a valuable opportunity to examine the occupational culture of officers working within a rural context. With some notable exceptions (Cain 1973; Young 1993), research and reflection on rural policing culture remains largely unexplored in Britain.

Although I mainly observed IMU and CAT officers, I also accompanied those from specialist units, including the Prostitution

---

[18] IMU shifts operated at the following times: 'earlies' (7am to 4pm); 'lates' (3pm to 12am); and 'nights' (10pm to 7am). There were some exceptions to this. For example, if a late shift fell on a weekend, a number of officers (on a rotation basis) were required to work a 'supernoon' stint, which ran from 4pm until 3am. CAT officers also worked a nine-hour shift but, generally speaking, began work no earlier than 8am and finished no later than 11pm.

Unit; the Football Management Unit; the Proactive Team; and the Rural Crime Unit. Throughout the research, I participated in an array of routine policing activity. These included observations of organized drug raids; the running of custody suites; formal interviews between the police and suspects; and occasionally tasking and coordinating meetings between LPU Commanders and their superiors. I attended football matches with officers involved in suppressing football violence; went to court with officers who were giving evidence against defendants; and once completed a two day rural policing course. For the most part, however, I accompanied uniformed officers as they went about the daily business of performing police work.

These observations form the backbone of the study that follows, but are supplemented with a series of audio-recorded group discussions and interviews with over 60 officers. Although some of these comprized those in supervisory and senior positions, the vast majority of participants were the rank and file. My aim during the interviews was to capture officers' perceptions of their job and immediate policing environment, as well as their understandings of change agendas. In order to explore the 'success' of reform initiatives on the internal culture, I also conducted biographical interviews with a sample of female, minority ethnic, gay, and lesbian officers. Finally, in assessing the endeavours made to reform the organizational culture, I analysed various internal Force documents relating to matters of diversity and equality.

A more reflexive discussion about my ethnographic experience with the police can be found in the back pages of this book. Before sharing these observations of policing culture a caveat is required: in reproducing the fieldnote and interview extracts for the purposes of this book I have been concerned to preserve the anonymity of Northshire Police Force and its personnel. As such, all of the names of individual officers are fictional and some details of the research environment have likewise been altered.

PART II

Police Culture in Motion

3

Dominant Culture Interrupted

It has long been recognized that the informal ideologies which comprise the police identity have the potential to exert considerable influence over the working environment of police organizations, and impinge on relations between officers from different social backgrounds. However, the transposition of identity politics onto the policing terrain implies that the stability of police culture can no longer remain taken for granted. Not least in the wake of the Macpherson Report (1999), British police forces are under increasing pressure to understand themselves as sites of diversity.

This chapter tracks the ways in which Northshire Police developed policies aimed at managing the contemporary demands of greater diversity. It explores how the extension of recognition for minority groups has shaped the interior culture through examining the ways in which such efforts resonate within the occupational ideologies of officers working inside the organization. In so doing, two broad and opposing perspectives on the working environment are presented. The first is characterized by resistance and resentment towards the institutionalization of diversity, and is articulated principally by white, heterosexual, male officers. A contrasting standpoint, held by female, minority ethnic, and gay and lesbian officers, reveals the persistence of a dominant white, heterosexist, male culture. In order to understand this tension, I argue that the narratives of decline and discontent articulated by the adherents of the former operate to subordinate the spaces of representation for emerging identities and aim to preserve an increasingly endangered culture. In juxtaposing these two positions, my analysis does not seek to homogenize the perspectives and experiences of officers. I acknowledge the need to reflect nuances within police culture (see Foster 2003), but am concerned primarily to emphasize the dominant narratives that arose in police responses. By exploring this discursive environment I aim to offer a multidimensional understanding of an organization that has consciously attempted to transform its internal culture, and advance an account of how the prevailing accent on diversity is reconfiguring traditionally inscribed cultural expressions of the police. It is first necessary to provide a picture of the character of the organization prior to the reform effort.

The 'Old Regime'

The shift in Northshire Police's approach to diversity coincided with the arrival of a new Chief Constable and almost entirely new team of senior officers in the mid 1990s. At this time, the character of the organization was considered by one such officer to be 'a deeply worrying, conservative organization—almost the police force that time had forgotten'. Externally, the idea of community and race relations was focused around a single department and was marginal to the philosophical and operational priorities of the Force. Internally, the dominant composition of the organization centred almost exclusively on the white, heterosexual, male officer. Very few women, members of minority ethnic groups, or (openly) gay and lesbian officers, occupied posts—and particularly supervisory positions. Furthermore, biographical interviews conducted with a sample of minority officers revealed that their low statistical presence had devastating cultural repercussions. For most, their experiences of discrimination under what they termed 'the old regime' were unequivocally a consequence of their social difference amidst the dominance of a white, heterosexist, male culture. The principal themes in respect to this are presented below.

Standing out

Because of the low presence of marginal groups within the organization, many female, minority ethnic, and gay and lesbian officers felt they were highly visible and easily marked out. One black officer expressed her sense of vulnerability in the following terms:

I always used to hate walking into the canteen, because when I walked in there, I felt all eyes are on me. And it was such an uncomfortable, oppressive feeling. [. . .] I stood out—everyone knew who I was.

Feelings of visibility also extended to other minority officers, especially those who had been successful in gaining promotion or obtaining a place in a specialist unit:

In the late 1980s, I got promoted. I went on the mounted branch, and later firearms. My gender there was always an issue. I knew that there weren't any female sergeants on the mounted branch—nationally even—and I stuck out like a sore thumb. Even on the firearms I was always being looked at, examined (Female Inspector).

A pivotal aspect of this hyper-visibility was the associated feeling that the work undertaken was open to exaggerated scrutiny by colleagues. Many respondents described having to 'prove themselves' in order to acquire acceptance by their shift or unit. Female officers have routinely been perceived by their male counterparts as physically and emotionally weak (Young 1991; Heidensohn 1992) and have traditionally defined their occupational role as either *police*women or police*women* (Martin 1980). As the same officer recollects:

I always had a choice to use the weapon the men use, or a smaller one. I couldn't ever go for the smaller weapon because I felt my credibility was on the line. I couldn't go for anything that made me look less capable than a man.

This heightened sense of scrutiny was most profoundly experienced by gay officers who recalled occasions where they were met with suspicion, and exclusion, until they demonstrated their masculine traits—namely through showing willingness to 'back up' fellow officers in incidents or uncomfortably adopting the heterosexist and macho culture of their colleagues (see also Burke 1993; Miller *et al* 2003). One gay officer described how for three years he invented a 'dual life', which included a girlfriend, in order to conform with the prevailing heterosexual culture.

Individualized experiences

Minority officers were the prime objects of overtly derogatory comments and discriminatory behaviour. Each respondent, sometimes painfully, recalled numerous occasions where they had been targeted by colleagues and supervisors because of their ethnicity, gender, or sexuality. Homosexual officers experienced intense forms of exclusion, as the following testimony demonstrates:

I had a lot of comments and homophobic behaviour directed against me personally. When I first joined and when in the firearms. And that was particularly difficult for me in that it was a job I really loved, wanted to stay. But it was a very difficult environment to stay in, very machoistic, particularly male dominated, heterosexual male dominated. And it was obvious what difficulties I was going to face really. I had a new uniform box through with a new uniform, and you would have things written across the box, homophobic things. [. . .] And things you would find in your locker, girly magazines or KY Jelly [lubricant], and my address details would have things written all over it (Gay Police Sergeant).

Other recollections of the internal environment revolved around instances of physical and sexual harassment. These manifestations of discrimination have long been experienced by women working within police organizations, and reflect the patriarchal sentiments of police culture (Fielding 1994; Brown 1998). The following account provides another illustration of these early patterns of discrimination:

There was lots of harassment on there too—physical assault but with a sexual motive. You deal with it in different ways. The first person who assaulted me, I hit. A senior officer, he took issue with me. And it was basically, yes I have hit you—but what have you done? I was married, I was a new female sergeant, and I'll tell my husband, and he'll flatten you. That was my way of dealing with it. I just didn't feel like I could report it (Female Chief Inspector).

Minority ethnic officers similarly worked in an environment where highly racialized terms were pervasive and tolerated:

We went to a university complex to attend a reported smashed window. When speaking to the caretaker my colleague said, 'Would you be able to give a description of the people who did it'? The caretaker said, 'No', and my colleague said, 'Well, would you be able to tell if they were Pakis or not'? And that was in my probation. I was coming up against those kinds of barriers and attitudes in my probation, so I knew it was going to be a real rough ride for me (Asian Police Constable).

After working in a station where the terms 'nigger' and 'wog' were frequently employed by officers throughout the rank structure, another black officer described how she was physically assaulted by her white male colleagues. Although the incident was presented as an 'initiation ceremony', for her, the assault was a consequence of her ethnicity. Ironically though, she does suggest that her gender may have softened the levels of racism she experienced:

I mean I saw what my male black colleague went through, mine was slightly different. There was a hatred for him, a black male officer. It was really like 'how dare someone like *you* come into this white organisation'? He had a very difficult time as a black officer. He was treated very badly.

'Troublemakers'

Overt verbal and physical discrimination were routinely experienced by minority officers, yet all respondents described the mindset of the organization as being one in which discriminatory behaviour 'simply did not exist'. Upon reporting their experiences to supervisors, many described how they were merely turned away or brushed aside. Frequently, officers who did complain were considered 'troublemakers' and physically moved to another shift—and in some instances another station. This point was especially salient in the experiences of one female Asian officer. After complaining about ongoing racism and sexism, she describes the following:

After I put a complaint in I got moved. *I* got moved! And then when the complaint was supposedly investigated, I wasn't told of the outcome or anything. I felt now that I had a label of my forehead saying 'troublemaker'. So when I was moved to Old Town it was like 'Oh! So she's the one who made a complaint.' I felt ostracised and singled out, and I feel that the label has followed me ever since.

Another incident was recounted by a lesbian officer who explained how she was moved to an all male shift in order to prevent her from working alongside female colleagues. For some minority ethnic officers, their discrimination was only exacerbated by experiences of intolerance at the hands of the public. Some black officers recalled how they were regularly called 'Bounty Bar' and 'Coconut' by minority ethnic populations.[1] On the occasions where minority ethnic officers experienced overt racial abuse by white members of the public, it was felt that colleagues failed to support them:

I have been in incidents where I have been racially abused, spat at, ignored, and there has been up to ten of my colleagues who haven't even battered an eyelid. It's like 'Well. It's ok to be racially abused because I should expect it because of the colour of my skin.' Nobody, my white colleagues has ever intervened, understood (Black Police Constable).

I have provided only a snapshot of some of the major themes raised by officers in discussing the discrimination they faced. For many,

---

[1] This terminology was explained to me by one minority ethnic officer, 'It's basically saying you have black skin colour on the outside, but you are white on the inside'.

these experiences of discrimination were a result of their social difference amidst the dominance of a white, heterosexist, male organization and the indifferent character of the Force at this time. The unabashed displays of discrimination have their foundations in the structural and cultural character of Northshire Police at this time. Although the impetus for change was generated by the new senior management team upon their arrival, the publication of the Macpherson Report in 1999 fundamentally augmented the reform initiative. In the contemporary policing context matters of diversity have, at least at the level of rhetoric, become integral to the Force.

Changing Culture

In recent years Northshire Police has embarked on a top-down reform effort, aimed primarily at improving both the working conditions of personnel inside the organization and the delivery of an effective and equitable service to the various publics outside the organization. In the first instance, senior officers embarked on constructing a new Force Diversity Strategy. The range of initiatives introduced under this rubric has generally fallen into three areas. The first concerns a review of the organization's guiding principles, and is demonstrated through a multitude of policy documents and statements. The second involves a commitment to diversifying the composition of the workforce, whilst ensuring that diversity training is made a compulsory part of police education. The final area of reform involved a renewed emphasis on improving the service that is delivered to members of the public within the Force area. The core components of the change programme are presented below.

Structures for diversity and guiding principles

In the immediate aftermath of the Macpherson report, A Task Group for Diversity was set up by the Chief Constable in order to approve, and ensure implementation of, initiatives relating to diversity. Bringing together senior officers from Northshire Police and representatives from the racial equality council and minority ethnic community, the remit of the group was to identify areas and implement actions for improving the service and career opportunity for members of minority groups. A Cultures Subgroup was also established to examine the implications of the Macpherson Inquiry for the Force, and comprised senior members from the police, community organizations, and academics. What is significant here is that the conscious establishment of the subgroup demonstrates that police culture was considered problematic by senior officers *themselves*, and that they were prepared to open up their organization for scrutiny. In addition, a new Diversity Structure was put in place to ensure that 'race and diversity issues are kept as a priority'. Within this, each territorial division were required to set up Divisional Diversity Panels. Managed by a senior command team member, the sphere of activity of each panel was to discuss and give practical effect to local diversity issues. However, the establishment of internal support associations organized around ethnicity, gender, and sexuality arguably symbolizes *the* foremost change to the arrangements for mainstreaming diversity. Launched in 2000, the Multicultural Police Network (MPN), the Female Support Association (FSA) and the Lesbian and Gay Police Group (LGPG) represent the main associations within the organization.[2] Along with providing support for their members, the stated aims of the associations are: to enhance knowledge and educate the police service about diversity matters; to advocate reform within the organization; and consult on Force policies and documents.

The integration of diversity into the philosophical and operational character of the Force is further demonstrated in relation to various documents and policy statements. Successive Race Equality Schemes specify Force and local police authority plans for meeting the requirements placed upon them by the Race Relations (Amendment) Act 2000, and accordingly define the organizational vision with respect to diversity. Internally, the scheme sets out the nature of its commitment to diversity through the application of its Equal Opportunities Policy:

Northshire Police is committed to being an equal opportunities employer and to the creation of a working environment free from any discrimination and harassment, particularly on the basis of sex, gender reassignment, race, colour, nationality, ethnic or national background, disability,

---

[2] The groups are local versions of national staff police associations including: the National Black Police Association (NBPA), British Association for Women in Policing (BAWP), and the Lesbian and Gay Police Association (LAGPA) respectively.

sexual orientation, or religion. We will always strive to have a culture where everyone is valued, and where differences are welcomed.

An Equality of Service policy statement is then provided in relation to the delivery of policing to the various populations that make up the county:

Northshire Police is firmly committed to ensuring that no members of the public will be treated less favourably because of their colour, race, nationality or ethnic background, sexuality, gender or disability.

The principles underpinning these two statements have been further developed into an Anti-Discrimination Code of Practice which all officers and staff are required to sign up to. A number of expectations are set out in the code, but all personnel are particularly required to

- treat all colleagues and members of the public appropriately, fairly and without discrimination;
- recognize that the way to treat people fairly and without discrimination is not to treat everyone as the same, but to recognize and respect diversity in order to determine appropriate need;
- vigorously challenge racist, sexist, and homophobic language and behaviour;
- understand that a person can be subjected to discrimination and harassment on the basis of their race, gender, religious, or political beliefs, disability, age, and sexual orientation;
- treat all those with whom they come into contact with dignity and respect.

The explicit official interdiction of discriminatory conduct became a prime policy focus. Expressions of racism were especially deplored, and a strong disciplinary line taken against any such slurs. These new philosophies have been supported, moreover, by various practical efforts to promote diversity within and beyond the organization.

Enhanced recruitment, progression, and training

A commitment to diversifying the composition of the workforce and ensuring the career progression of minority officers was placed high on the organizational agenda. In working towards a representative police force, a set of recruitment objectives were established. A commitment to recruit more women and ethnic minorities was particularly outlined, and the Force embarked on high profile recruitment campaigns to increase the number of applicants from minority backgrounds.[3] A Proactive Recruitment Officer was appointed to target recruitment from within local minority ethnic communities, and new mandatory ethnic classifications were introduced to monitor all aspects of employment—including applications for employment and promotion and information on those who leave the Force. Flexible working practices were similarly introduced to encourage career longevity and progression, particularly for female officers.

Within recent years, there has been a gradual rise in the number of female and minority ethnic officers in Northshire, some of whom have progressed to occupy supervisory positions. According to an internal Diversity Monitoring Report, there are currently almost 40 sworn police officers from minority ethnic backgrounds within the organization, some of whom have progressed to occupy supervisory positions. Women police now constitute almost a quarter of the workforce at around 500, and there has been an unprecedented rise in the number of female sergeants, inspectors, and superintendents. From a demographic viewpoint, however, minority ethnic and female staff continue to be overshadowed by the dominant composition of the organization; out of nearly 2,300 sworn officers, over 1,800 are white, heterosexual, males. I should emphasize that these figures were borne out during the observations where I overwhelmingly accompanied white, heterosexual, male officers—heterosexual in so far as I did not meet any officers in the two research sites who were *openly* gay. Due to their low numbers in Northville and Southville, I only occasionally had the opportunity to accompany female officers and I was never able to go out with officers from a minority ethnic background. In some contrast, processes of civilianization appears to have contributed to a greater presence of females working inside the organization; out of nearly 1,100 support staff just over 600 work in roles, ranging from staffing enquiry desks and administration support to dispatch control and intelligence analysis. In addition, out of the 55 Police Community Support Officers (PCSO) working for the Force, over

---

[3] Most notably, through advertisements in the local press and the use of recruitment exhibitions to better attract minority ethnic recruits.

30 are female.[4] The picture is less healthy in relation to minority ethnic personnel, where 8 work in support roles and similar numbers are PCSOs.[5]

Finally, attempts were made to better educate officers on the cultural and racial backgrounds of heterogeneous populations. Diversity training was made a mandatory part of police education, and 2004 saw the creation of a new Police Race and Diversity Learning and Development Programme. With a focus on matters such as the Sex Discrimination Act 1975, the Race Relations Act 1976, the Stephen Lawrence Inquiry, and *The Secret Policeman*, prominence is placed on 'recognizing and respecting diversity'.

Improving service delivery to minority groups

In line with the Equality of Service policy statement described earlier, the revision of operational policing policies and practices assumed a prominent place on the reform agenda.

Closer consultation with minority groups and community policing

In the wake of the Macpherson Report, Northshire Police attempted to establish closer consultation with minority groups. The Task Group for Diversity led by the Chief Constable actively sought to increase liaison with several local interest groups, including representatives from the racial equality council and other locally based groups concerned with other forms of hate crime and domestic violence.

Attempts to transform the way policing organizations relate to their public constituents were supported by a general move towards 'community policing'. Community policing, as Tilley (2003: 315) reminds us, stresses 'policing *with* and *for* the community, rather than policing *of* the community' (see also Fielding 1995; Brogden 1999). The following *Quality of Service* declaration demonstrates the current policing style in Northshire:

Northshire Police and Police Authority are committed to delivering a community based policing style characterised by high quality services focused

[4] This new variant of the 'police family' are support (civilian) staff and are becoming an increasing fixture of contemporary policing provision (Crawford 2003). Broadly speaking, they have limited powers and deal primarily with trivial 'antisocial' behaviour.

[5] But I would draw attention here to what some have flagged as the risks of recruiting mainly women and minority ethnic police staff into the jobs which have lower pay, conditions, and status (see HMIC 2004: 12).

on priorities identified through systematic consultation, engagement with communities and responsiveness to customer need.

Underpinning this is the idea that members of the public should be treated as though they are users of and stakeholders in a public service—and central to this has been the redefinition of the public as police 'customers' (see Walters 2000). To support this style of policing Community Action Teams (CAT) were created to work alongside Incident Management Units (IMU). While the latter are designed to manage those incidents that require an immediate response or ones within short timescales, the former are involved primarily in community work. As noted, to supplement this reassurance policing endeavour, the Force also recruited Police Community Support Officers (PCSO).

The revision of operational policing policies which could have an adverse bearing on minority ethnic communities was elevated as a pressing concern. In response to the recommendations of the Macpherson Report, mandatory ethnic monitoring processes in stop and search encounters were adopted. In order to meet the challenges of policing a multi-ethnic society, information about rights and entitlements in over 30 languages were held in custody suites, and interpreters were employed to assist with police interviewing of suspects, victims, and witnesses.

A new approach towards victimization

A concerted 'proactive approach' towards minority groups as victims of crime was also adopted. The improved recording, investigation, and prosecution of hate crime was particularly emphasized.[6] Hate crime officers are now diffused throughout the organization and are responsible for five key areas of crime: racist, religious, homophobic, transphobic, and disability.

A revised policing strategy towards female victimization was another way the Force assembled questions of diversity to new policing agendas. The adoption of examination suites for victims of rape and sexual assault were accompanied by improved training for officers. Several mechanisms were also established to support victims of domestic violence. In line with other British police forces, Northshire Police adopted a model of policing domestic violence which directs officers to arrest the assaulting partner

---

[6] See Dixon and Gadd (2006) for a broader discussion of the concept.

where there is evidence of an assault (see Heidensohn 2003). These endeavours have been supplemented by a new domestic violence incident form called DVIR.[7] The log requires officers to gather relevant evidence and intelligence on the perpetrators of domestic violence, and enables the Force to monitor and target offenders more closely. By following the prompts in DVIR officers are able to make an early 'risk assessment' and, if necessary, a 'tailored safety plan' for the victim. Each division has also introduced a Domestic Violence Liaison Officer and, as noted earlier, the Force consults with local interest groups in this area.

Disseminating the New Organizational Ethos

Silverman (2001) suggests that the spatial arrangements of organizations are an important indicator of their intentions, priorities, and overall character (see also Hallett 2003). The dissemination of the Diversity Strategy was communicated internally and relied on a number of organizational props. Diversity-related noticeboards, e-mails, general briefings, and memorandums were employed. It was particularly interesting to note how architecture was used as a means of conveying the message: from the use of posters promoting the 'celebration of cultural difference' through to messages officially abhorring discrimination being printed on Force mouse mats and coffee cups. These subtle measures pertaining to cultural difference aptly capture the ways in which the formal face of the organization has become saturated with notions of diversity and its recognition.

Although local in its implementation, the change programme instituted in Northshire emulates the new diversity culture characteristic of the broader policing landscape. The promotion of respectful interactions within increasingly diverse contexts lies at the core of this endeavour. However, in what ways do those who inhabit the traditional police culture perceive the new realities? And how does being perceived as the embodiment of the diversity terrain shape the experiences of minority officers? What emerges, in attending to these enquiries, are two broadly opposing standpoints on the working environment.

---

[7] In the case of an arrest, officers are required to complete a Domestic Violence Investigation Record. If officers make no arrest, a similar form entitled the Domestic Violence Intelligence Record is then completed.

Narratives of Decline and Discontent

During the course of the fieldwork, it soon became apparent that a recalcitrant perspective has emerged from white, heterosexual, male officers towards the new realities. The revised emphasis on diversity was considered excessive and unwarranted. On certain aspects, it was vehemently resisted and resented.

Demise of the job

A clear awareness of the official hard-line against discrimination permeated the organization and, in line with the study by Foster *et al* (2005), one of the striking features of the research was the broad *absence* of overt racist language among officers. This reflects an important change, both in relation to the ostentatiously racist talk encountered by minority officers under the 'old regime' and previous studies (Smith and Gray 1985).[8] Yet the absence of discriminatory language is a consequence of a heightened awareness of the disciplinary line being taken against such slurs, and is not reflective of a genuine change in assumptions and understanding of issues of discrimination. As the following set of comments from Northville demonstrate:

Collin: Nowadays, you have to be so careful with what you say . . .
            [murmurs of agreement]

Tim: You'd be out of a job . . .

Collin: It's political correctness. It's all gone, it has gone mad.

Martin: You are taught . . . it's like half caste and gypsy, you can't even say them anymore. [Sarcastically] Now it's 'mixed heritage' and 'itinerant'. The words they use is like . . .

Tim: Now you can't even say 'nitty gritty' because it refers to the black slaves at the bottom of the slave boats or something. But it's daft.

Neil: It's like, I was on the air [the radio] the other week and I was trying to say mental asylum. I stopped myself and started stuttering. I couldn't think of the correct word . . .

Susan: [Laughing] The funny farm, fruitcake—nut house!

Neil: Yeah! But I just couldn't think of what the politically correct word was.

Group discussion

[8] See Fitzgerald *et al* (2002) who, in replicating the classic study by Smith and Gray (1985), also found a marked decline in the use of overt racist language.

The current organizational emphasis on identifying and challenging discriminatory words has required officers to manage their daily narratives in a way previously unseen. This is to be achieved principally through learning which words and phrases are censured, and which ones are to be appropriately used in relation to those groups given prominence in the current climate of diversity. However, as the extract shows, officers may change their everyday parlance to avoid any potential disciplinary repercussions, but the repositioning of anti-discriminatory language is considered excessive and vacuous.

The general absence of overt discriminatory language indicates a marked change in police culture, but officers repeatedly complained about what they saw as excessive 'political correctness'— that is, a perceived robust governmental and organizational attempt to restrict or change everyday attitudes and behaviour. A principal objection was that the organizational ambience had intruded on the immediate environment in that seemingly harmless remarks could now be interpreted as discriminatory by 'touchy' colleagues (see also Foster *et al* 2005). In managing this, officers developed spaces which allowed them to engage in behaviours considered potentially ominous in the revised terrain:

Andrew: Now, there is always this constant demand. We are a PC [politically correct] Force now. . .

Simon: You do. You have to be so politically correct and everything else.

Andrew: But within the confines of four walls, you are four or five people that can get on and have a laugh without offending people.

Simon: That is sometimes more important because you need to be able to vent steam somewhere. You can't do it in public, you can't take it home with you. . .

Andrew: You can get it out in the open here in a safe environment. We all have confidence and trust in one another. It's important to have that bond as a team.

Group discussion—Southville

As I explore below, the emergence of what I would term *white space*—that is, spaces where the white majority feel comfortable enough to resist and subvert aspects of the diversity agenda— finds resonance with comments espoused by minority officers who argued that the performance and execution of discrimination has undergone transformation in the wake of the Diversity Strategy.

At the same time, officers were anxious about being declared 'racist' by the organization (see also Foster *et al* 2005) and subsequently had accusations of racism at the forefronts of their minds. The following interview with a white male police sergeant in Southville reveals the sensitive nature of this:

Bethan: It is often said that Britain is a multicultural and diverse society. Do you think that has affected the way you police? Perhaps you could talk around your own experiences, locally?

Stephen: I can honestly say that I don't know a racist officer, sexist officer. Yes jokes are cracked—the same as anywhere jokes are cracked—but I don't know anyone who discriminates against anyone. And I am saying that honestly. I know this interview is supposed to be anonymous, but I honestly don't know a racist officer.

This extract, and others like it, demonstrates Stephen's anxiety when the words 'diversity' and 'multicultural' are invoked. Upon hearing the terms, he immediately associates them with the topic of police racism. This extract offers an indication of what some officers understand by the term diversity, but more importantly what the *implications* of diversity are. As the extract makes clear, the issue of diversity is firmly associated with becoming accused of being racist.

Most officers believed that the police service in general is viewed negatively by the public for their 'race relations'. For many, damaging portrayals of the police in the (national and local) media were primarily to blame for constructing an image of endemic police racism. It was considered largely unjust to label the police as racist, and many officers adopted the bad apple theory of police racism. Much as in the research conducted by Foster *et al* (2005), the notion of 'institutional racism' aroused considerable resentment:

Robert: It annoys me. Institutional racism may be in the Met, but it ain't here [murmurs of agreement] . . .

Warren: They have made a mess of their own backs down there . . .

Robert: In my dealings with blacks. When I was in the Westcity Force [*large police force covering a large multi-ethnic terrain*] we had a place we called 'Little India', because it is predominantly Indian. And I have dealt with officers who you would probably say had a racist element. But they dealt with them as fairly as anybody else. So when the Force says to me about 'institutional racism', and the blacks pick up on it, it has made our job 10 times worse because you are coming from a point of defending

> everything you do. I'm not racist, I'm just trying to do my job. It has become such a political bloody nightmare. There is nobody here openly racist. If London, that's London.

James: It's crap . . .

Warren: It's all down to political correctness at the end of the day. It all boils down to that the world has gone crazy. The law has turned on us [. . .]

Robert: We've had our teeth taken away from us. Because of all this, the police are having to walk an invisible tightrope.

Southville

This extract underlines another central theme regarding the way in which minority ethnic members of the public are viewed within the contemporary policing climate. It was widely claimed that minority ethnic people, because of their heightened political status, deliberately used their ethnicity in order to neutralize the effects of routine policing—a discourse, I argue, mobilized to reinforce the idea that minority groups are problematic. The Macpherson Report was considered to be the driving force behind the new climate of police critique (see also Foster *et al* 2005). At the extreme end of the spectrum, officers articulated robust resentment towards the Stephen Lawrence Inquiry, with some suggesting that Stephen Lawrence's parents had exploited his death in order to benefit, both generally and financially. Somewhat disturbingly such narratives are reminiscent of sentiments made in *The Secret Policeman* (see McLaughlin 2007a: 160). During one interview, a white male sergeant in Southville even made the following false allegation:

> What people don't say is that Stephen Lawrence, which all this has come out of, that Stephen Lawrence was up for attempted rape or rape. He was up on bail for it. [Sarcastically] let's forget about that charge.[9] (September 2005)

It would be inaccurate though to suggest that the Stephen Lawrence Inquiry had significantly affected officers in Northshire. Rather, it was often viewed as relevant to those larger forces which are responsible for policing large multi-ethnic populations. Nevertheless, the inquiry and its resulting report, was

---

[9] According to an article in *The Guardian* (17/09/99), Dwayne Brooks (Stephen Lawrence's friend) has been implicated in a rape case—but with no formal conviction.

broadly denigrated as being responsible for ruining the policing environment.

Clear antipathy was expressed towards what was viewed as the 'constant reaffirming' of diversity-related issues. Consider the following comments made by a white male probationer in Northville towards the diversity training:

I only have such a short service, eight months in, but I have had so many diversity courses, and they are nailing the lid in the coffin and stamping on it. It is just driving us insane. They go through all these different things, and they labour the point and labour the point. At the end of it I was thinking, 'For God's sake, I wasn't racist at the start of this, are you doing this for my benefit or yours? It's just pathetic. Let me go home.'

Many officers felt 'insulted' that the diversity training assumes the police are inherently racist and require specialist training—a sentiment which can be linked to the wider defensiveness mentioned earlier about being branded racist by the organization. Nevertheless, this culture of anxiety generated from within the organization resulted in officers expressing resentment towards what they saw as minority groups who seemingly exploited their new status for personal gain.

The erosion of white advantage

It was vehemently argued that recruits to the police should only obtain employment on merit—and not by virtue of their ethnicity, gender, or sexuality. An equal opportunities policy on recruitment and promotion operates within Northshire, but officers invariably chided a situation in which perceived schemes of affirmative action and positive discrimination was serving to marginalize white male officers from employment and internal promotion opportunities.[10] The following exchange during a group discussion in Northville captures this widely supported sentiment:

Martin: It's the positive discrimination effect, it discriminates against white. . .

Gary: If people from the ethnic background or female background or whatever this non-white male background is, if they want a job as a police officer they will come off their own steam, and not

---

[10] Currently, any such policy (also referred to as 'positive discrimination') is not legally permitted in Britain.

high profile leaflet campaigns or recruitment caravans parked on Tesco [*large supermarket chain*] car park . . .

Bruce: That's right. Imagine: mother, father and eighteen year old white lad outside Tesco thinking, 'I would love to be a policeman. Can I go and have a look in the caravan mum'? And he gets there, and it's just ethnics and females.

Howard: Pakistani lads can't run: I know this from the TA [Territorial Army]. Genuinely, Pakistani lads cannot run, they are known for it. And to get them up to the minimum standard they had to drop the standards for the entrance test. Now if that isn't affirmative action . . .

Gary: It has gone too far, you're putting ethnic minorities on a pedestal—you're creating divisions before you even start. The Force is deterring potential candidates because they are white males.

It was also claimed that minority groups had an unfair advantage in acquiring internal promotion. On one occasion in Southville, a white police constable who had failed a sergeant board for a third time returned to the station and declared to his immediate shift, 'If I was a black lesbian with a wooden leg you would be calling me Sergeant today.' This type of comment reflected and reinforced a discourse that minority officers are the recipients of special treatment within the revised organizational climate.

Outside the organization, it was also believed that minority groups had an unfair advantage as victims of crime. This was especially salient in relation to crimes with a potentially racial motive:

Claire: But they [the organization] give it priority, but even if the IP [injured party] says, 'I've had my vehicle damaged, and I think this is racial', it's suddenly put to the top of the—whoof! But the little old lady, who is the same, is still at the bottom. She could drop dead before she sees an officer . . .

Catrin: It's wrong isn't it?

Claire: But because they are from a minority, they go straight to the top. Wow. And everybody's bottom starts twitching and sirens go off.

Group discussion—Northville

The new proactive approach towards the victimization of marginal groups has two components: the first calls for the improved recording, investigation, and prosecution of hate crime, while the second asks officers to be more understanding in their dealings with such victims. The comments made in the above extract demonstrate an irritation and sense of unfairness about the prioritization of racially motivated crimes. Somewhat paradoxically, the finely tuned awareness about the improved approach towards victimization ensured that some officers *dealt* with such incidents in a professional manner—and is a point which highlights the continuing disparity between police discourse and practice (see Waddington 1999*a*).

Front-line officers have a clear sense of the uniqueness of their role. This self-understanding engenders feelings of solidarity and perpetuates the opinion that they are set apart from others within the organization (Young 1991). The expansion of civilian employment was another source of contention among the rank and file. Although my research focused primarily on sworn constables, I did note some themes with respect to how civilianization is currently shaping police culture.[11] In particular, officers bemoaned the appointment of 'civvies' working in dispatch control and custody suites, and likewise articulated opposition towards the recruitment of PCSOs. The principal objection was that these groups lacked any 'real' understanding of the special rudiments of the police role. A perceived decline in sworn police numbers underpinned feelings of resentment towards civilian personnel, but this view only served to fuel the more widely diffused regard that change processes were an assault on the traditional constable as the bastion of policing.

A 'dying breed'

Police resentment was most profoundly directed towards the internal support associations. Throughout the research, officers expressed vigorous resentment of, and suspicion towards, the MPN, FSA, and LGPG. The associations were denigrated for erecting a cultural barrier within the organization and maintaining an 'Us' versus 'Them' mindset. The discontent felt towards this

---

[11] Because many support staff worked in offices and units which were centralized and away from street level police stations, there was a low presence of police staff and PCSOs in the two research sites. In Northville, four civilian staff (one male and three females) worked in administrative roles, including staffing the enquiry desk and intelligence support. At the time of the fieldwork, no PCSOs were employed at this station. Only two police staff (one male and one female) worked in Southville. However, towards the end of the fieldwork period, two female PCSOs began their probation at the station.

feature of the diversity landscape is encapsulated in the following set of comments made by a white male officer:

I wish I had an association. Can I have an association? How about a white, heterosexual, male association, where we can sit and discuss at our private meetings that they can't come to? It's like an 'Us' versus 'Them' culture isn't it? You join your gang, and we'll join our gang.

Interview—Northville

Confusion about the remit of the associations contributed to the idea that they were furthering political and individual objectives (such as gaining promotion for example). Officers placed a greater emphasis on the MPN in erecting this perceived cultural barrier, and the robust opposition towards this association indicates that the feelings of marginalization have become *racialized*. In their daily narratives, the MPN was regularly described as a 'political pressure group' or 'splinter group' as opposed to an association. The following extract provides due illustration of these issues:

Bethan:	Another issue I would like to talk about is your thoughts on the introduction of the internal cultural associations. So, you have the MPN, FSA, LGPG . . .
Jeremy:	It's rubbish . . .
Bethan:	Do you have any experiences of these associations?
Jeremy:	I think it is rubbish. You have got the Police Federation which should cover everyone. Why have your blacks and gays and lesbians got their own Federation?
Donna:	Your black police . . .
Jeremy:	Your ethnic groups, why have they got their own groupings? Disability, yes they need it. But they should get them through the Fed.
Warren:	White, Heterosexual Male Association . . .
Matthew and Jeremy:	[sarcastically] Oh! I'll have to join that one . . .
Colin:	Basically, regardless of whether you are disabled, your creed, colour or religion, you should go through the Fed. You should *not* need other organisations and splinter groups. [. . .]
Desmond:	I fear for some of the motives. Like you said, with the black one for instance . . . I'm just wondering that sometimes, some people—their motives are less than honourable. And I think that's what you

have got to be careful of, especially because they are such powerful groups. The black association, whatever they might be, those are the real power groups aren't they? The political pressure groups [. . .]

Colin: With all of these diverse groups forming now, the rest of us lot are becoming a dying breed. We are becoming the inferior ones, the white heterosexual male.

Group discussion—Southville

The Police Federation was considered to be the only legitimate interest group as its core remit was to represent individuals *as police officers*. This indicates a profound lack of deeper understanding that while police officers do face similar dilemmas (in the course of their duties and pressure from management, for example), some experience distinctive problems as a result of their ethnicity, gender, and sexuality. What is of significance here is that the discourses of exclusion captured in the above extracts cannot be considered authentic; as noted earlier, white, male, officers continue to form the prevailing group within the organization.

Moments of questioning

These narratives of decline and discontent point clearly to the dominance of a dissident white, heterosexual, male perspective, but it would not be entirely accurate to portray officers as culturally homogeneous. Recent theorizations support the contention that there are possible subcultures contained within what is usually presented as 'mainstream' police culture (Foster 2003). Along with differences between and within police forces, there are also various conflicts amongst individual officers. As I stated at the outset, my purpose in this chapter is to emphasize the dominant narratives which arose in police responses to the emergent accent on diversity. Lending support to these new ways of envisaging police culture, however, the research did capture instances when rank and file officers transcended the core values of police culture and accommodated aspects of the new organizational ethos. For example, there were several notable disagreements between officers in relation to the support associations. The next exchange is part of a heated discussion between white officers about the place of the LGPG within the organization:

Warren: Obviously they have brought these associations in because these people feel inferior to everyone else and, in these groups, they get more support. We are all [his emphasis] police officers after all, and they should feel part of . . .

James: But what about my support? Where has that gone? They've got the Fed. They don't need anyone else. It's, it's . . .

Heidi: That's not the point James, the point is. Right: if you were gay and you were coming into work and experiencing problems, who do you go to? Would you go to the Fed who possibly doesn't understand, or do you go to the other gays in the job?

James: No but, but there should be a point of contact in the Fed . . .

Darren: But if you were gay and had the choice, which one would you go to?

James: No, you contact the head office of the Fed . . .

Warren: But would they understand?

Darren: What if you were a closet gay and didn't want to speak to somebody in the Fed, but someone who is like you?

James: I just don't get it. I don't have a problem. My only problem is that it's not all equal.

Group discussion—Southville

There was also evidence to suggest that young officers critically reflected on the beliefs of the older generation of officers, as the following respondent put it:

The officers who make remarks, they are mainly the older generation—officers with about eighteen years' service. It is the original generation that is the problem. You still hear them saying the words 'coloured' and 'faggot'. Our generation, we are different from the last one. We don't use derogatory words. We are much more modern, have modern views. We are more tolerant.

From the fieldwork I also recall an occasion where an officer considered to comprise this dominant police culture expressed criticism towards his colleague for stopping and searching a young black man. However slight, the questioning of established sentiments is important because it indicates that sections of the dominant composition have begun to unlearn and reject aspects of the seemingly monolithic police culture.

Yet, while we may be witnessing the beginnings of multiple policing identities, the prevalence of the resentful discourses put forward by officers indicates that the impact of the revised organizational ethos has not been decisive. It is worth pausing for a moment to reflect on some of the issues that the currency of these discourses in the occupational milieu raises about the role of language in police culture. As Shearing and Ericson (1991) point out, police talk makes up an integral part of the received commonsense of their culture; it serves as an invaluable source of information for the socialization of officers, and provides cues for police behaviour. Moreover, lay discourses are invaluable for instituting, solidifying, and reproducing social formations and inequalities—particularly racism (Wetherell and Potter 1992; see also Nayak 2005). As the extracts make clear, the police discourses of resentment are peculiarly tied to an unspoken understanding of whiteness, and are part of the invisible grammar through which radicalization becomes inscribed.

The authenticity of the aforementioned tales of exclusion was severely undermined by the emergence of an opposing standpoint which revealed a markedly different working environment. Minority ethnic, female, and lesbian and gay officers stand forth as visible emblems of the new diversity paradigm and, for the most part, continue to be repositioned as 'outsiders' within (see Holdaway 1996).

Durable Discrimination: Minority Perspectives

One way of examining the 'success' of recent endeavours to transform the organizational culture can be found in capturing the contemporary experiences of officers from minority backgrounds. While the Diversity Strategy was considered to have made some changes to the interior culture (a point I explore below), it was believed to be largely hampered by the persistence of a white, heterosexist, male culture that was resistant towards the revised ethos.[12] Notwithstanding the multitude of initiatives introduced to improve the working environment, many officers continue to feel excluded.

New exclusions

There was a broad acceptance that instances of overt discrimination had significantly declined in the wake of the diversity emphasis. Yet,

---

[12] It is worth noting, however, that some respondents believed that the formal change programme was largely cosmetic (see also Cashmore 2002).

for many, this apparently critical development merely acquiesced to more subterranean forms of exclusion. The following comments demonstrate this current species of discrimination:

Bethan: What kind of issues come up today for gay officers, do you think?

Simon: It is still homophobic comments and inappropriate comments the majority of the time. But it's weird, I don't see it as any out-right homophobia as in real, active or physical or anything like that. It is usually your subtle, low level type of harassment (Gay Police Constable).

There are still pockets holding us back. There is a subversive culture, a feeling: people generally don't feel part of . . . On the face of it, it may appear like, and say the right things, and tick the boxes, and use photographs. Now it happens on a more informal basis (Female Inspector).

I was a victim of institutional racism. Racism can be used in many different ways to degrade you—it doesn't have to be in your face. When you hear it and see it, and it's in your face you can deal with it, but when you can't see it, and it's being done, you can't deal with it. Racism has gone underground now in the police service and people don't, they won't say it to your face. They choose their audiences carefully (Black Police Constable).

What these officers are describing is an interior environment where forms of discrimination are pervasive, yet subtle—a proposition which finds salience with recent works which have located 'stealth' or 'covert' racism within police organizations (Foster *et al* 2005; Holdaway and O'Neill 2007; McLaughlin 2007*a*). This new guise of discrimination, it was believed, reflected the entrenched dominance of a white, heterosexist, male culture. This composition continued to espouse intolerant views, but merely 'chose their audiences' when expressing them. As noted earlier, manifestations of discrimination accordingly occur in what I would term white space—that is, spaces where the white majority feel comfortable enough to resist and subvert aspects of the diversity strategy. The proposition of white space was alluded to by another officer:

I can go into some shifts and do a presentation, and on that shift you have got white, male officers—and they are *all* [his emphasis] white, heterosexual, male officers. And they'll feel like it is a safe environment to come out with comments. But they don't know who is walking in the door. You don't know the sexuality of anyone. It's not like race or gender is it? (Gay Police Sergeant).

As Holdaway and O'Neill (2007) explain, the elusive nature of discrimination has important implications for those wishing to make a complaint against colleagues. In defence of this, officers draw upon a range of indicators which, for them, signal a prejudiced temperament. One Asian officer in Northshire felt that colleagues who were awkward, or silent, around her could not be considered trustworthy:

It's [discrimination] more underneath, without a doubt. Underneath. Because I have seen it, heard it and witnessed it on my own shift even. Where people have been talking or whispering, and as soon as I come in the room, they stop. But I have heard because the door was open; 'You watch Simea, you have to watch your P's and Q's around her, keep her at arm's length. Be careful what you say.'

Other officers detected a potentially racist disposition through the stereotypes frequently drawn upon by their white colleagues:

Some of the shift was talking about an Asian offender who had said to the sergeant, 'I bet your house isn't as big as mine.' And one of the lads said, 'It's because he lives with his entire family. They do that don't they? They have loads of family living with them.' And I'm thinking, 'Who are *they*? And what is wrong having family living with you? Is that how you regard people of different ethnic origins?' (Black Police Constable)

The broad consensus was that while changes had been made at the surface level, there was a subversive culture of resentment and discrimination 'bubbling underneath'. For another minority ethnic officer, this is manifest in the dominant attitude towards diversity:

I don't think having diversity courses and all this matters. You only have to look at the attitudes of people who go on these. They are typical, 'Oh we don't want to go on that', and 'Why should we? Why do we need to know all this'? 'Waste of time.' Officers still now to this day feel that there is too much emphasis on being politically correct.

A further indication of the relatively untouched character of the organization related to the lack of understanding from colleagues of the difficulties faced by minority ethnic officers in their work. After arresting a white male for a public order offence, one female Asian officer felt unsupported by white colleagues:

When I took this particular lad into custody he called me a 'Paki' nine times until the custody sergeant said anything—and then he only says, 'What is all this Paki business about?' I had to remove myself from the cells because of the conflict.

The current genus of discrimination is not only a feature of police organizations. As Miles and Small (1999) observe, the formal interdiction of racism within broader society has transformed the way in which it becomes executed. Expressions of racism are increasingly performed through coded schemas in which the parlance employed is heavily loaded with meaning to attribute particular social groups with a set of—usually undesirable—social characteristics. This proposition finds resonance within the policing terrain, as the following interview with a black male constable demonstrates:

On parade now, he [the shift sergeant] says in front of everyone, 'Did you know that the majority of people who commit robberies are black.' And he would look at me. He was looking straight at me! I challenged him, but he started coming out with all these statistics. On the face of it, it was all innocent like, but he knew.

The proposition that exclusion is increasingly accomplished through less explicit channels also finds resonance in the everyday experiences of those officers from other marginal backgrounds, as the following extracts illustrate:

Everything is aimed with a remark. When I came back off holiday from Tenerife, he [colleague] kept saying, 'I bet you shagged loads of girlies.' But he was saying it in such a way that he knows, but all the time testing your reactions. [. . .] He looked across the car and said, 'You're like Stephen Gately [gay pop idol] aren't you?' I looked at him, and he said, 'No! I don't mean you're like Stephen Gately, you just look like him.' But I don't look anything like him, and he knows it (Gay Police Constable).

It's the little things. You go to a meeting, and you are the only female in the room. Or I get emails saying, 'Dear gentlemen'. You still hear people talking about officers being 'he'. You become hard to it, you learn to just deal with it (Female Inspector).

Tokenism and scrutiny

Some officers felt that their gender, sexuality, and ethnicity was being used a token by the organization in their quest to be seen to be 'doing diversity'. This was particularly salient in relation to minority ethnic officers who had been promoted to a senior rank or specialist department. One black male constable couched this situation in the following terms:

When I was promoted, I was really pleased to be promoted, but I also felt used because of my race. I know that I have been used as a token—I see where I have been used. But I have always thought that I got the jobs on my ability.

Many described an irony of tokenism in that successful promotion would be viewed sceptically by other officers, but equally, that failure to obtain promotion would somehow 'confirm' that minority officers are not up to the job:

You can't win. If I get the promotion I know people will think, 'He only got it because he is black—the organization needs to tick boxes.' But if I don't get it, they will think, 'He's obviously not good enough' (Black Detective Constable).

This sense of a heightened visibility has long been experienced by minority officers (Heidensohn 1992; Burke 1993; Holdaway and Barron 1997) and in Northshire continues to go hand-in-hand with an increased pressure to perform. Another female sergeant maintained that the only way to gain recognition and credibility was to have a high performing shift. These feelings were also experienced by rank and file officers. One minority ethnic officer stated that all aspects of their work were being subjected to scrutiny and criticism by colleagues and supervisors. These individual accounts may reflect individual perceptions, but they nevertheless demonstrate that minority officers believe their social difference may pose problems for them.

Silent members and hierarchies of difference

The discourses of exclusion put forward by what remains to be the dominant white culture revealed considerable resentment towards the internal support associations. This proposition is further supported by my conversations and interviews with minority officers, some of whom are members of the associations. It was unanimously felt that being a member of an association had a stigma attached to it, as one a female constable put it:

I think one of the reasons I haven't become involved in the FSA is because of the predominantly straight, heterosexual, white male attitude towards it. And I think, I don't want anything used against me. I look at the way they [members of the FSA] are thought about in the Force, and I don't want people thinking of me like that. People, white males, look at you and you become a target then don't you?

The impetus behind the formation of internal police associations was closely related to the charge that the mainly white and male Police Federation was not best placed to promote racial equality within police organizations (Holdaway and O'Neill 2004). Because of the pervasive sentiment that the associations were serving to marginalize the white, heterosexual, males, I decided to put this perception to one lesbian officer who is involved in the LGPG. Her reply suggests that the Police Federation is still being run along white male precepts:

Bethan: How do you think the white, heterosexual male officer views the associations? A number of officers have said to me for example, 'Why can't we have a white, heterosexual male association'? What are your views of that?

Rachael: That is the comment that is always thrown at us. And my reply to them is, 'You have, it's called the Police Federation.'

Members of the associations believed that their immediate colleagues, and some supervisors, resented the occasions when they were required to leave their shift early to fulfil an association commitment. This had the effect of drawing further attention to their social difference, and had regularly served to discourage some members from asking for time off to attend meetings—a point which perhaps explains the low turnout for group meetings. All of the associations have an abundance of what I would call *silent members*—that is, those who are formal members but who do not routinely participate in the activities or day to day running of the associations.

The new organizational ethos states equality to women, minority ethnic, gay, and lesbian officers, but there was a view that some marginal groups had made more progress in attaining recognition than others. One senior officer I spoke with painted the following picture:

On a scale of 1–10, our recognition towards race and ethnicity is probably an 8 or a 9. We have made huge strides there. Gender is at about a 6. We have some way to go, but we are getting there. But being gay or lesbian, that is down at a 2 or 3. And I worry about that (Male Chief Inspector).

It is evident that some kind of cultural transformation has taken place in relation to minority ethnic groups. This is reflected principally by the general absence of overt racist discourse and conduct among officers, and the visible defensiveness around 'race' issues. Several female and gay officers nevertheless expressed concern that the prominence placed on issues of ethnicity and racism had failed to be extended to sexuality or gender. For many, sexism and homophobia continue to be implicitly embedded in the organizational culture (see also Foster *et al* 2005), albeit in a more diluted form in the wake of the new diversity emphasis.

As Brown (2007) observes, the prominence placed on racism within the diversity climate not only eclipses the requirements of gender equality, but also ensures the survival of a gendered occupational world. Officers in Northshire shared a set of norms and values that were consistent with a dominant white, heterosexual, male composition. These informal ideologies manifested themselves in a particularly *male* form of banter, or 'canteen culture' (Smith and Gray 1985; Fielding 1994). As the next instance shows, female officers tended to accommodate the attitudes of their male colleagues:

When we got back to the station, we all went through to the canteen and started eating. Linda, a female Sergeant, was already in there and we started talking. The other eight officers, who were all male, were sitting around other tables. They were flicking through FHM magazines, and holding up pictures of semi-naked women to each other.[13] This was accompanied by highly sexualized language. Linda, who was having a relationship with one of the officers, glanced over at me and rolled her eyes in a 'boys-will-be-boys' way.

Fieldnotes—Northville

Female supervisors who asserted their authority over their male constables were sometimes disparaged. After asking one officer why he had not yet attended an incident from earlier on in the day, one female sergeant in Southville was later described as a 'jumped-up bitch' for seemingly 'throwing her weight around'. Explicit discussions about sexual encounters—real or exaggerated—were routine and the use of sexualized language

[13]   FHM is an acronym for 'For Him Magazine'. This is a popular magazine for men and covers a range of items to do with sport, 'women', cars, and fashion.

was tolerated. The taken for granted ethos of robust, heterosexual masculinity within the research sites served to exclude some female members of the organization:

I went into the office to talk to Megan who was doing some paperwork at her desk. She said that she wanted to go into the other room to use the computers because hers was down, but she didn't want to go in there while 'all the lads' were in there. This was probably exacerbated by the noisy displays of bravado coming from the parade room.

Fieldnotes—Southville

On one occasion an officer who had dyed his hair blonde was jokingly called a 'poofter' by his shift colleagues, and another officer routinely answered his mobile telephone by humorously stating, 'Hello—this is the gay hotline.' Officers who travelled in the station carrier (informally termed the 'fun bus') engaged in an exaggerated heterosexist form of culture in which women leaving the local pubs and nightclubs were subjected to voyeuristic gazes and comments by male officers. The dominance of a heterosexual culture was likewise apparent in the policing of casual sexual relationships amongst men. These relationships took place in public areas and became firmly embedded within police cultural knowledge as deviant. In Northville, one such area had been informally nicknamed 'Anal Lane' by officers and was routinely targeted during patrols.

New Contestations and the Preservation of Dominance

The institutionalization of diversity has altered the interior culture of the organization in some important, and contradictory, ways. Paradoxically, several minority officers espoused *similar* comments to their white, heterosexual, male counterparts in subordinating the diversity agenda. Any such criticism came almost universally from female officers and can be explained by reference to some renowned features of police culture. Women police experience intense pressure to 'prove themselves', and in order to gain the acceptance of their male colleagues they invariably adopt the characteristics of the prevailing culture (Martin 1980; Young 1991; Heidensohn 1992). I would also add that many minority ethnic, female, and gay and lesbian officers shared, with their white, heterosexual, male colleagues, comparable perspectives on being a 'bobby'. Yet of particular value here is to acknowledge minority officers' sense of how the working environment *has* been transformed in recent years. Notwithstanding the aforementioned accounts of exclusion, it was considered that the formal accent on diversity has made some noteworthy mileage in significantly reducing overt forms of discrimination and mainstreaming equality. There was a proposition among some that the organization was now characterized by an ambience where discriminatory language and conduct could be actively challenged. For example, one gay officer, for example, depicted the general 'spirit of inclusion' which had come to envelope the workplace, while another minority ethnic officer described how he felt 'empowered and represented' within the new organizational climate. These new-found feelings of confidence among minority officers indicate the ways in which the revised organizational ethos is beginning to modify the interior culture. The police organization is an environment where alternative cultures are emerging to challenge old ones. New contestations have evolved not only from minority officers, but also from current generations of white, heterosexual, male officers who have the potential to confront and question established sentiments. In many ways, the emergence of new identities reflects the increasingly fragmented condition of policing culture (see also Loader and Mulcahy 2003).

It would be erroneous, however, to overstate the extent to which these emerging identities have displaced the dominant police culture. The occupational environment is increasingly competitive and hostile. The widely articulated resentment articulated by the prevailing white, heterosexual, male composition towards the increasing recognition of minority groups indicates that the challenges to the 'old' police culture remain partial. The narratives of resentment and discontent represent, I contend, an aggrieved attempt of a hitherto hegemonic culture to retain its privileged position; they operate to *preserve* an increasingly endangered culture by subordinating the spaces of representation for emerging identities.

These local narratives are similar to the hostile reaction by white Metropolitan Police officers in the aftermath of the Macpherson Report (see McLaughlin 2007: 154), but they also illustrate a broader dialogue at work. In particular, the police reaction find resonance with what has been identified as a 'white backlash' to the politics of multiculturalism (Hewitt 2005; see also McLaughlin and Neal 2004). In a similar vein, the notion of *ressentiment* has been used to conceptualize white sentiments towards multiculturalism (Mann and Fenton forthcoming, 2009) and, I suggest, is useful for understanding the resentful police response to the extension of equality. In essence, this French term is most easily translated as 'resentment', but has been afforded wider sociological significance to describe an ongoing and entrenched sense of resentment which becomes directed against others who possess desired goods and values (Scheler 1961; Meltzer and Musolf 2002). A sense of *ressentiment* arises in response to perceived inequalities in social circumstances, and is characterized by feelings of loss, envy and injustice. A presupposed sense of entitlement fuels these feelings and becomes manifest through proclamations of anger and bitterness towards the bearers of the desired goods (Mann and Fenton, forthcoming 2009). In order to reassert a sense of superiority, those experiencing *ressentiment* embark on an enterprise to devalue the envied goods. In this way, it is an effective tool in the creation and reproduction of identities.

The recalcitrant comments articulated by the majority of white, heterosexual, male officers find clear parallel with the themes of *ressentiment*. As demonstrated, officers certainly experience a sense of decline and loss in the policing climate. Yet complaints about the apparent demise of workplace banter and restrictions on everyday language reflects, I argue, a broader ambivalence and nostalgia about values that were previously mainstays of the dominant white, male, culture. The narratives also depicted robust resentment towards the apparent 'special treatment' of minority officers. Once again, these comments reveal a profound sense of insecurity against the *possibility* of white, heterosexual, male officers having to compete with black, female, and gay or lesbian colleagues on occupational grounds—particularly in gaining promotion. The narratives of resentment espoused by the dominant majority also construct a condition of victimhood—as exemplified in the prevalent discourse that the white, heterosexual, male officer was becoming a 'dying breed'. The clear antipathy expressed towards the internal support associations reveals, moreover, the ambivalence and anger felt towards the *potential* acquisition of new power and status by minority officers—and as the robust hostility articulated towards the MPN makes clear especially minority ethnic officers.

Concluding Remarks

My aim in this chapter has been to examine how social, political, and organizational reconfigurations around questions of diversity crystallize in the dispositions of police officers. It seems clear from the narratives presented here that the extension of recognition for hitherto marginalized groups sits uneasily within the culture of the ordinary rank and file. In defence of threats to their increasingly beleaguered identity, white, heterosexual, male officers have emerged as prime propagators of a resentful discourse which operates to devalue the revised accent on diversity and preserve the traditional culture. Moreover, the hostile comments put forward by officers indicate that the salience of exclusion and othering has extended into the post-Macpherson era.

There is of course a danger of presenting police discrimination solely as rank and file pathology (McLaughlin 2007; see also Waddington 1999), but there unequivocally remains a resilient residue of dispositions which undermine the requirements of the diversity terrain. Yet, in broader terms, it is precisely those narratives of demise and discontent put forward by the dominant majority which also indicate that the sentiments which comprise police culture are becoming—at the very least—*interrupted* by the salience of identity politics within policing.

4

Classic Themes, Altered Times

In revisiting police culture I aim to provide an account of the values, beliefs, and outlooks which officers bring to bear on their work. This task requires exploring the ways in which greater social diversity in the policing environment has shaped the cultural expressions of the rank and file. But it also involves returning to the classic themes from the police culture literature. What are officers' motivations for and aspirations upon joining the police? What are their perceptions of 'the job'—its status, rewards, and challenges? How do officers relate to peers, managers, and different strata of the public? What are their dispositions towards different categories of crime and policing styles?

In this chapter I leave aside questions of ethnicity, gender, and sexuality and consider how much of the classic themes have survived the period of transition. Notwithstanding the changes that have occurred in policing, officers espouse remarkably similar cultural characteristics to those found in earlier accounts. The informal assumptions continue to exercise considerable influence over routine police work. However, while the characteristics identified by the classic ethnographers are evident in the occupational thinking and practices of current generations of police officers, I also observed several important differences. In particular, police culture can be shaped by the local context in which officers work. The ethnographic fieldwork was conducted in two different geographical areas: one urban and one rural. Officers mainly shared a related set of assumptions and practices, but it is noteworthy that the *substance* of each theme had the potential to carry different meanings and emphasis. In the main, though, these differences were nuanced rather than outstanding and in broader terms underline the powerful endurance of police culture.

From 'Beirut' to the 'Mary Celeste'

The interactions and cultural characteristics described and analysed in this chapter occur within distinct geographical and social contexts. It is important, then, to set the stage of these two policing environments.

Northville LPU is situated in the Northern policing division and is one of the busiest stations in the Force. A typical IMU shift consists of anything between ten and fifteen officers, while eight officers work on the CAT.[1] It is a station where many young officers are posted to serve their probationary period, although there is also a notable presence of older and seasoned officers. Along with the IMU and CAT, the station also houses a Prostitution Unit and a Priority Crime Unit. Its patch covers an urban geographical terrain which is densely populated. In recent years, Northville has become increasingly multi-ethnic. Official census data indicates that black and minority ethnic populations make up 29.9 per cent of the area's demographic profile. Comprising mainly those of Pakistani, Indian, and Black Caribbean ethnic origin, there is, in addition, a significant travelling populace, and small Polish, Iraqi, Italian, and Vietnamese communities. With this urban landscape comes a high level of social and economic deprivation. Northville is characterized by long-term and intergenerational unemployment; low income and wealth; low educational attainment; and poor health and housing.

For those officers working there, Northville is a particularly rough and disorderly area; one that is brimming with criminal activity. The following exchange was captured during a group disussion with IMU and CAT officers and reveals their thoughts on the policing environment:

Bethan: What is Northville like as a place to police? What types of problems does it pose from your point of view?

Matt: It's Beirut isn't it? That's what we call it. . .

Simon: I don't think there is a type of crime we don't deal with. Burglary, drugs. . .

Gary: I don't think you'll find a better place to police than Northville—there is everything here. You've got private residential estates,

---

[1] The IMU comprised of five separate shifts (1-5) while the CAT ran along one shift.

council estates, industrial estates, main roads, side roads, alleys, walkways. . .

Matt: Prostitutes, drug dealers, prostitutes, drugs, vehicle crime, house burglaries. . .

Roger: And that's just on The Reservation Estate [everyone laughs]. If you come here as a probationer you will learn everything.

Matt: It is quite a small area but here, here you've got everything. . .

Roger: There is. I don't think there is nothing missing from here.

Simon: It's just a big lump. You never know what you are going to be given when you get shouted up. Before I came here, when I was going through tutor college people would say to me, 'Where are you stationed? And I'd say 'Northville', and they'd go, 'Oooohhhh'. . .

Gary: What have you done wrong? Who have you upset?

[Participants laughing in agreement]

Matt: It's a sin bin. . .

Gary: You learn quicker that's for sure. You learn or burn. You sink or swim.

Matt: That's the hardest thing about being a probationer in Northville because it is that intense. If you can't arrest enough people or do enough crime in Northville, you're plainly not getting out of the station!

Roger: It's like a fish in a bucket isn't it?

Matt: Oh it's just crazy, crazy. If you swing around you'll hit a wall somewhere eventually. It's dead easy.

Nearly all officers were essentially visitors to the area in that they merely commuted into Northville for their work, but lived elsewhere in more affluent areas. From my observations, the typical tasks facing officers were dealing with domestic violence; neighbour disputes; and low-level antisocial behaviour involving youths; traffic accidents and stolen vehicles; suicide threats and missing persons; drug-related offences and prostitution; minor public order incidents; and an array of organizational commitments, such as completing paperwork.

Southville LPU, conversely, is positioned at the far corner of South Northshire. Covering a patch of almost seventy square miles, the LPU is responsible for policing a large and mainly rural geographical terrain. It is sandwiched between two surrounding counties: Long City, which is densely urbanized, and Green Downs, which is rural. Officers serve a number of satellite stations in surrounding villages, but the majority work out of the station in Southville. In contrast to their urban counterpart, it was usual for the IMU to operate with a maximum of four officers, while four officers worked on the CAT. The station also comprised a Rural Crime Department which was managed by one police officer, and a member of civilian support staff.

By official standards, the areas covered within the LPU are some of the most affluent in Northshire. Operating largely as a commuter village, many of those living in Southville are high-earning senior officials, executives, and other professionals. Most of the houses are privately owned with a standard market price higher than the national average, although the area also comprises several social housing estates. The population is over-whelmingly white at 98.2 per cent, but a small number of people of Pakistani, Indian, Black Caribbean, and Chinese ethnic origin also live in the area. Southville is characterized by vast spaces of fields and attractive woodland; farms; small clusters of houses and large gated mansions; and a combination of fast open roads and narrow, winding country lanes. Unlike their urban coun-terparts, officers in Southville spoke favourably of their work-ing environment. Owing to the attractive rural landscape, it was common to hear officers describe Southville as a 'pleasant place to police'. Many officers lived locally and the local population were viewed as pro-police and cooperative, as the following extract demonstrates:

Andrew: On the whole, I love working Southville [murmurs of agreement]

Will: Me too, I wouldn't want to work anywhere else.

Bethan: What's good about it?

Andrew: The fact that you just come to work in a beautiful area. . .

Will: You're not dealing with rubbish all the time. The people you deal with are nice to you. Their views on the police in general aren't great, but as an individual, they are great.

Don: Not like those you were with up North, Beth. We get paid the same as them, yet they spend their lives getting abuse and run ragged. This is one of the very few areas in the Force where we police by consent.

The volume of work was clearly lower, but the primary tasks facing officers were analogous to their urban counterpart.

However, there were some uniquely rural aspects such as dealing with escaped farm animals; investigating the theft of tractors and other farm equipment; and responding to reports of stolen horses and badger baiting.[2] Because of its relatively quiet and tranquil nature, officers nicknamed Southville the 'Mary Celeste'. However, this epithet also arose from the broader perception that it was a peculiar place to work. Firstly, given both its rural nature and remote, southerly position on the Northshire Police map, officers believed that the LPU was the forgotten part of the Force. Common sentiments had it that Southville was the 'tail end' or 'little Italy' of Northshire Police, and many officers felt isolated and disconnected from the wider Force. Secondly, the fact that the LPU borders the urban sprawl of Long City raised several issues for officers in terms of the nature of local crime problems. Notwithstanding the tranquil nature of Southville, crime work occupied a central position in officers' value systems—and it is here that one clear distinction emerged between the two policing areas. While the crime problems facing officers in Northville were viewed as *internal*, the problems in Southville were considered to be *external*. It was widely stated that the LPU was under constant threat from young, low status, male 'outsiders' who originated from the less affluent regions of Long City. Outsiders were believed to be responsible for the serious crimes which took place on the patch—particularly residential burglaries and theft of high performance cars. In the wake of anxieties about crime in the area, police feelings of otherness became racialized.

There is, then, a marked contrast between the geographical, social, and economic arrangements of Northville and Southville. In light of these differences, do the cultural expressions of the police differ within these two locations? Or, conversely, can the cultural characteristics be found across both sites? In broader terms, what aspects of police culture are enduring?

Imagining Policing

As Manning (1977) observes, police culture encompasses the images that police have of their role along with their assumptions

---

[2] The IMU and CAT would deal with escaped farm animals (they caused potential mayhem on the main roads) but the rural crime office would deal solely with many of these other types of crime.

about their external reality which, in turn, underpins and informs conduct. In the current context, where traditional conceptions of policing are being challenged, an exploration of officers' understandings of their role is paramount.

The moral mission

A heightened sense of mission towards the police role has long been identified as a core feature of police culture. The function of policing, as Reiner (2000*a*: 89) notes, is conceived as 'the preservation of a valued way of life, and the protection of the weak against the predatory'. During the research, officers expressed great pride in the mission of police work, and celebrated its uniqueness, and potential to make a difference. It was asserted that being a police officer was different from other occupations, with many officers couching it in terms of a vocation or calling—as the following exchange between officers during a group discussion in Northville demonstrates:

Bethan: What were your motivations for becoming a police officer? Why did you join the job?

Jake: I know it sounds corny, but I really wasn't happy with the way things were in society. People were being mugged, raped, burgled and I thought I could make a difference. I wanted to make a difference to society, to help people . . .

Rowan: I joined for the same reasons. I didn't join to go on the CAT to be honest with you. I really joined to go out and lock up people. I think because my dad was in the job as well. You know, you hear the stories, and it sounds exciting and interesting . . .

Jake: It's something different to everybody else's job you know?

Rowan: I wouldn't want to sit in an office for forty years. That has no appeal to me whatsoever. It's nice to be outside, and it's nice to feel that sometimes you are making a difference. You see people being taken advantage of and it really winds me up, and I can do something about it from the position I am in. . . .

Sam: It's not a job though is it? It's a lifestyle [others agree]. You can't go home and think, 'I am not a police officer.' You go home, and you are who you are.

Bill: It messes up your home life a vast amount though. Bringing the job home is something I always get in trouble for with my missus.

Jake: I don't think it is just us who are in the police. It's the families as well, isn't it?

A residue of the sense of mission is its concern for the victim (Reiner 2000*a*). This moral perspective on the police role contributed favourably to current service orientated approaches to policing. On one occasion, for example, all patrols in Southville provided their immediate and prompt attention to a report of an autistic child who went missing from one of the area's supermarkets. Although the child was eventually discovered by a member of the public, officers displayed a strong desire to search for the infant, and were supportive and sympathetic towards the mother who was, understandably, panic-stricken. Equally, however, the moral values associated with the culture also made imperative the controlling of their 'patch'—and of certain people. In their own estimation, officers were the thin blue line which stood between chaos and order. Importantly, this exaggerated assessment of their role had an underlying influence on policing styles and practices. Mirroring an abundance of earlier research (Westley 1970; Cain 1973; Brown 1981; Smith and Gray 1985), officers saw themselves, first and foremost, as crime fighters.

Proper police work

From my observations officers spent only a small amount of time on tasks which had a distinctly criminal element. However, detecting and catching offenders was elevated as the core justification for policing:

Bethan: What do you think policing is for today?

Geraint: To get criminals off the streets . . .

Mike: To lock up criminals.

Shaun: I still like to see them locked up because that is the thrill of the job I joined for. . .

Mike: Proper policing. . .

Shaun: The bosses are trying to change minds now. We have to be customer-focused, to ring the IP [Injured Party], but all they do is moan . . .

James: I have to be honest. I don't think that is my job. I am not a social worker. I'm not there to mollycoddle people. I am there to detect and prevent crime, to keep the streets safe.

Group discussion—Southville

In contrast, responsibilities such as completing paperwork and attending incidents which involved a service element were not considered authentic policing experiences. Incidents which failed to conform with dominant conceptions of 'proper' police work were accorded an inferior status within officers' sense of a crime hierarchy. Domestic violence incidents and neighbour disputes were routinely relegated to the lower end of this hierarchy. From the fieldwork, however, these incidents formed what officers actually dealt with on a day to day basis. And, as I have made clear, the enhanced resolution of domestic violence is emphasized in current governmental and police organizational agendas.

The orientation towards crime fighting interfered with prevailing initiatives to redefine the police role. Community policing has accrued broad currency within policing discourse (Fielding 1995) and the recasting of the public as police 'customers' has been central to this development in Northshire. During the research, an initiative called Customer Focus was being promoted within the organization. On one occasion, a superintendent attended Northville police station to tell officers about the new policy. He used a shop analogy which posed the police as shopkeepers and members of the public as customers—the point being that officers should be helpful, courteous, and provide a service to their customers. The following fieldnote captures the rank and files immediate thoughts in relation to this:

After the meeting, the shop analogy was caricatured and parodied by the officers in the parade room. Comments [in American accents] like 'Do you want fries with your stop and search record', 'I'm sorry we don't accept giros' [state benefits] and 'Here's three points on your licence, have a nice day now', were just some of the banter flying around the room.

The principle of treating members of the public as though they are customers was profoundly inconsistent with the police conception of what real policing was all about. As the following comments make clear, officers were particularly critical of regarding suspects and offenders as customers:

Bethan: One of the statements that Northshire Police says is that it delivers a service which 'reflects community needs' and is 'customer-focused'. What are your views of that?

Ron: We're not fucking Sainsbury's [large supermarket chain]

[Everyone laughs]

Scott: Northshire police is not a business and never will be. We don't have customers—we have complainants and offenders. It's as simple as that.

Gareth: The world has just gone politically mad. It's not, like Scott says, yeah there are members of the public out there, but the wording the bosses use is totally out of sync with the real world. . .

Ron: Management speak . . .

Gareth: I don't think it reflects what we are. We are an emergency service rather than a, what am I trying to say. . .

Scott: A corporate entity . . .

Gareth: Start talking about customers, you expect us to kiss feet.

Group discussion—Northville

Of significance here is that the scepticism articulated towards viewing the public—and especially offenders—as customers stands up in sharp contrast to the Force Quality of Service Commitment as outlined in Chapter 3. The above extract also demonstrates officers' cynicism towards the management emphasis on such initiatives. It is well known that an internal chasm exists between the rank and file, and senior officers (Ruess-Ianni and Ianni 1983; Graef 1989). In my view, this chasm has been exacerbated by new pressures on organizations to rethink the police role. In particular, cynicism towards bosses was aggravated by what the rank and file saw as the irrelevant and inane 'management speak' which surrounds the revised policing philosophies.

On an operational level, community policing stresses 'policing *with* and *for* the community, rather than policing *of* the community' (Tilley 2003: 315). This new way of envisaging the police role has become increasingly prominent to the change programme in Northshire. As noted, to support this style of policing Community Action Teams (CAT) have been created to work alongside Incident Management Units (IMU). Some officers acquiesced in the ideologies underpinning community policing, but the overwhelming majority saw the activities of the CAT as marginal to the work of the IMU. During my observations, it soon became apparent that a symbolic separation existed between the IMU and the CAT. Officers who adopted the new community role were disparaged by their immediate response colleagues. Invariably, community officers were referred to by the IMU as 'station cats' or the 'tea and sympathy brigade', and the formal acronym of CAT similarly became reworked within their informal vocabulary to denote 'Coffee And Tea' and 'Can't Attend This'. In contrast, CAT officers generally portrayed IMU officers as unsophisticated 'slaves to the radio'. However, this conflict was only subtle and throughout the research I noted a high degree of team work between both units; as one CAT officer in Northville put it, 'The way I look at it is that the IMU wrestle the alligators while we control the swamp.'

It would be inaccurate to portray those working on the CAT as subscribing wholeheartedly to the principles underpinning community policing. Across both sites, CAT officers invariably perceived themselves as members of a 'mini proactive team' with the remit to control crime and gather intelligence on the local criminals, and many displayed the characteristics of the new centurion (see Reiner 1978). In furtherance, one officer in Southville suggested that to work on the CAT for a period of time was beneficial for securing promotion to sergeant as it demonstrated a preparedness to 'Jump on the reassurance policing bandwagon'. Paradoxically, the preoccupation with crime control led to some CAT officers *themselves* disapproving of the new policing initiatives. The following fieldnote was recorded during a shift with the CAT in Northville:

Sergeant Adams asked Warren to go out into Dale Port and do some work for 'Operation Door to Door'—an initiative which requires officers to go door to door in the LPU and offer practical crime safety advice to members of the public. Warren and I got into the car and I asked him what the job entailed. After giving me a brief overview, he said that it was a 'crock' and he and the rest of his shift had nicknamed it, 'Operation Bullshit'. [. . .] A call came over the radio about a public order incident in the town centre. Warren expressed much disquiet about the fact that he was 'stuck doing this bullshit' and could not attend. He put very little effort into the task and went back to the station as soon as it began to rain slightly.

More broadly, the widespread preference for crime fighting served to challenge probationary officers' outlook towards certain incidents:

The job was to attend an incident where two female neighbours were shouting at each other in the street. The argument had become very heated and a shoe had been thrown at Miss Jones by Miss Roberts. When Simon, a probationary officer, and Tim arrived much of the shift were already there and were trying to calm the situation. Frank said to Simon, 'Here you are. This is your chance to get some experience of a dispute.' Simon and the rest of us went into the house. In dealing with the incident, Simon was very attentive and sympathetic to Miss Roberts who was saying that Miss Jones's children had been harassing her and her family. [. . .] Over an hour later, when Simon, Tim, Warren and I got back into the car, the following general conversation developed:

Tim: You did well there Simon but I thought you were never going to get rid of that.

Will: The thing with that type of incident is that it's rubbish. It's bullshit.

Tim: It's just people who can't look after their own lives and need us to come in and sort them out. Don't engage in conversation with them, just take down what's needed and get out of there.

Will: With that type of incident, just bat it out and move on to doing what we joined for.

Fieldnotes—Northville

This type of incident formed a staple part of daily police work, but was regularly presented to probationers as 'bullshit' by experienced officers. Incidentally, the episode also demonstrates how a common way of thinking continues to be communicated and learned within police culture (Van Maanen 1973; Fielding 1988).

It would be inaccurate, however, to portray all officers as subscribing to the crime fighter image of policing. As several works demonstrate, operational policing encompasses a multitude of different styles and orientations, from peace keeping to order maintenance (Banton 1964; Bittner 1967; Wilson 1972; Reiner 1978). During the research, I observed differences in the *context* in which the crime fighting approach was invoked. In Southville, officers remarked that the public liked to see them 'out and about' and, during patrols, would drive past schools, churches, and affluent houses to engage in public reassurance policing—or 'flying the flag' as they called it. In attending relatively minor incidents, a relaxed and easygoing approach was adopted. Officers took their time to deal with the problem, and a straightforward incident would be long and drawn-out—sometimes deliberately so. However, there were numerous occasions when officers adopted a hostile and crime control approach to policing. An understanding of why officers espoused a community policing style in some instances, and a crime-fighting stance in others, related to the *types* of people and crimes which held significance within their cultural knowledge. Based on a notion of 'outsiders' as core perpetrators of local crime, officers directed their suspicion towards young, low status, minority ethnic males whose appearance was incongruent with the white and affluent surroundings.

Much as in the study by Reiner (1978), I noted variations between individual police orientations and styles. In both sites, some officers enjoyed addressing the mundane problems of everyday policing and approached interactions in a responsive, as opposed to adversarial, manner. These instances indicate how officers are now afforded the space to support and develop new policing styles (see Foster 2003). In the main, however, it was female officers who adopted a more service-oriented approach to their work—and this was in any case eclipsed by the prevailing emphasis on crime fighting. The preoccupation with crime reflected the dominance of a masculine ethos within the occupational culture and it is to this I now turn.

A Masculine Ethos

As a wealth of research has shown, masculinity is a theme which infuses the police identity (Martin 1980; Smith and Gray 1985; Westmarland 2001b; Crank 2004). In addition to devaluing 'softer' approaches to policing, powerful undercurrents of masculinity encourage an aura of toughness and celebration of violence.

Discourses of violence

A masculine ethos, absorbed by the imagery of conflict and danger, was one of the most prominent features of the occupational culture. While actual occurrences of dangerous and confrontational encounters were rare, officers routinely told each other, and me, stories which glorified violent and confrontational encounters with members of the public. The transmission of these 'war stories' (Punch 1979) occurred during the quiet times of the shift, and served to reinforce the aggressive element of the culture. Consider the following episode which I recorded during my time in Northville:

2.45pm

I walked into the parade room to begin the late shift. Officers were sitting around and eagerly listening to Shaun and Justin animatedly relaying an incident they had been involved in the previous night. From what I could gather, they had been in some kind of fight with four men on their way home from work. As I sat down, Justin said, 'Here you are Beth, here's some excitement for you' and, along with Shaun, began to tell me what had happened:

Shaun: Last night after the shift, I was giving Shaun a lift home and as we approached Vicars Lane, we got hit by a car full of 'scrotes'. I got out and could immediately tell that the driver was pissed. . .

Justin: The ones in the back must have recognised us because they started saying, 'It's the fucking Feds get them.' With that, they all got out of the car and it all kicked off. Shaun and I started rolling around with them. I was getting kicked to the floor but, before I went down, I managed to punch one of them in the face—I think I broke his nose!

Shaun: I was just thinking, 'Right, I can take these two if Justin takes the other two.' One tried to headbutt me—but he missed—and I just launched at him.

[. . .] The offenders had managed to get away, but because Justin and Shaun had provided a detailed description of the offenders, the rest of the shift were confident they would find them and be able to give them 'the treatment'.

This incident was big news and was circulated within the station for some time afterwards. A few weeks later, I even wrote the following entry in my research diary:

People are still talking about the fight Shaun and Justin had with some men after their shift had finished. Today I saw Nigel from shift three in a local supermarket, and he asked me if I had heard the story. I replied that I had, but he told it to me again anyway.

A discourse of violence operated as an invaluable source of information for the socialization of new recruits, as the following incident in Southville demonstrates:

Jacqui gave Bob, a new probationer, a lift to one of the village stations. As part of his training, he had been stationed at the cells in Main Town for the last few weeks. In the car, I asked him how he had found his stint in the cells. Bob said it was 'boring' because there had been no scraps [fights] down there. When he left the car, Jacqui laughed and said, 'I see Bob is trying to become one of the boys, trying to be all macho. He is probably trying to make up for the fact that he is the new boy.'

Fieldnotes—Southville

Excitement and action

Police narratives celebrated a confrontational approach to policing and this created and reinforced a thirst for excitement and action. A popular expression used by officers before embarking on their patrols was, 'Are you ready to go out and play'? The following episode captures how a preoccupation with violence, excitement, and action became manifest in practice:

1.15am

We all went into the canteen. Just as everybody was eating, an IR came over the radio for police assistance on Park Street—a part of the student union at the local University. The Area Control Room (ACR) said that there were approximately two hundred drunk students out on the streets, and that their presence posed a potential public order threat. Officers in the canteen (nine—all male) immediately became really excited, grabbed their coats and started to run towards the 'fun bus'. As they were running, Justin was humorously shouting, 'Let's go student bashing!' We all got into the carrier and it was clear that they were genuinely excited about this incident, and all simultaneously started putting their leather gloves on. John, David and Don were laughing and saying that they should have put snooker balls in their gloves for extra impact during the fight. One officer said, 'Students—it will be all, 'I know my rights. You can't touch me.'

It was very much an atmosphere of humour, bravado and looking forward to a fight. The call definitely offered officers a chance for excitement given that the night had been really quiet. But just as we were over half way there, the ACR came back on to tell officers the job was cancelled—the students were merely leaving their end of term ball and were dispersing. This offered major disappointment to the officers and they started saying how 'boring' the ACR were.

Fieldnotes—Northville

However, an important distinction is to be drawn between police discourse and practice. It is debatable whether the officers would have actually fought with the students in this incident. Following Waddington (1999a), I would suggest that the overt displays of aggression were merely bravado—a 'backstage' aspect of the role mobilized to protect their occupational esteem in the *absence* of action and excitement. Nevertheless, this episode exemplifies the way in which excitement and the anticipation of physical confrontation was revered within rank and file culture. On occasion, moreover, the desire for conflict did set the rationale for practices. The prospect of action recurrently engendered a prompt and heavy police presence at incidents involving a public order element. These occurred mainly on deprived housing estates, especially in Northville, and where relations between the police and sections of the community were already strained. Mirroring the research conducted by Smith and Gray (1985), officers valued responding to emergencies and tended to drive at high speed to incidents which did not necessarily require an immediate response. The latter illustrates how police technology can become implicated within the occupational culture (Holdaway 1983). Officers criticized police vehicles for being

'too slow', while simultaneously expressing a desire to participate in high-speed car pursuits:

A black Honda with tinted windows drove quickly past in the opposite
direction. Tom suddenly shouted 'That's mine'! He then slammed on the
brakes, did a wheel spin in the middle of the road, and drove over eighty
miles an hour until he could see the car in sight. He was saying, 'Go
on, try and lose me', before asking me if I had ever been in a car pursuit
before. However, the car pulled over. The occupant was a middle-aged
Black Caribbean woman who was apologetic and polite to Tom. He
explained to her that he had stopped her because she was going too fast.
She apologised again and was free to leave. Walking back to the car, Tom
said, 'No! Don't be nice. Why can't they be arseholes? I don't mind getting
naughty with arseholes.'

Fieldnotes—Southville

During group discussions, I asked officers to describe their
ideal working day. Their responses overwhelmingly centred
on action-packed activities such as catching burglars and drug
dealers; engaging in car pursuits; and breaking up public order
incidents. Conversely, incidents requiring a less zealous police
response were only rarely mentioned. The centrality of a masculine ethos which celebrates confrontation and excitement is most
forcefully brought to the fore when one imagines the possibility of
officers animatedly relaying stories about their exploits on a community policing task, or a time when they have assisted a vulnerable member of the public. On the contrary, some officers were
known as the 'shit magnet' for their propensity to be called to
seemingly boring incidents.

Organizational Realities

As several commentators note, police work is characterized by an
underlying tension. The strain is between expectations of what
police work involves and its daily realities (Van Maanen 1978*b*;
Manning 1977; Crank 2004). In Northshire, various organizational requirements challenged dominant conceptions of the job.

The paper burden

The effective completion of paperwork is an essential feature of the
police occupation; it provides a formal record of policing practices
and provides and essential 'foundation for transparency' (Foster

2003: 231; see also Fielding 1988). The paperwork completed by officers is mobilized to secure prosecutions and in this sense influences who enters the criminal justice system (McConville *et al* 1991).

During the course of the research, officers failed to recognize these wider issues. Instead, 'paperwork' was the subject of the most forcefully expressed criticism of the job. It was denigrated for preventing officers from carrying out their preferred role as crime fighters and engaging in, mainly adversarial, outdoor activity with certain factions of the public. It was also criticized for precluding officers from supporting their colleagues out on the streets. The following was typical of the sentiments expressed:

Tim: I haven't been in the job that long but, to me, it's totally not what I expected. It's like you do a job for ten minutes, and then sit around for hours doing all the paperwork. You've got the paperwork coming out of your ears . . .

David: Instead of going out there and fighting crime, people are pushing you to be a secretary. Paperwork is deemed more important a lot of the time, and it gets you down. You can't get out there and do what you joined for.

Gary: I have made the argument that we should get a civilian in to do it for us—or one of the girls in the office could do the bits that we don't need to do.

Malcolm: For six weeks I was released from paperwork and posted to Westville. And I have to say, they were the best six weeks I'd done in the job. You could go out and look for crime, deal with problems.

Group discussion—Southville

Officers who adopted a conscientious approach to paperwork were criticized for somehow abandoning their 'proper' policing responsibilities:

Jim: he best bobbies, the ones that go hunting for it, those are usually the ones with the most outrageous paperwork tray . . .

Gary: [Laughing] Yeah, that's me. I'm sorry boss, but it's more important.

Jim: But the ones with no paperwork, you usually find they are the bone idle ones—they clearly don't get out of the station.

Group discussion—Northville

The notion that paperwork is marginal to the police role served as an important source of information for the socialization of new recruits, and provided cues for police behaviour. After attending a road traffic accident, a probationer came back to the station and diligently began to prepare an incident report. Upon noticing this, a seasoned officer stood over him and said, 'Bloody hell, you're keen aren't you? Don't worry; we'll soon knock that out of you.' Looking somewhat embarrassed, the probationer laughed and then put the incomplete paperwork back into his drawer. Whether excessive paperwork duties were real or imagined, enormous antipathy was expressed towards this organizational requirement. At the time of the research in Southville, a new domestic violence incident form had been launched and aroused considerable criticism. The resentment felt towards the form served to reinforce the long-standing perception that domestic violence incidents are both troublesome and time-consuming.

Several reasons may explain the opposition towards paperwork. Firstly, doing paperwork challenges the imagery officers have of the police role. Most officers continue to invest in the exhilarating aspects of policing and perceive paperwork as encumbering the accomplishment of this idealized representation. Secondly, aversion to paperwork also reflects officers' antipathy towards education and, in some cases, their own limited educational achievement (Young 1991; see also Fielding 1988).[3] Finally, and as an earlier extract illustrates, completing paperwork was considered to be feminine. It was, by some accounts, a job for the women.

The 'numbers game'

The imposition of performance indicators within police organizations is a key component of current managerialist agendas (see McLaughlin *et al* 2001). In line with other British forces, Northshire Police are under pressure to achieve 'results' in the form of detections and arrest. Within the occupational culture, however, the requirement to meet performance targets was another contentious issue.

---

[3] Throughout the research, I encountered very few rank and file officers who held a university degree—most had reached the level of secondary education only. Officers tended to have a mixed view of university students, ranging from arrogant and stuffy to lazy and polluting. One officer was rebuked by his colleagues because he held a degree in philosophy. He had been nicknamed 'The Vicar' for displaying relatively left-wing intellectual views; as one officer told me, 'Peter is a member of the Looney Left—he should have joined the church, not the job!'

Officers asserted that a substantial proportion of operational police work could not be quantified (such as undertaking high visibility patrols for example) and consequently failed to be appreciated in organizational terms. The formal accent on numbers was also criticized for impinging on relations between the police and the public, as some officers in Southville put it:

Noel: The job is getting harder. All they want is statistics, statistics, statistics . . .

Mike: It's the numbers game . . .

Noel: They want me to ticket Mrs Smith on the road instead of asking her to move on. They want me to whack her for the figures and then when I need her help with something she says, 'No. You gave me a ticket' [. . .]

Valerie: Quality of service has gone. Now it is quantity of service. Are we giving the public a service, or are we actually going out there and getting as much crime as we can just to get our figures? What do they [management] want—quantity or quality? Because I don't think you can have both.

Group discussion—Southville

As Smith and Gray (1985: 342) remind us, however, police contempt of 'figures' results from the perception that evaluation of performance in terms of numbers are an attempt by management to keep their autonomous movements accountable. Although the performance regime was heavily criticized, it also, somewhat paradoxically, provoked a mindset in which arrest carried enormous kudos. On one occasion, two IMU officers had a heated argument over which one of them would 'get the numbers' for an arrest they had both been involved in. Officers always boasted of their arrest rates and, within their informal vocabulary, those arrested were referred to simply as 'bodies' or 'hits'. Most of the time, securing an arrest served a personal victory rather than fulfilling a public service. It was likewise considered a 'bonus' if the suspect possessed any outstanding warrants.

Another consequence of the performance regime was that officers targeted certain people and areas which were considered to provide them with a greater opportunity of attaining results:

David had been set the following targets in his Performance Development File (PDF): three intelligence entries on NPIN (Northshire Police Intelligence Network), ten detections with a minimum of three arrests, submission of five stop and search forms, and the issuing of five Hort.1 forms ('producers'). I asked him how easy it was for him to meet these targets. David said they were all relatively simple, especially the 'producers' and the stop and search forms. All that needed to be done was to drive over to some of the car parks where the local 'druggies' hang out, or to the local council estate to see who was around. If he saw somebody who was 'known' to the police he would then say to them, 'We have had a number of burglaries in the area and I would like to search you for any material'; as he put it, 'If they say yes, then you can submit a form. If they say no then you bring them in, and you have satisfied one of your arrests.'

Fieldnotes—Southville

On another occasion I accompanied officers from Southville and another station on an organized drugs operation which focused on several public houses. Officers spent over two hours searching people who 'looked likely' for drugs, but none were ever found. Once we got back into the carrier, the sergeant told the group that they could simply not go back to the station empty-handed. One of the officers suggested that they go over to Mill Park, an area renowned as where young people went to smoke cannabis and take recreational drugs. However, the park was virtually deserted and officers were forced to return to their station without any 'prisoners' or detections. This line of reasoning was also noted in Northville where officers would focus on certain locations and people to boost their arrest rates. Police attention was invariably directed towards low status males and other 'police property' (Lee 1981) groups. In broader terms, the external imposition of performance indicators reflects the increasingly punitive stance of the government towards crime and, as Crowther (2000b) notes, especially the 'crimes' of the residuum.

The imposition of performance indicators hinders the extent to which new modes of policing can be put in place. In organizational terms, arrests and detections are an indicator of success and consequently accrue rewards. Yet in the wake of the organizational adoption of community policing a tension emerges. While officers are encouraged to be community-oriented and 'customer-focused', the emphasis on attaining results operates to reinforce the existing and pervasive crime control mindset.

Civilianization

One of the main changes to have occurred in British policing is the expansion in civilian employment (Newburn 2003; HMIC 2004). However, the civilianization of Northshire Police

Force was another source of criticism among the rank and file. In particular, officers bemoaned the appointment of 'civvies' in the ACR. Civilian personnel were criticized for lacking any 'real understanding' of the apparently special rudiments of the police role and they were accorded little status. This sentiment was also exemplified by comments officers used to describe their sworn colleagues who were now working in offices and other non-operational posts; they were, as one officer put it, 'civilians on police wages'. This type of attitude was likewise apparent in the renaming of the Public Service Desk (PSD) where a number of sworn officers worked. Within the informal vocabulary, the PSD had been nicknamed 'Pregnant, Sick, and Disabled'.

Officers articulated robust opposition towards the recruitment of Police Community Support Officers (PCSO) into the Force. From their perspective, the limited powers available to PCSOs meant they could not be considered 'proper police'. A perceived decline in police numbers underpinned these feelings of resentment towards their civilian colleagues, as the following comments demonstrate:

Graham: They can only really be the 'eyes and ears' for us so we can get on with doing real policing . . .

Jake: But they get £15k a year. I would rather they employ one real police officer than two PCSOs. But apparently they are going to employ another sixty of them just in Lowerbrook Division . . .

Kate: But the kids, they all know that they've got no powers and make fun of them. So now they are too frightened to go out on their own and rely on us to come and get them!

Jake: I have been off duty and I have seen PCSOs walking down roads that are access only. There is a garage, a couple of houses and a graveyard! How on earth do they see that as policing?

Andy: But they are not proper police. The uniforms look like something from the Thunderbirds! 'Yes Officer Plastic' . . .

Graham: Plastic Police. . .

Jake: But they'll make the police redundant.

Group discussion—Southville

Front-line officers have a clear sense of the uniqueness of their role. This engenders feelings of solidarity and contributes to an idea that they are set apart from the public and others within the organization. In the current terrain, where policing is becoming increasingly diversified, some new dynamics have emerged; the proverbial *vertical* distinction between the rank and file and management has been accompanied by a *horizontal* division between 'real' police and 'plastic police'.

Managing Policing Realities

The occupational perspectives developed by the police represent the solution to 'coping with the reality of the job' (Van Maanen 1978*b*: 117). Officers in Northshire soon discovered that instead of engaging in exciting criminal pursuits and being respected by the public, their work was largely unrewarding and monotonous. It involved what many characterized as 'mopping up' after people, mainly after the event and usually in the face of public contempt. Officers accordingly developed a profoundly cynical and pessimistic view of their social world. This outlook was reinforced by their critical involvement in dealing with the darker side of society, and from the associated sentiment that the morality they were attempting to defend was rapidly becoming eroded.

Beleaguered minority

The conception of the police as a 'beleaguered minority' is germane for understanding the cynicism I encountered. An upshot of the mission perspective within police culture is that the rank and file come to see themselves as a small minority in the large fight against crime; as Reiner (2000*a*: 90) puts it, police develop 'a hard skin of bitterness, seeing all social trends in apocalyptic terms with the police as a beleaguered minority about to be overrun by the forces of barbarism'. Much as in earlier works (Banton 1964; Reiner 1978; Holdaway 1983) officers continue to view their social world as though it is on the verge of chaos:

David: We've got how many thousands of people living in the LPU? And we just can't cope. We are run ragged all the time. We are overrun. . .

Scott: We are overrun. Out there, we are outnumbered.

Richard: From a probationer's point of view I think that we are out of the frying pan and into the fire. You do fifteen weeks' initial

David: training, and it just does not prepare you for what you are fa-
        cing at all . . .

David: Your uniform is only just on and it's, 'Get in the car and go and
        deal with them twenty people fighting' [. . .]

Howard: We're always chasing different problems. We are going round
        putting little plasters over massive gaping cracks, just juggling
        problems.

David: Fighting fire with a thimble of water aren't we?

Group discussion—Northville

Officers working in Southville had a lighter workload than their urban counterparts, but this omnipresent pessimism was also a central feature of their occupational consciousness:

Wayne: This is a thankless job to be honest. No matter what you do, you
        don't get any encouragement. It's a hard job we do out there.
        And down here we are working with skeleton staff and no
        resources. We are pushed to the hilt trying to protect the patch,
        but it's a thankless task . . .

Jacqui: How great would it be to see an Inspector coming onto a shift
        and working alongside you? They don't know what its like out
        there. They lose sight of what we are facing because they don't
        go out there and do it . . .

Chris: People don't realize what we have to deal with. When the wheel
        comes off down here, it's downhill all the way.

Group discussion

More generally, officers in both research sites refrained from saying out loud the word 'quiet' for fear it would prompt a sudden burst of incidents.[4] As Reiner (2000*a*) notes, the discourse of the police as a beleaguered minority is often mobilized to secure increased powers and extra resources. In Northshire, feelings of harassment underpinned numerous complaints about apparently deficient resources, including malfunctioning radios and depleted staffing levels, which hampered operational policing.

---

[4] After commenting on how quiet a shift had been I was frequently met with the response, 'Sshhh! don't say the Q word. If you say that, all hell will break loose'. At the same time many officers said that my presence on their shift had seemingly 'jinxed' the excitement and activity which normally took place.

Conservative ideologies and the futile delivery of justice

The cynical feature of the police perspective became directed towards an abstract notion of 'the law' and the wider criminal justice system. Emulating earlier works (Reiner 1978; Graef 1989) officers robustly chided soft laws and lenient judges for ostensibly hindering the police in their assignment to combat crime:

Walter: There was a time when I had pride in this job. But when you constantly get kicked and keep getting back up. I am at the stage now where I just do what I have to . . .

Philip: I think the problem came in with the Human Rights Act because it really is designed not for the victim, but for the offender to be quite honest.

Fraser: Gone now—there is no justice for the victim. Now it is all for the offender. 'What can we do to stop you taking drugs? What can we do to stop you nicking cars'? It's all about them. Forget the victim. Forget the people who have just been raped, burgled, and robbed. It makes you sick. . .

Ian: But you arrest them and the criminals get their card out, 'Can you ring my solicitor.' The solicitor turns up, raking in the pennies. The criminal justice system is bullshit. . .

Philip: Let's look at the criminal justice system as a whole. Scrotes go into this so-called prison system and their cell. They have got everything; a TV, a sink, a bed, all mod cons. And what's happened to the IP [injured party]? It's a disgrace. The criminal justice system is a joke. Full stop. . .

Ian: Then they get minimal sentences. And once they are inside, they are just learning more stuff, chilling out with their mates . . .

Philip: Then they come back out on the streets, and find better ways of getting away with it.

Group discussion—Southville

The local courts were criticized for excessively favouring the criminal and eroding all the painstaking work officers put in to keep 'the streets' safe. Defence lawyers were vehemently denigrated for finding loopholes in the law and allowing suspects to walk free from court. But as Holdaway (1983: 72) reminds us, the police have an aversion to lawyers because they are in a position to challenge their practices. These ideas about the futile delivery of justice underpinned a robust 'law and order' stance on crime. During one group discussion in Northville, the subject of policing by consent arose and provoked the following response by one officer:

Mark: There is not enough respect for the police. I know it sounds harsh, but fear works. Fear of being locked up, fear of a sentence, even fear of the police. Policing by consent doesn't work, policing by fear will. People are not afraid of the police anymore, and I think people need to feel scared.

Officers' worldview included a simplistic, decontextualized understanding of criminality. It was routinely asserted that 'boot camps' and the death penalty should be reinstated. These authoritarian ideologies were accompanied, moreover, by a conservative *political* persuasion (see also Baker 1985). The research in Southville coincided with the 2005 general elections and many officers overtly articulated their preference for the Conservative party, whose political package at the time contained policies that resonated with the existing norms and values of rank and file culture.[5] A few officers I encountered were also practising evangelists and espoused a particularly moralistic position on the world. Although officers championed a moral way of living and placed much weight on family ideologies and marriage, these conventional mores were not necessarily followed in practice; a notable number of officers were involved in extra-marital affairs with their colleagues.

The classic work of Skolnick (1966: 59) understands police conservatism as a cultural response to the uniqueness of the job; as he puts it, 'the fact that a man is engaged in enforcing a set of rules implies that he also becomes implicated in *affirming* them' (emphasis in original). The police conservatism I observed in Northshire led to pervasive support for the dominant ideologies of society and officers displayed considerable hostility towards people who challenged conventional morality.

Public as stupid, greedy, fallible . . .

Although officers espoused a powerful desire to protect the public they also paradoxically expressed profound cynicism towards the

---

[5] These included the promise of extra police powers, an expansion of the prison system, and more severe prison sentences, the reduction of police paperwork, and the enhanced recruitment of sworn police officers (as opposed to civilian Police Community Support Officers, for example).

unreliability and criminality of the public. In particular, they resented the public for being unappreciative of the work they did 'out there'. Against the backdrop of the current rhetoric of consumerism in policing discourse (Reiner 2000) the public were criticized for being excessively demanding. Consider the following comments which were made by CAT and IMU officers during a group discussion in Southville:

Jack: But you stop a member of the public now and they are like, 'How dare you stop me.' And they write in and complain.

Alistair: It's their village—and *we* work for *them* [his emphasis]. That's their attitude.

Philip: I remember turning up at a job and the woman said, 'My boys are here'—as if she owned us! I don't think so missus. But she has got the ear of the Chief so you can't say that. You just have to touch your forelock and get on with it.

Group discussion—Southville

During interactions, officers were aware that some members of the public wished to manipulate their authority by exaggerating the nature of the incident or by lying to them (see also Rubinstein 1973; Van Maanen 1978*a*). Officers held the attitude that they had 'seen it all before' and in their practices tended to disregard what 'civvies' told them. In line with the observations made by Manning (1977: 26) I too noted that people were seen as 'stupid, greedy, fallible, lustful, immoral and hypocritical'. This is evident in following incident where I accompanied two IMU officers in Northville:

The ACR dispatched Paul and Nick to a job. A car had crashed into the side of a terraced house in Hope Street, and had driven off. [. . .] A few bricks were missing from the house and there was glass all over the pavement. They cleaned up the mess and both surmised that the car was stolen. Two minutes later, the ACR passed all officers the details of a car that had just been reported stolen. Paul let out a sarcastic groan and suggested that the person who reported it was probably the driver of the car that had hit the house. He turned to me and explained, 'He was probably drunk and faked the theft. This job makes you so cynical. You get to think the worst of everyone—even your own mother.'

As McLaughlin (2007*a*) reminds us, the views the police hold of the public are influenced by their contact with them. Officers are particularly inclined to display cynicism towards their 'regulars', and this becomes manifest in an outwardly detached and unsympathetic manner when interacting with such groups. In the next instance, two IMU officers in Southville were dispatched to an incident involving a man who was threatening suicide by walking in the middle of a fast road at night time. Their response shows how police cynicism can set the rationale for interaction:

11.30pm

On the journey there, Bill and Anthony were immediately very sceptical about the man's suicide bid. They surmised he was probably drunk, wanted some attention and a taxi ride home from the police. [. . .] An ambulance crew had already arrived, and because the man had minor cuts on his hands, he was sitting in the back of the ambulance. Bill suddenly realised he recognised the man from a month or so ago when he had threatened to do the same thing. The officers became even more dismissive, and openly told the ambulance crew that the man only wanted some attention and that they had better things to do. Anthony contacted the ACR and made out that the man had sustained *serious* injuries to his hands, and as a consequence, the man would be going into hospital for the night. They told the ACR there was nothing else they could do, so could they close the incident down.

Interactions with suspects were clearly fraught with distrust, but victims of crime were likewise handled with scepticism. In responding to incidents involving theft and burglary, officers were immediately doubtful of those who requested a crime number as it denoted, for them, a potential inside job.[6] People who had been physically assaulted were similarly treated with less sympathy if they brought up the subject of 'compensation'.

Dark humour

The cynical element of the police outlook became further expressed through officers' predisposition to joke about the personal tragedies they routinely encountered. Various fieldnote extracts would demonstrate this, but I think the following is most pertinent:

Mathew and Jeremy were called to a domestic incident at Old Road. After his girlfriend had ended their relationship, a man in his late twenties had locked himself in their house and tried to kill himself by drinking bleach

---

[6] Having a crime number means that the incident has been officially logged by the police. In the main, insurance companies require a crime reference prior to investigating a claim. One officer described crime numbers as a 'gateway to riches'.

and taking an assortment of pills. In order to gain entry to the house, Jeremy smashed a back window through with his baton and opened the front door for the rest of us. We eventually entered the bedroom where the man was lying semi-conscious on the floor. The stench hit us straight away: there was vomit all over the floor and around his mouth. Mathew and Jeremy were trying to lay him on his side while repeating his name to bring him round. All the while, the girlfriend was screaming hysterically and Mathew asked me to take her out of the room [. . .] He was taken to the hospital by the ambulance crew. [. . .]

At 5pm, we were sitting in the parade room when the ACR contacted Mathew to say that the man from the 'bleach incident' had done a runner from the hospital, and could he confirm what the man looked like, including what he was wearing. At this point, all the officers began to snigger as he sarcastically replied to the ACR 'he is very *clean* shaven', 'his clothes are *clean*'. Later on in the shift, Sergeant Lewis asked Mathew how the domestic incident at Old Road had been resolved, to which he jokingly replied, 'Don't you mean the *'Domestos'* incident?[7]

Fieldnotes—Southville

In Northville I was once shown a photograph of a young boy who had been shot through the head. Pointing to the gaping hole, the officer said to me, 'It's like Derek [colleague]: in one ear and out of the other'! As Westley (1970) notes, there is little opportunity in police work to celebrate humanity. This observation is developed by Waddington (1999*a*), who proposes that police humour, however dark and misguided, is a valuable tool for releasing the tensions associated with the working environment. I should note that the importance of humour is also recognized by officers themselves:

Mike: I think it takes a special person to take all the pressures of this job. You have got to have a warped sense of humour to cope with it—If you didn't laugh, you would cry.

Group discussion—Northville

Police humour also became expressed in less depressing ways. In addition to routinely telling jokes, officers also liked to play pranks on each other. In Southville an IMU officer once radioed through to his colleague and told him to come back to the station because there was a 'gorgeous blonde' waiting to speak to him. Upon eagerly returning to the station, however, Simon was met with a golden retriever dog which had strayed onto some farm land and needed

---

[7] 'Domestos' is a brand name for a household bleach/cleaning fluid.

to be taken to the local kennels. Humour is indeed an important coping response but, as Powell (1996) argues, it fulfils a broader function; it fosters a sense of solidarity among officers and has the potential to devalue organizational goals. As many of the extracts demonstrate, humour and parody were significant elements in subordinating aspects of the reform programme.

Maintaining Dominance

A range of other cultural responses underpinned interactions with the public, including the desire to maintain control over, and extract respect from, members of the public. It is not unlawful to be impolite to the police but, throughout the research, people who challenged officers' authority provoked a repertoire of reactions.

In Northville, the need to maintain dominance was pivotal to the development of an informal procedure called the 'attitude test' which officers applied when interacting with the public. In order to pass the attitude test, people were required to display deference through, for example, being polite, apologizing, or admitting their guilt. Below is an instance of the attitude test in operation:

Gareth stopped a black Peugeot which was being driven by a young Asian man. Gareth took the car keys out of the ignition and asked the man to stand outside the car. The man did what he was told and assumed a subordinate role, just nodding and agreeing with what Gareth was saying. The general conversation centred around the following:

Gareth: I stopped you because you were going too fast over the speed bumps.

Driver: I'm sorry officer. I was trying to get home to watch the second half of the football. Are you following the match?

Gareth: [Ignoring him] If I wanted to, I could keep you here and make you miss the rest of the match.

Driver: I'm sorry, I won't do it again.

Gareth: I'll let you off this time—but be careful, there are young kids on this estate.

When we got back into the car, I asked him why he took this course of action. Gareth replied, 'He was alright. He passed the attitude test. Basically, I treat people how they treat me. If they apologise straight away and don't get arsey, then they won't get a ticket. If he would have been cocky I would have given him a producer—just to be a pain in his arse.'

Fieldnotes—Northville

Removing keys from the ignition of cars was noted in many of these types of encounters, and further demonstrates the police desire to exert control over the situation.[8] Like the study by Foster (1989) officers also sought to 'wind people up' in order to create an explosive situation which could potentially result in an arrest:

Nigel and Jack were called to an incident at a local Chinese restaurant. The owners were complaining that a man and woman had eaten a meal, but did not have enough cash to pay for it. The man had written a cheque, but it was completely illegible, and he was being argumentative with the staff. After arriving at the restaurant the man, who looked much dishevelled, told the police he was a diagnosed schizophrenic and that he needed to go home to pick up his medication before he could write the cheque. Jack recognized the woman he was with as a prostitute and became even more sceptical of the man's character.

[. . .] The man was becoming quite irate and Nigel and Jack took him outside. The man was shouting at them in frustration, but they were laughing in his face and being contrary to everything he was saying. The man was getting even more upset and was shouting louder. At one point he began to walk away and Nigel grabbed him by his coat and pushed him against the wall. After a threat of being 'locked up', the man backed down and started to apologize for his attitude. [. . .] In the car afterwards, the officers were laughing at the situation and Jack said, 'I couldn't believe it when he backed down, I was just about to do a section 5 on him. I was gutted—stupid fucker was nearly playing the game.'

Fieldnotes—Northville

On some occasions, failing the attitude test resulted in the actual arrest of an individual. This occurred mainly over weekends when people who were drunk and leaving local nightclubs were being 'mouthy' to officers intervening in minor public order incidents. What is notable in these cases was officers' use of section 5 of the Public Order Act 1986. This piece of legislation provides arrest powers for relatively trivial offences and was extensively employed by the police to enforce their authority and engage in what Box (1987: 58) calls 'vigilante justice'—that is, where the police charge people for offences to which they have no real defence. In the main, though, there was little intention of arrest.

---

[8] As McBarnet (1981) notes, however, this widely used practice is essentially unlawful because it detains an individual.

Rather, officers wished to merely stamp their authority and, in so doing, win a 'moral victory' over those with whom they came into contact (Choongh 1997; see also Muir 1977).

Saving face

This 'contempt of cop' (see Waddington 1999*a*: 154) response was most readily invoked when officers had an audience, such as members of the public and colleagues. It was on such occasions when officers felt the most need to 'save face' by maintaining and displaying their authority. Officers considered the act of being sworn at as the ultimate threat to their authority:

Peter: Most officers challenge it [swearing] . . .

Scott: Yeah, that's a big problem for me. I'm a big one for that. If someone swears at you, then they're coming in—I don't get paid for that. They wouldn't do it to a bus driver . . .

Gareth: If there's an audience, there's no alternative.

Jake: If there's an audience, you've got to save face. You've got to take them away . . .

Scott: Give them a chance to apologise. If they make the wrong decision they'll get locked up and if they do, then they've learnt a lesson.

Group discussion—Northville

This philosophy was noted during observations, as the next extract shows. It was a Friday evening and a group of IMU officers were driving around in the 'fun bus' when a middle-aged woman, who was staggering along a pavement, caught their attention. Ken, who was driving the carrier, pulled up next to her and asked her what she was doing:

The woman was fairly drunk and started saying 'Oh just fuck off. I've had a couple of drinks if that is OK with you lot.' Ken immediately jumped out of the carrier, stood very close to her face and threatened that, because of her language, he could 'bring her in' under Section 5 of the Public Order Act if he wanted to. The woman went quiet and apologised. With this, Ken got back into the van and started to drive off. As he was doing so, the woman shouted, 'Fuck off pigs'—at which point all the rest of the shift started saying, 'Ooohhhh.' Ken slammed on the brakes and turned around in the middle of the road and sped back towards her. He jumped back out and said, 'What did I just say to you about swearing'? Just then a large man came running up the road and told Ken he was her husband, and that they had just had an argument in the pub. He was saying that he was a firefighter and started to give Ken his collar number [*he was trying to find a common bond*]. Before getting back into the carrier Ken warned him, 'Keep your missus under control or she is coming in for the night.' After they moved on, he said to the rest of the shift, 'I don't give a fuck what your collar number is mate—just shut your fucking missus up.'

Fieldnotes—Northville

Although officers considered swearing to be grounds for arrest, it is worth noting that profane language was pervasive within *their own* everyday vocabulary. Swear words were regularly employed, moreover, when interacting with marginal and low status groups. As Crank (2004) explains, police swearing during formal encounters grabs the attention of their adversaries, establishes social distance, and accordingly alienates the subject of their interest.

Involvement in minor public order offences was less frequent in Southville, but the cultural norm of maintaining authority was also evident:

Duncan noticed that a car had driven through a red light. He activated the lights and siren, and pulled the car over. He asked the driver if he knew why he had been stopped, to which the driver replied that he did not know. Duncan asked, 'What colour were the traffic lights when you drove through'? The man said, 'They were on amber', at which point Duncan said, 'No. They were on red.' When the man contested this point, Duncan said, 'You can either admit that you drove through the light when it was on red, or we can argue this in court.' The man then admitted he had driven through the red light and that he was sorry—after which he was then free to leave.

Along with the threat and actual imposition of a range of penalties, officers attempted to maintain their dominance in less overt ways (see also Smith and Gray 1985). During routine patrols it was common practice for officers to slow down and stare intensely at certain groups—particularly youths and those previously 'known' to the police—in order to assert their authority. After an arrest, officers would sometimes deliberately delay interviewing suspects in order to 'let them stew' for a while. Officers also exploited the anguish felt by people brought into custody—and particularly those with addiction problems. I recorded the following conversation after officers arrested a prostitute. They saw the arrest as a prime opportunity to gather some intelligence about where she was buying her heroin from:

Clarke: Don't worry—she'll talk to us when she starts rattling.

Bethan: What does rattling mean?

Clarke: It is a word we use to describe what happens to someone when they haven't had a fix of heroin for a while. Their whole body starts rattling like a skeleton.

Gloria: You can always tell the heroin addicts because they ask for about ten sugars in their cup of tea—they have a really bad sweet tooth.

Clarke: When they are rattling, they just want to get out of here—which is good for us because we can get the information out of them.

Other informal tactics were employed to intimidate prisoners. On one occasion, a young black man had been arrested for suspected drugs offences but, from the police perspective, he was being uncooperative. The officers retaliated by saying they would 'pop him open' (meaning he was going to be intimately searched for drugs) unless he provided the information they needed.

Of course, not all officers acted in this way and I noted that some took a less confrontational approach. During the policing of a football match, members of the crowd began to jeer at officers who were forming a line across the pitch. When some officers were becoming visibly aggravated, the sergeant assured them, 'Don't let them rattle you. We are getting paid for getting wet, they aren't'! Similarly, as a couple of officers put it during a group discussion in Southville:

Nathan: Unfortunately, there aren't any offences against lippiness and arseholes. You can't do anything about it, because you will just worsen the situation. You just have to ignore it and not rise to it . . .

Mike: A lot of the time, they are just trying to get a reaction out of you, and wind you up . . .

Nathan: You have to put a professional head on and ignore it.

Responses of this kind originated principally from older and more experienced officers who had become accustomed to some of the remarks and behaviours directed towards the police. And I did note that younger officers who displayed the characteristics of the 'new centurion' (Reiner 1978: 230) were inclined to react aggressively to challenges to their authority.

The police are an integral part of the criminal justice system and, as a result, come to see themselves as intimately bound up with the delivery of justice and punishment. The pervasive sentiment that the criminal justice system fails to punish offenders accordingly justifies the operation of the kinds of informal punishment I observed. But what is of central importance here is that the use of *culturally* defined procedures undermines formal attempts to redefine the public as police customers; the informal means used by officers demonstrate the persistence of an overtly controlling approach towards members of the public.

Isolation and Loyalty

As visible symbols of state authority, the police are prone to become socially isolated from the outside world (Banton 1964; Skolnick 1966; Reiner 1978). Following an abundance of earlier works, many officers reported feeling alienated from the general public. In defence of this isolation, they developed a strong sense of togetherness with their colleagues. Feelings of solidarity were further exacerbated by the anticipation of hostility and danger.

A stigmatized identity

Van Maanen (1978*b*) observed over thirty years ago that the police are a somewhat defiled and stigmatized group. Northshire officers were only too aware that their position as police isolated them from the wider society. Consider the following comments made by an IMU officer in Northville:

Howard: When is the last time a police officer turned up and gave you good news? 'I'm sorry your son is dead', or, 'You are coming with me down the nick.' We don't deliver lottery wins. People see the uniform and they know we are bad news.

This sense of separation was heightened by officers' pervading sense of danger. In the deprived urban context of Northville, officers believed the local population were particularly hostile:

Derek: We aren't liked in a nutshell. There are no two ways about it. Drive through any estate, and they will stop and stare at you, spit at you. They hate us. . .

Sam: They do. They throw insults, stare and try to intimidate you [. . .]

Howard: People are always trying to fill you in . . .

Scott:　It all comes down to that. You've always got to be wary that someone's going to have a go, and try to fill you in.

Group discussion

Intensified by feelings of detachment this danger consciousness engendered the proverbial 'Us' (the police) versus 'Them' (the public) mindset. The following fieldnote, which was recorded during the policing of another football match, demonstrates how the element of danger can reinforce the sense of 'Them' within the police outlook:

The fans were getting louder, and one officer was recording their behaviour on a camcorder. At one point, the fans were stamping their feet, chanting and throwing items onto the pitch. One of the young officers asked me if I had ever been involved a fight with football fans before. When I replied that I hadn't he said, 'It's really scary. Imagine being weighed down with loads of equipment, not being able to see properly and having 10,000 angry men shouting at you saying, "You are next. I am going to kill you." It really is you against them.' Because they anticipated a fight after the match, all the officers stuck together throughout the evening.

This anxiety about public hostility was not experienced as intensely by officers working within the rural terrain of Southville. The mainly 'respectable' populace were considered to be pro-police and, in many respects, officers viewed themselves as working *for* this section of the population. However, the omnipresent disquiet about 'outsiders' meant that potential violence and physical risk also assumed an important place within their occupational consciousness. The apparently low staffing levels only intensified these feelings of insecurity:

Tim:　Morale is very low down here. It is such a rural, isolated area and danger is a major factor that is constantly being overlooked by senior management.

Rob:　Travelling criminals, they know we are thin on the ground. They know it takes twenty minutes for our nearest back-up to get here. We are alone down here . . .

Tim:　You've got outsiders coming over all times of the night. That is dangerous—for us and the public.

Group discussion

It is worth noting that senior officers working away from Southville disagreed with these assertions. Complaints about 'travelling criminals' and 'outsiders' were often mobilized by officers in their requests for extra resources, but were subsequently turned down by police managers who were sceptical about the actual threat posed by such groups. This apparent betrayal by management only served to reinforce officers' sense of isolation.

Shift solidarity

It has long been acknowledged that the isolation and sense of danger experienced by the police generates peculiarly strong feelings of togetherness with fellow colleagues (Skolnick 1966; Brown 1981; Holdaway 1983; Graef 1989). During the research, officers expressed clear interdependence with each other. Group loyalty was especially potent between officers on the same shift, and was no doubt encouraged by the predominantly white, heterosexual, male composition of such shifts. Feelings of solidarity were articulated in the following terms:

Bethan: What do you think influences the way you do the job?

[. . .]

Jack: The biggest influence on you is your peers though . . .

Ian: Yeah, definitely. It sounds really sad, but when you come into work it's very social. I see more of the lads than I do of my own family! And in a way you all become like family don't you?

Matthew: It's very social. My shift, and here, the team spirit is phenomenal. I once got a three month attachment to another squad, and I didn't want to leave my shift!

Ian: It's fantastic, a group of people who really give a monkeys about you.

Matthew: And you come back in after a good job that everyone has been involved in, you come back in and think, 'Good job. Team work'. . .

Jack: You talk everything out as a team.

Group discussion—Northville

Officers had a clear awareness of what characteristics were important in a colleague, as the next extract demonstrates:

Bethan: As a police officer, what qualities do you think makes an ideal colleague?

Simon: You like to think of your colleague as a good friend. We are all good friends, and the police are a family at the end of the day . . .

David: Yes, yes . . .

Simon: Someone you can turn to in confidence, and someone who is
             going to back you up. Someone who you can trust and who is
             going to be there if you need them . . .

David: Somebody you can talk to and have a laugh with.

Donna: We are all in the same boat doing the same job. And you like to
             think that we are all singing from the same hymn book . . .

Simon: The ideal colleague is someone who is the same as you
             basically.

                                              Group discussion—Southville

On one level, solidarity is beneficial for the organization because
it produces a high degree of team work and, throughout the fieldwork, officers displayed enormous willingness to support their
colleagues during potentially dangerous incidents. But, as several
writers observe, an in-group perspective can encourage the protection of colleague infringements of procedure (Westley 1970;
Skolnick and Fyfe 1993). During my observations, I noted various
instances of occupational deviance.

Officers routinely engaged in what Cain (1973: 42) has identified
as 'easing' behaviour. Owing to the low presence of supervisors
and vast rural landscape, the practice of easing was particularly
rampant in Southville. On one occasion, the IMU officers I was
accompanying attended one of the many parties which were being
held in the station's police bar. The officers and I participated in
the spirit of the party for over an hour; we ate sandwiches, drank
soft drinks and talked to the guests—most of who were serving
and retired police officers. During another shift, some CAT officers noticed a member of the public waiting outside one of the
locked satellite stations. Because they did not want to deal with
the inquiry, they drove past the station, hid around the corner and
went back once the coast was clear. In both sites, officers would
run personal errands (including picking up cat litter, prescriptions
and visiting the bank) while informing the ACR they were 'committed' to a previous incident.[9] Officers were dependent on each
other for concealing these instances of minor deviance from the

---

[9] On the face of it, these instances of 'easing' demonstrate that not all officers
shared a thirst for action or worked with the dominant crime control model of
policing. It is worth emphasizing, however, that only *certain* types of crime—and
people—were viewed within this framework.

attention of supervisors and, as a result, the norms of solidarity were sustained and reproduced.[10]

As Manning (1978*b*) observes, solidarity is a cultural characteristic closely related to police lying and secrecy. The lies told by the police results, he suggests, from the tension between formal organizational rules and expectations, and the realisms of daily police work. The following episode shows how police deception played out during the course of the research:

> We were sitting outside the rear of the station in the sun. Everyone was talking about the high speed car pursuit that Keith and Frank had been involved in a couple of nights earlier. Keith was driving and had taken a bend in the road too quickly, and had subsequently crashed the car. Nobody had been hurt, but the car had some damage to it. Nevertheless, and as is apparently usual in these circumstances, Keith and Frank were required to go to police Headquarters to be debriefed about the incident. When they were relaying the incident, the other officers were telling them to omit certain facts from their account when they visited HQ—including the speed at which they were travelling. The colleagues offered them advice on how best to answer any potentially incriminating questions and Keith assured them they had already omitted the 'worst bits' from the initial report.
>
> Fieldnotes—Southville

Another instance in Northville demonstrates how defensive solidarity covered up deviant practices. After using excessive force to arrest a local man, an onlooker asked one of the constables for the arresting officers' name so they could make a complaint. Another officer quickly stepped in and replied that they did not know the arresting officer because he was from a different station to theirs. This was untrue because all the officers who were present worked in the same station—and many worked on the same shift. Deception towards members of the public and supervisors represented a culturally supported norm. It should be emphasized that the lies articulated by officers were mainly small scale, or 'white lies' as officers saw it (see also Manning 1978*b*). They were perceived as doing little harm, and some were even viewed as being in the public interest. On one occasion, for example,

---

[10] However, there was a limit to what acceptable easing behaviour was. On one occasion, some officers got caught sleeping in the parade room during their night shift. This was heavily frowned upon by the other shifts as it meant they had left their patch wide open to 'outsiders'.

a grandmother reported to the police that her granddaughter had been physically assaulted by her partner. Upon being arrested, the perpetrator angrily demanded to know who had contacted the police. To prevent any future repercussions for the grandmother and the granddaughter, the officer replied, 'It was just a passer-by who heard all the shouting coming from your house.'

Group loyalty was an integral feature of rank and file culture, but various conflicts and fractures were nevertheless evident (see Fielding 1989). In addition to conflicts between ranks, the organizational emphasis on performance created an atmosphere of competitiveness between and within *shifts*. After informing one Northville officer I would be accompanying a different shift the following week he replied, 'We fucking hate them. They are always picking up our scraps and getting the numbers for it.' An entire shift in Southville were also disliked because its members were seemingly 'bone idle' and neglectful of their patch. Other officers disliked working with their immediate colleagues due to a simple 'personality clash'.

On Patrol

Police culture is characterized by a distinctive interpretation of the different people and places that officers encounter (Rubinstein 1973; Holdaway 1983; Fyfe 1991). In Northshire, officers demonstrated an impressive, detailed knowledge of their respective areas. In their own estimation, a good bobby is a 'streetwise' one. At the mundane level, this virtue is revealed in recognizing a stolen car, knowing who has just been released from prison, and other pieces of information conducive to police work.

On the ground, certain places stood out in officers' cultural knowledge as relevant to the contingencies of policing. First and foremost, there were those places associated with certain forms of crime and deviance. Social housing estates and other dreadful enclosures (Wilson 1972) were known for where 'rough' populations lived and for generating a high volume of domestic violence calls. Public houses were earmarked for their potential to trigger public order incidents and drink driving offences. Several haunts were associated with youth subcultures and drug takers, while other areas became linked with 'deviant' sexualities. In Northville, certain streets were notorious for prostitution and in both sites several locations were renowned for casual sexual relations between men. Finally, concealed from the scrutiny of supervisors, various places were marked out for rest and refreshment whilst on duty—or 'brew stops' as officers called them.

Officers displayed a strong protective interest towards their 'patch', and engaging in patrol work was considered to be the pinnacle of their role (see also Holdaway 1983). In the quiet moments of the shift—of which there were many—officers liked to engage in proactive patrolling. This practice was accorded high value within the culture because it closely resembled traditional metaphors of the police as crime fighters and investigators. Proactive patrol allowed officers to act on their own initiative and develop information on crime and its spatial location (see also Crank 2004). But, more importantly, this form of patrolling was the principal means through which officers located suspicious persons.

The art of suspicion

In his classic study of the police, Skolnick (1966) identified suspicion as an integral feature of the working personality. In Northshire the ability to identify potential offenders was equally pivotal to the police identity. Officers found it difficult to articulate the practical basis for their suspicion, with some suggesting it was analogous to a sixth sense or 'instinct'. The next extract records a late shift where I accompanied two IMU officers in Northville. They were on their way to the local Salvation Army to enquire about a man who had been missing for a number of days, when the following happened:

Don suddenly pulled up next to an old red Nissan car which was parked on the corner of a road. The car was placed awkwardly on double yellow lines and had one of its headlights on. Because it was empty, Don got out of the police car and started to look carefully around the vehicle. As he was doing this, Paul turned to me and said, 'Don is a big traffic offences guy—he has a real instinct for it.' [. . .] When Don got back into the car, I asked him why he had decided to stop and examine the Nissan. He replied, 'It's hard to explain. To you I bet it appears like a normal, run-of-the mill car but, to me, I see a car parked dangerously on a corner with one light on and it has joy riders written all over it.'

As Sacks (1972: 285) observes, in patrolling their areas the police learn to treat their geographical domain as a 'territory of normal appearances'. Their patch is infused with regular 'background expectancies' (ibid) and the task of the officer is to become sensitive to those occasions when these expectancies are in variance or, more simply, 'out of place'. The notion of incongruence as a source for police suspicion found enormous support during the observations. Consider the following incident in Southville:

As we drove past Main Street, Duncan noticed the 24-hour garage in complete darkness. Surmising how unusual this was, he stopped the car, turned it around and sped back towards the garage. Duncan warned me that the darkened garage might be a sign of a robbery because it gave the impression it was closed for the evening. He parked the car up around the corner, pulled his torch out and approached the main hatch as I followed. As we got nearer, however, a woman who was sitting inside the garage came to the window and said that everything was fine—apparently there was just a small problem with the electricity. Duncan kept asking her if she was sure everything was alright until he was satisfied nothing untoward was taking place.

Officers developed an extensive dictionary of indicators which, for them, signalled a person's possible involvement in crime. I noted how certain characteristics, or cues, in the working environment stimulated suspicion and became a basis for public contact (Rubinstein 1973; Brown 1981). People who avoided eye contact with officers, displayed nervousness or gave conflicting accounts of their whereabouts, were vulnerable to police questioning, and stop and search powers. On-the-spot decisions in policing their environment were routinely determined by over-simplified conceptions officers held about particular social groups and situations. This stereotyping invariably resulted in patterns of differentiation along distinctions of class, age, gender, sexuality, and ethnicity. For instance, the presence of several teenagers or young men in dilapidated vehicles stimulated police suspicion, as did men who were parked up in areas associated with casual sexual encounters. In Northville, the operation of a red-light district meant that women who were walking by themselves late at night came to be viewed as potential prostitutes. Lone male drivers in areas renowned for prostitution were similarly seen as 'punters'. As Choongh (1997: 44) argues, individuals who are recognized by the police because of a previous event or conviction are the 'permanently suspect'. Lending support to this, the ultimate prompt for stimulating police suspicion was whether the person was already 'known' to the police. Officers also retained enduring stereotypes about the involvement of minority ethnic men in local crime. However, the *practical* policing of such groups was contradictory and uneven. In Northville, anxiety about being labelled racist sometimes led to the avoidance of proactive encounters with members of minority ethnic groups. A less ambiguous scenario was evident in Southville where poor and low status minority ethnic men were regularly subjected to police intrusion because they were seemingly inconsistent with the white, affluent surroundings.

The theme of suspicion cut across both locations with striking similarity, but there were some nuanced differences in the who, when, and where it was performed. These finer distinctions underline, I suggest, the manner in which suspicion is driven by the everyday characteristics of the occupational environment. In attending to their respective areas, one clear difference emerged within the culture; the problems Northville posed for officers meant that, for many, their task became one of *containing* the area. In Southville, conversely, officers perceived themselves as *protecting* the patch from outsiders and accordingly policed their rural landscape in an incessantly defensive state.

Enduring Themes of Police Culture

A wealth of research has identified recurring characteristics within police culture over time and space. There were interesting sources of variation between the occupational perspectives and practices of officers working in Northville and Southville—and these variants clearly capture the importance of local dynamics in shaping culture. Ultimately, however, such differences were subtle rather than outstanding and officers shared a related set of assumptions, beliefs, and practices which transcended the contrasting terrains. As noted in Chapter 1, current scholarship argues for a pluralized conception of police cultures (Chan 1997; Foster 2003; Sklansky 2007). This is important for interrogating its assumed homogeneity, but I maintain that there still is a police culture whose defining elements are to be found across different policing contexts. The discourses and interactions described and analysed in this chapter expose the powerful endurance of cultural characteristics noted by earlier works. A collection of dominant features persist around the sense of mission and preference for crime fighting, informal working practices and defensive solidarity, the celebration of masculine exploits and willingness to use force. Notwithstanding the considerable refashioning of police work that has occurred between my research and the classic studies, these features remain virtually untouched by policies and initiatives aimed at changing everyday assumptions and behaviours.

The endurance of these proverbial characteristics must surely point to broader questions about the very essence of the police role. What is it about policing that promotes these orthodoxies in cultural expression? It is well accepted that police culture derives from the common tensions which are inherently associated with the job of being a police officer. As Skolnick (1966) explained over four decades ago, these tensions are the potential danger facing officers in their day to day encounters, the authority (coupled with the capacity to use force) they bring to bear on such encounters and, finally, the pressure to be efficient. It remains the case that police work comprises these basic rudiments which, in turn, maintains and reproduces the cultural tendencies. Reiner (2000*a*: 87) arrived at a similar conclusion when he argued, 'police culture survives because of its elective affinity, its psychological fit, with the demands of the rank and file condition'. Yet the timeless qualities of police culture also derive from other stable elements of the police role. As Loader and Walker (2007) make clear, the police mandate may now be characterized by a myriad of functions, but maintaining and reproducing the social order remains pivotal. The operational logic of street policing inexorably requires officers to draw upon their cultural preferences and sensibilities to fill the gap between law in books and law in action. It is perhaps obvious that this is only facilitated by wide latitude that continues to be afforded to the police.

Prevailing change initiatives, especially ones that focus on diversity, cannot possibly transform these universal and stable features of the police role—and in fact may only serve to exacerbate aspects of the occupational identity. Nevertheless, notions of diversity are pivotal to current reform agendas. With this in mind, I want to now examine how the salience of ethnicity, gender, and sexuality within policing has influenced the way officers think about and interact with their diverse publics.

5

Policing Diverse Publics

In addition to exerting considerable influence over the internal character of police organizations, police culture can also shape the service that different members of the public receive. Debates about police culture have been principally concerned with the relationship between the police and certain sections of the population. The apparent racial discrimination within policing has been explored, along with other social divisions such as gender and sexuality. However, the British policing terrain is characterized by a new politics of policing diversity. Political sensitivity surrounding policing has changed remarkably since the classic studies and a new generation of officers inhabit a moment where they are expected to better serve all sections of society. The reform programme in Northshire focused primarily on the revision of operational policing philosophies and practices which could undermine the delivery of an effective and equitable service to minority ethnic, and gay and lesbian communities, and women. Has this recasting of diversity changed the way officers think about and interact with those groups currently emphasized in policing agendas? Is policing culture responsive to, or at odds with, the new realities?

In this chapter I consider these questions and examine how the accent on diversity has shaped the perspectives and practices of officers as they policed their diverse publics. I show that responses to the altered policing landscape are contradictory and uneven. In the wake of the diversity emphasis, aspects of the occupational culture are being revised and unlearned. We are witnessing, in particular, the beginnings of multiple policing identities and styles. Yet there also remains a resilient residue of characteristics which undermine the requirements of the new policing paradigm. For the most part, police culture continues to impact adversely on minority groups in ways identified in earlier research. I begin my analysis with an exploration of how the informal ideologies which comprize the police identity currently interact with gender, before going on to discuss sexuality and ethnicity.

Policing *for* Women?

Research and reflection on gender and police culture have chiefly examined police perceptions of, and responses to, women as victims of domestic violence and sexual crimes. However, the political agenda towards women as users of policing services has transformed considerably in recent years and various initiatives have been introduced to better serve this section of the population (Heidensohn 2003).

Domestic violence: new practices, old assumptions

Being a victim of domestic violence is one of the key avenues through which women encounter the police (Stanko 1985; Hoyle 2000). Yet there has been no shortage of evidence that police responses to such incidents have been inadequate. Facilitated by wide ranging discretionary powers, the police have routinely avoided arresting the usually male perpetrators and have likewise disregarded such incidents as 'rubbish' (Holdaway 1983; Edwards 1989; Young 1991). Today, police organizations are under greater pressure to change in a direction which emphasizes quality of service for victims of domestic violence. As Heidensohn (2003: 569) notes, this has involved two shifts; firstly, police organizations are expected to take domestic violence incidents seriously and, secondly, officers are being asked to be 'supportive and sensitive' in their response to such incidents. In Northshire, the improved resolution of domestic violence incidents was placed high on the reform agenda. One of the main changes was the adoption of a policy which directs constables to arrest the assaulting partner where there is evidence of an assault.[1] But the question remains; in what ways have these new requirements changed police narratives and practices in this area?

In the instances that were observed, the police *did* mainly arrest perpetrators of domestic violence. Most officers were acutely aware of the revised stance towards these incidents and had integrated it into their policing practices. However, within the occupational consciousness 'domestics' were still considered to be troublesome and unimportant (Holdaway 1983; Smith and Gray

---

[1] This is a local interpretation of a *national* trend (see also Hoyle 2000; Heidensohn 2003). Nevertheless, the introduction of pro-arrest policies has, for the first time, shifted domestic violence incidents into the sphere of law enforcement.

1985).[2] Responding to these incidents formed a large part of what officers actually dealt with on a day-to-day basis, but they were nevertheless regarded as marginal to what many celebrated as meaningful police work. The following exchange during a group discussion in Northville provides an illustration of this:

Ben: You join the police and spend your lives dealing with domestics don't you?

Edward: It is the same places, same faces every single day. And that's another frustrating element because we are just mopping up after people again and again. [. . .] The gaffers are big on domestics at the moment, and because of that, we are not being able to do the things that interest us . . .

Andy: The problem now is that we are going out dealing with those types of incidents. And fair enough, technically a crime has been committed by these inebriated people, but we've got paperwork to do for that, and we can't go out and catch the burglars, the rapists and the dealers. We are dealing with drunken domestics—it's crazy.

Officers informally referred to these disturbances as 'crocks of shit'. During patrols many loathed being dispatched to a domestic violence incident, and it was also common for some officers to simply ignore requests from the ACR inviting any available patrol to attend one.

From the police perspective, several features make 'domestics' unappealing. It was believed that attending domestic violence incidents are notoriously difficult because of their private nature; as one officer in Southville put it, 'I would hate it if someone came round my house whilst having a barney with the missus and interfered—it's our private business.' Officers also complained that domestics were frustrating because of their failure to lead to any conclusive results (see also Altbeker 2005). It was believed that attending these disturbances was futile because the female victim withdraws, or denies, the initial complaint.[3] From my observations, women

---

[2] As Waddington (1999*b*) points out, for the rank and file 'domestics' can also include disputes between an array of family members—and can equally extend to arguments between neighbours. For the current context, however, I am referring to the violence which is perpetrated largely by men against their (sometimes estranged) wives or partners.

[3] This does find some substance. A classic study by Horton and Smith (1988) found that victims of domestic violence rarely wanted their partners arrested. As others remind us, however, fear of future acts of violence and economic hardship may also explain some women's reluctance to pursue complaints (Edwards 1989; Hoyle 2000).

who failed to 'help themselves' were given little sympathy. In the following incident, I was accompanying a young IMU officer called Nathan. He was particularly authoritarian and displayed many characteristics of the new centurion:

The report was of a woman being beaten on a street by a male who, it was believed, was her boyfriend. When Nathan and I arrived at the scene, there were four other male officers there from a different shift. They were standing around a young woman who was crying and whose arm was covered in blood. One of the officers was sympathetically trying to coax the name of her boyfriend out of the woman, but she was telling him to go away because she did not want to name him. Another officer became impatient and was saying things like, 'Look love, you are going to have to help yourself'; and, 'Only you can get yourself out of this situation' while another told her, 'We can't stand here all night.'

It was agreed that there was nothing that they could do while she was with-holding the boyfriend's name from them. The first officer appeared genuinely frustrated at the prospect of not being able to help the young woman, but the other officers displayed a striking lack of sympathy and virtually blamed the woman for her position. Walking away, Nathan called her a 'stupid slag', and said that she deserved her abuse if she was not going to help herself.

Field notes—Northville

A popular discourse circulated among the rank and file was that they did not have a legitimate role to play in domestic violence incidents. Officers invariably described themselves as 'referees', as opposed to professionals intervening in a legit-imate crime. Yet effective police intervention in domestic vio-lence incidents is crucial to the protection of women (Stanko 1985) and, as we have seen, is of central importance to current policing agendas.

The construction of domestic violence incidents as rubbish, low status work reflected the persistence of the masculine ethos. In line with earlier works, officers held stereotypical assumptions about conventional gender roles, behaviour and family ideologies when attending these incidents (Grimshaw and Jefferson 1987; Edwards 1989). On one occasion two male IMU officers dis-played empathy towards a man who had assaulted his wife after discovering she was having an affair. More generally, it was often explained to me that there were 'always two sides to every story' in the case of domestic violence.

As the next fieldnote shows, police responses to domestic vio-lence incidents continue to be informed by masculine sentiments.

After going to a primary school to pick up her son, a woman discovered her child sitting in her ex-husband's car. Following a heated argument, she rang the police and explained that her former husband was breaching his agreement because his 'custody had been suspended'. David, a CAT officer, and Ian, an IMU officer, attended the scene:

The woman was extremely upset and shaking. The headmaster took us through to his office so she could explain the situation better. The woman told David and Ian the full story, and also said that her ex-husband kept coming round to her house late at night and looking through her window. She was also receiving 'silent' phone calls in the early hours and suspected it was him. Ultimately, however, it emerged that his custody rights had only been temporarily suspended, and there was no formal injunction against him contacting the woman or their son. Because of this, David explained that he could only go and 'have a word' with the dad, and ask him to go through his solicitor in the future.

On the way there, it was clear that David and Ian sympathized with the father. They called the woman a 'fretter', and surmised that it must be hard for the ex-husband not being able to see his son. They also agreed that, because he had left his wife for another woman, she was probably trying to turn the child against his father.

We arrived at the house where the father and his new girlfriend lived. During the interaction, the atmosphere was one of 'I-am-on-your-side-mate', and David and Ian were apologetic to the man for the intrusion. The father was discrediting his ex-wife by saying she was 'mental' and 'unfit to be a mother'. Ian brought up the subject of the silent phone calls and the late night visits. Although the man turned bright red, he denied them. The officers did not challenge him, but merely advised him that he needed to be careful in his actions because his ex-wife could 'use it in court'. No action was taken, and the officers told the ACR to record it as a 'no-crime domestic'. In the car, and commenting on the attractiveness of the new girlfriend, David and Ian said, 'Bloody hell—he has upgraded hasn't he? No wonder he left his wife.'

Fieldnotes—Southville

As I mentioned in Chapter 3, the revised stance on domestic violence incidents have placed an onus on officers to record key information relating to the case so that specialist officers can make an early risk assessment and, if necessary, a 'tailored safety plan' for the victim. In the above incident, the particularly male way of viewing the situation interfered with the quality of service afforded to the victim. Despite describing to officers behaviours which appeared to amount to harassment by her ex-husband, this information was not seized upon by the officers. As a consequence, the potential for future conflict was overlooked.

A central function of the police role is to enforce respectability but, as Waddington (1999*b*: 61) reminds us, 'respectability is gendered'. Victims of domestic violence were invariably defined according to a set of stereotypical assumptions about their femininity which, in turn, related to their deservedness as recipients of police protection. Much of the time, the perceived moral character of the victim interfered with the degree of sympathy and professionalism displayed by officers. Officers were rarely sympathetic to women viewed as contributing to their victimization. Their response was particularly deficient if the complainant was 'rough' or had a 'history' of domestics, as the following incident in Northville demonstrates:

An IR came through about a domestic violence incident on the Hammond housing estate. A woman had been heard shouting out of a top floor window that her husband had hit her. David and Sergeant Jones recognized the address and said, 'Oh for fuck sake, not that daft cow again.' Apparently, the police had been called there on a number of occasions.

When we arrived at the location, the woman was standing on the front doorstep and was arguing with her husband. She appeared to be drunk and was shouting to the police that her husband had hit her—but her husband was denying it. About seven officers had now turned up, and merely stood around and listened to the woman as she started to cry and shout. She was shouting that her young nephew was dying in hospital, and that her husband had hit her for coming back late from visiting hours. She kept repeating the sentence, 'The system stinks' and, as she was saying this, she began to stagger over to where we were standing. At one point when she fell over, her blouse lifted up and exposed her stomach and underwear. By now all of the (male) officers were looking on in amusement, and laughing amongst themselves. One officer said to another, 'If she doesn't fucking shut up, I am going to knock her out myself', while another said, 'I'm going to lock *her* up if she doesn't shut up.'

Sergeant Jones eventually went into the house to talk to the husband. After a while he came out and said apologetically to the other officers, 'I am going to have to lock him up—Logan will have my arse if I don't' [Logan was the Superintendent who was responsible for reiterating the current organizational drive on domestic violence incidents to the rank and file]. However, Jones told his colleagues that the woman had come home drunk and probably 'wound up' the husband, who had subsequently retaliated. Jones and the other officers saw the arrest as an 'arse-covering exercise'.

This episode demonstrates that police practices are not entirely independent of societal pressures and legal rules (see Chan 1997). Yet, as the extract shows, officers are merely concerned to 'cover their arse', rather than protect and support female victims. In the wake of the reform initiative, then, an important tension emerges. While some police behaviours have changed accepted ways of thinking have persisted. The role of Sergeant Jones is also important here. As Marks (2005) intimates, middle management is key to police culture; they are the people who can translate new ideas from senior officers into reality. As we see though, Jones openly undermined the revised organizational drive and his discursive response only operated to authenticate the widely diffused regard that domestics are 'crocks of shit'.

Furthermore, despite the general change in police behaviour, some officers continued to impose a temporary solution, such as separating the parties (Stanko 1985; Smith and Gray 1985; Edwards 1989). The next extract was recorded during a night shift. I was accompanying Rob, an IMU officer in his early thirties, when the following call came in:

2.15am

A woman with head injuries had been found at a house on the Norton Park Estate. Rob recognized the address and said it was where an alcoholic called 'Fat Charlie' lived and was known to the police for his drinking binges. Given that the evening had so far been quiet, five patrols turned up to the incident.

We entered a dilapidated house which was dimly lit. Lying on the sofa was a large man who was drunk. A woman was lying on the floor by the kitchen and paramedics were trying to get her to talk. Rob—who had encountered the couple on previous occasions—asked Charlie what had happened, and why the woman was covered in blood. He mumbled that they were separated and that she had come around to his house to have a go at him. He explained that she was really drunk and, as she was leaving, she had fallen over and knocked her head on the wall. The officers, and the paramedics, appeared not to be taking the incident seriously and made remarks to each other about the 'stench' of the house and the woman.

[. . .] The police eventually decided they would take the woman to her sister's house a few doors away so she could sober up. About five officers carried her through the back alley and into the house. I went back to the house with Rob where he decided that Fat Charlie was 'harmless', and that he probably didn't hit the woman. Rob notified the ACR that it was some kind of 'drunken accident' and could they clear it off the computer.

Paradoxically, what these extracts also show is how domestic incidents can initially offer the prospect of excitement.[4] Officers raced to the scene if there were public order implications—particularly if the male perpetrator was still present at the scene and behaving in an aggressive manner. Officers saw such occasions as an opportunity to use their physical strength (see also Westmarland 2001*a*) and I did note that an unnecessarily large number of patrols would arrive at the location. However, when it became apparent that there was little chance of confrontation, officers soon lost interest and tried to 'bat' (pass on) the incident onto an unfortunate colleague.

The new organizational response to domestic violence has been supplemented by the creation of a domestic violence incident form called DVIR. In the case of an arrest, officers are required to complete a Domestic Violence Investigation Record. If officers make no arrest, a similar form entitled the Domestic Violence Intelligence Record is then completed. The form was launched during my time in Southville and was vehemently criticized by officers. One of the problems was its 'invasive' character in that it required (predominantly male) officers to ask sensitive questions to (predominantly female) victims who had just experienced domestic violence. This complaint found some support from my observations. The form required women to answer in detail various questions about recent and past experiences of physical or sexual assault. Victims were quizzed about their mental health, and were also asked to provide detailed information on any children in the home.[5] One of the overarching problems of the form was its inference that the information provided may be passed on to other formal agencies—including social services. These features made the police-victim relationship strained. In most of the cases I observed, victims of domestic violence displayed enormous anxiety as to who would receive the information and what would be done with it.

However, the greatest complaint officers made about DVIR was its lengthy and time-consuming character and there was a perception that the form was 'pointless'. Of course this undoubtedly

[4] An Immediate Response (IR) status is attached to these incidents and, as Westmarland (2001*a*) rightly observes, what is seen as 'rubbish' actually represents a significant distraction from the tediousness of routine patrolling.

[5] This information included their age, schools attended, doctor's details, and whether *they* had been victims of assault within the household. Officers were also required to talk to the children in order to assess their safety and risk of victimization.

reflects the broader hostility towards paperwork, but several issues are nevertheless pertinent for the current context. The antipathy felt towards DVIR reinforced the long-standing perception that domestic violence incidents are troublesome. Moreover, the association of these critical incidents with the filling in of a long and intrusive form compromised the 'customer focus' officers were supposed to display in these cases. Some officers avoided filling in the form at the scene of the incident. Instead, they merely noted down key details (such as the full name, address, and date of birth of the victim) and completed the form at a later time—and sometimes at a later date. The problem here is that the use of *culturally* defined procedures could fail to provide an accurate picture of the victim's situation and, therefore, policing needs.

Sexual crime and the despised gender

Current policing policy likewise emphasizes the sympathetic and professional treatment of victims of sexual crime (Heidensohn 2003; see also Jones *et al* 1994). In line with other British forces, Northshire Police has adopted new examination suites for rape victims and has also enhanced police training in this area. Officers expressed clear abhorrence towards perpetrators of sexual crimes such as rape but, during some incidents, I noted that the perceived character of the victim interfered with their assessment of the situation. In particular, several officers retained enduring assumptions about victim precipitation (Edwards 1989; Page 2007). On one occasion in Northville two male officers were dispatched to a rape incident involving a woman in her early twenties.[6] Although they were initially very caring and sympathetic towards the victim, this was soon replaced by scepticism after it emerged she had reported a similar incident on a previous occasion. The victim also told officers she had been on a date with the perpetrator, and that she had invited him back to her house. Officers continued to take down the relevant details of the assailant, but the comments which were later expressed in the car made clear their cynicism towards her role in the event. These classic

---

[6] Ordinarily a female officer from their shift (who had received specialist training) would have been dispatched to such an incident. However, this officer had been on light duties and, because it was 5am, had just left to go home. She was later called back to the station by her sergeant and subsequently arrived at the location to replace the male officers I was with.

ideas about victim precipitation found striking resonance, moreover, when dealing with women who worked as prostitutes.

As Jefferson (1993: 28) notes, prostitutes are 'the one overwhelmingly female manifestation of the criminal Other'. Although some officers understood that working as a prostitute was a way of surviving poverty and drug addiction they were invariably viewed with disdain. Prostitutes were targeted during patrols, but their victimization received less attention. As Edwards (1987) reminds us, working as a prostitute carries enormous personal risk and, in Northville, prostitutes were subjected to sexual and physical violence by their clients. However, officers expressed the view that the violence experienced by these women was something as an 'occupational hazard'. After describing to me an incident in which a woman had been raped at knifepoint, one male CAT officer stated, 'However, it was a prostitute and you always have to be wary when they cry rape. Sometimes it is just to get back at a punter that hasn't paid them.' Women suspected of working as prostitutes were always viewed with suspicion, and this affected the quality of service that more 'respectable' women would have been given. I recorded the following incident while on night duty with two officers from the Prostitution Unit:

A young woman approached the car and told Ray and Keith she had just been 'touched up and mugged' by a man. After trying to drag her down a side street, he had grabbed her breasts and then stolen £20 from her. With no sense of urgency, the officers told her they would drive up the road to see if they could see the man. However, once the woman was out of earshot, they explained to me that they would not bother going to look for the man because she was a 'known pro' [prostitute]. Ray suggested, 'With them, you can't believe a word they say. It was probably a punter who refused to pay her.'

Ideas about prostitutes closely interacted with the patriarchal and misogynistic aspects of the occupational culture. For example, officers working on the all-male Prostitution Unit called themselves 'whore hunters' and, more generally, prostitutes were referred to using a range of derogatory epithets, including 'slag', 'scrubber', 'bint', and 'slut'. Officers working on the unit stated that their philosophy surrounding prostitutes was one based on 'helping and assisting' the women. Yet this narrative stood in sharp contrast to the practices of officers as they went about policing prostitution in the area. The following extract demonstrates an interaction between these officers and a known prostitute:

Eddie radioed through to Ross and Paul and told them to look out for Vicky Roberts—to which they groaned because she is their most prolific.

Eddie had just seen her getting into a car with a punter and wanted them both arrested. He recited to Paul and Ross the make and registration of the car, and we drove around the streets searching for it. After a short while they spotted Vicky walking up the road. Paul drove past her, turned into the side street, switched the car lights off and waited for her to come towards the unmarked car.

Paul wound the window down and told her to get into the car. She immediately recognized him and shouted, 'Fuck off I've done nothing.' She started to run but Paul jumped out and chased her. After he caught her, he marched her back towards the car. A man standing outside a nearby pub saw the commotion and shouted to Vicky, 'Hey love, are you alright'? However, Paul shouted back to him 'It's OK—I am copper.' The man apologized and went back inside. In the car Vicky was crying, shouting and denying that she had been working that evening. At one point when she was shouting, Ross turned to her and shouted, 'Shut the fuck up. We know you have been working and you are coming in for it.' She was saying that she had only just come out of prison for breaching an ASBO [Antisocial Behaviour Order] and that she had been sleeping rough for a week while waiting to go on a list for housing. She was shouting that because they had arrested her she would lose out on a drugs programme and public housing. Even though she was crying uncontrollably, Paul and Ross appeared very blasé. Paul was looking at me in the car mirror and smiling. Vicky thought that Eddie had a personal grudge against her and told us that he had said to her, 'I am going to make it my personal mission to get you behind bars.'

In part, this kind of approach towards prostitution was a consequence of the profound cynicism felt towards the wider dilemmas of resolving prostitution. Officers felt a sense of disenchantment towards the cycle of arresting prostitutes, taking them to court, seeing them fined and then returning to the streets to earn the money to pay off the fines.

Signs of a new direction

It is of course crucial to explore those narratives and practices which exist outside, or in opposition to, the seemingly mainstream culture. In their dealings with women, I found evidence of the proverbial disparity between police talk and conduct. Most officers made negative remarks upon being dispatched to domestic violence incidents, but were generally sympathetic and professional in their treatment of victims. It is also worth re-emphasizing that while the discursive response to domestic violence remained remarkably unchanged, the new arrest guidelines has altered police practices in this area. Some male officers viewed themselves as 'hero-protectors' (Westmarland 2001*a*: 27) and displayed a clear desire to apprehend perpetrators. Unlike their male colleagues, female officers saw attending domestic violence incidents as a legitimate part of their role. I should note though that much concern was expressed about the desirability of the mandatory arrest policy. It was criticized for its potential to cause a 'backlash' against the victim by the abusive partner, and as another demonstration of the Force's desire to increase its detection rates. The following exchange between two female IMU officers sums up these complaints:

Sarah: I can't understand this, but we have a domestic policy where we have to put all violent perpetrators under arrest. But it worries me because a lot of the time, the woman doesn't want us to because they are frightened. . .

Carol: The women don't want him arrested—they want longer-term help on how to get out of the situation . . .

Sarah: They want support from us, and not just a bloody detection.

Carol: [Sarcastically] we are not here to help people—we are here to make Northshire Police climb the league tables. So we are like, 'Tough luck, you're going to have a battering when you get home, but Northshire Police have got their detection. Hey I'm happy—I've got a detection. The bosses up there are happy. You aren't, but hey' . . .

Sarah: You are either going to be dead under the patio, or get a good slapping because we have taken your choice away.

Group discussion—Northville

Considerable disquiet was expressed about the DVIR, but some officers in Southville understood the logic behind the new stance towards domestic violence. Consider the following exchange between two IMU officers:

Patrick: But it's the DVIR forms too. What do we have to do these for? There is no need to do a DVIR form, let's be honest.

Andrew: I can see the purpose of them. It's to assess the situation . . .

Patrick: But you can assess the situation in your pocket book without spending two hours doing a domestic form. It's pointless . . .

Andrew: I can see where all these things on domestics have come from. A lot of these things have come in because we have failed to do our jobs properly. I joined seventeen years ago, and the job I joined then was different. Now we know a domestic can escalate and the police have failed miserably in the past. There have been cases in the papers—and it must have been awful when we walked away because the victims were then thinking, 'The police have failed me again', you know?

Group discussion

It would also appear that the misogynistic elements of police culture are being challenged. On one occasion, a CAT officer told his IMU colleagues that a young woman who had been reported missing by her family was probably working as a 'smack-head' prostitute and getting 'spit-roasted' nightly. This remark was overheard by a male sergeant, who subsequently reprimanded the officer. These signs of progress demonstrate the complexity of the police identity, but they did not represent the norm. Moreover, the persistence of these problematic elements of the culture was found in respect to sexuality and ethnicity.

'Deviant' Sexualities

Despite some changes in the composition of personnel within Northshire Police, the Force continues to be made up of white, heterosexual, males.[7] In addition to impinging on relations within the organization, I also found that the taken for granted ethos of heterosexual masculinity influenced attitudes and practices towards members of the public whose sexuality was at variance with the prevailing norm.

The dominance of a heterosexist culture was most apparent in the policing of casual sexual relationships amongst men. These relationships took place in public areas frequented by gay men and became firmly embedded within officers' cultural knowledge as deviant. In Northville, this led to one area becoming stigmatized and routinely targeted during patrols:

The radio was quiet and Hayden drove down to Banal Lane, a public wooded area with picnic benches and a small car park. Officers often drove down here because it was known to be an area where gay men met for casual sex. Hayden told me that the area was 'well known for it' on the internet, and he himself had been on the website to 'suss out' any patterns, arrangements and details of the men. The area had been renamed 'Anal Lane' by officers in order to capture its association with homosexual encounters, and officers frequently came down here to try to 'catch them at it'.

Fieldnotes

[7] As noted elsewhere, I say heterosexual insofar as I did not meet any officers in the research sites who were openly gay.

From my observations, however, officers did not actually arrest any of the men discovered in 'Anal Lane'. Rather, the area was a source of fascination and amusement, with many officers preferring to humiliate and embarrass those who went there. This was also noted in Southville where one area had likewise become associated with non-normative sexualities. Police were always suspicious of lone males parked up in the area, as the following fieldnote illustrates:

9pm

Neil explained that he wanted to drive over to Wooton Common for a look round because, at night time, the Common became a gay meeting place. Several cars were parked up and many had lone men sitting in them. For Neil, a lone man in a car signified a 'cruiser'. He contacted the ACR and did a check on one of the vehicles. It came back to an address over twenty-five miles away and this aroused his suspicion because it was not local. Just as he was about to approach the car, a short overweight man in his forties came out of the woods. Neil shone his flashlight at the man, and asked him what he was doing in the area. The man was stunned and sheepishly murmured that he and his wife had been in an argument so he had come out for a drive. Neil began to question him further, but an IR came over the radio about an RTC [road traffic collision]. Neil cut the conversation short and we headed back to the car.

Back in the car Neil sarcastically said to me, 'You'd be surprised how many blokes come here after having an argument with their wives.' He then explained that when he stops men in the area he usually says to them, 'I would be careful round here at night if I were you. It's full of weirdoes and perverts.' He did this to let 'cruisers' know that the police were aware of what goes on in the area.

Lifestyles which challenged traditional norms of sexual conduct were constructed as deviant within the culture, and became the basis for interactions between the police and people perceived as 'cruisers'. As Young (1991) explains, homosexuality is viewed negatively within police culture because it fundamentally threatens the dominance of heterosexist masculinity (see also Miller *et al* 2003). But we could also explain their behaviour by reference to wider features of the police role. As Ericson (1982) argues, the police are prime enforcers of respectability and their official mandate emphasizes the control of public spaces.

Of central importance here is whether or not the police response to this section of the populace accords to, or jars with, the revised organizational ethos. In line with other British forces (Moran 2007)

Northshire Police has implemented various policies to better serve lesbian and gay people. Some of the more notable efforts include the positive approach taken to recruit and retain gay and lesbian officers, and the commitment to eliminating homophobia inside and outside the organization. In respect to the latter, the improved recording, investigation, and prosecution of homophobic and transphobic crime was placed high on the agenda. Yet the response I observed towards gay men reveals a clear disparity between the official and unofficial face of the organization.

Policing the Multi-ethnic Society: Antipathy and Ambivalence

There is a long history of persistent police harassment of minority ethnic groups in Britain (Lambert 1970; Holdaway 1996; Bowling and Phillips 2002). In the wake of the Macpherson Report (1999), however, police organizations are under considerable pressure to change the way they respond to the task of policing multi-ethnic communities. In Northshire, the equitable policing of minority ethnic groups was placed at the forefront of the reform agenda. The police are expected to provide a professional and considerate service to minority ethnic communities and this is to be achieved through respecting cultural difference and taking seriously the victimization of such groups, not holding or expressing racist views, or subjecting people from minority ethnic communities to discriminatory practices. How, then, have officers responded to their old adversaries in the new policing climate?

The view from 'Beirut'

Northville officers are responsible for policing an increasingly multi-ethnic population, but they complained that in comparison with other policing areas theirs was 'overrun' with different minority ethnic groups. The changing cultural scenario of Northville was articulated in the following terms during a group discussion:

Mark: Northville is a strange place. If you look at the north of the county as a whole, the area that Northville covers has probably got ninety per cent of your different minorities within that area. But other places, the officers there don't have any different cultures to contend with. Westcourt has got a growing Asian population, but Northville's is massive. It seems that year on year we are just getting overrun with your different minorities . . .

Tony: With your minorities, there are a lot of issues though aren't there? We have probably got *the* [his emphasis] biggest Iraqi community within the county. And you get their cultures which are frighteningly different than like . . .

Rebecca: Even with what we have had to get used to with Asians and culture and everyone else, they are all still lumped onto Northville aren't they?

The ethnic diversification of Northville was not celebrated within the culture. Instead, it was seen to have important and overwhelmingly negative implications for policing. Consider the following extract taken from another group discussion with a mixture of IMU and CAT officers:

Bethan: From your experiences, what do you think the most difficult aspect of policing is today?

Martin: Obviously diversity [murmurs of agreement]. All of the different ethnic groups in the community. It's definitely a big problem. Not really them being there, but things like communicating and their cultures. They do things differently don't they?

Howard: Definitely your different cultures. Someone said that there are one hundred and ten different nationalities within a one mile radius of our station, which I just find outrageous . . .

Gary: [Laughing] I knew it wouldn't take you long!

Howard: That was from immigration, and that is just ridiculous! You can't hope to communicate with all those people. And they have all got different ways of culturally dealing with things as well. An Asian gentleman will send his kids to the door to assault you, or will send his wife because they deem a woman to be a lower class citizen. So do you speak to his wife and agree with their system? Or play your system to theirs which would give you the upper hand? Or do you say, 'No I want to speak to the man, that's sexism'?

Ian: But they understand, and will play the game . . .

Howard: It's a really weird way of doing things, really odd. And you've got to understand different people to do it effectively. But with that many cultures out there it . . .

Graham: Confuses you . . .

Nigel: Well it does. I spoke to an Iraqi gentleman the other day. I called him over with my forefinger and said, 'Come over here.' Under interview he went off the scale [angry] because, apparently, that is how the Ba'ath party police used to call them over, with that gesture . . .

Scott: Like how are you supposed to know that?

Howard: It's the tiny things . . .

Scott: Have you seen the advert for HSBC bank? It's true . . .

Gary: 'Don't underestimate the importance of local knowledge.'

Scott: That is true in Northville. We have got everything here.

As I explore later, although officers considered the cultural and linguistic differences between themselves and minority ethnic groups to be problematic, the heightened political status of the latter was seen to be *the* primary difficulty facing police officers.

Classic stereotypes

Police work is largely influenced by oversimplified ideas about suspicious people and activities. In the past, ethnic minorities have been stereotyped as disorderly, anti-police, and inherently criminal (Cain 1973; Smith and Gray 1985; Young 1991; Chan 1997). Notwithstanding the efforts made to challenge these conceptions, it would appear that officers continue to associate some members of minority ethnic communities with certain forms of criminal activity.

Officers believed a large council estate called The Reservation was one of the most disorderly places within the LPU. The estate is home to a large black and minority ethnic population and, in the police mind, was 'brimming' with criminal activity including drugs and burglary; public order offences; prostitution; and gangs and guns. Young Black Caribbean men were particularly associated with these forms of crime, as the next fieldnote shows. I wrote it after one of my first ever shifts with two officers from the CAT. We were on our way to a supermarket to buy lunch when the following conversation developed:

Scott and Darren remarked that I had chosen a good time to do my research with them because there were a lot of black gangsters on their patch who were causing trouble for the police. They suggested that The Reservation Estate was the worst for gang crimes because of its high black population. Scott explained that most of the 'black lads' on the estate hated the police—even though they were responsible for most of the gang and drugs-related crimes in the entire policing division. Scott and Darren then started to mimic a strong Black Caribbean accent and parodied aspects of gang culture.

Before exploring this further, it is worth noting that referring to interactions with minority ethnic people in an exaggerated dialect was something I noted on several occasions. Although officers had an image of the estate as rife with crime, they approached it with a mixture of apprehension and resentment. Because of the heightened political status of ethnic minorities, the area was a site of anxiety. During routine patrols, some officers *avoided* the estate for fear of conflict with residents and, more importantly, any subsequent reprimand from the organization. This situation was resented by officers who thought that the estate was essentially 'untouchable' because of the sensitivity of the area (see also Foster 1989). In managing this tension, however, some officers deliberately patrolled the estate in order to assert their authority over the area. As I show later, this could cause antagonism between the police and some of the minority ethnic residents.

The stereotyping of black and minority ethnic men as inherently criminal was evident on other occasions. I was often told that the main drug dealers in the area were black males. Yet whenever I accompanied officers on organized drug operations, all of the houses raided actually belonged to white people. Nevertheless, the assumption that minority ethnic males were responsible for drugs crime could result in stop and search powers being exercised against this group. Consider the next instance where I accompanied Ian, a young CAT officer:

Shortly before 8pm, whilst patrolling near The Reservation Estate, Ian observes a woman wearing a short skirt and long boots leaning into the window of a purple BMW and talking to a black male in his early thirties. Ian's immediate suspicion was that the woman was a prostitute, and that the man was supplying her with drugs. Ian pulled over and did a check with the ACR and NPIN to see if a silver BMW had been reported stolen in the area. Both inquiries came back negative.

The BMW started to drive off, and Ian drove quickly behind it to pull it over. However, because it was an unmarked police car, the BMW failed to respond to any of the flashes from the headlamps. For Ian, this was a sure sign of guilt, and he called for other patrols to assist him. The BMW eventually pulled over and Ian jumped out of the car. He told me to wait in the car because, as he explained, 'These big dealers carry knives.' I watched the interaction through the car window. The man got out of the car and Ian started to search him, and then the car. Other patrols had now turned up and surrounded the car. Approximately five white officers assisted with the search. At one point, Ian came back to the car and said to me, 'He's definitely a dealer, but has got nothing on him—he's too compliant to be innocent.' Because Ian couldn't find anything, he issued the man with a 'producer'.[8] This was done purely to inconvenience him. Ian also put the man's details on NPIN so that if he was seen again in the area, other officers would know that he was a suspected drug dealer.

This episode reveals the persistence of classic stereotypes of black men in high performance cars as gangsters and drug dealers (see Smith and Gray 1985), but it also demonstrates the way in which stereotyping can set in motion something of a police swoop. In the current environment, where the problems of racial prejudice and unwarranted over-policing have been emphasized, the sudden and robust police presence no doubt increases the level of distrust and hostility towards the police. On another occasion, after being suspected of carrying drugs, two black males were separated and 'strip searched'. However, nothing was found and the men were free to leave. One of the suspects was extremely angry with the police and very much perceived the incident as racial harassment.

Within British society, some minority ethnic groups are regarded inferior to others. Modood (1992) argues that there is marked hostility towards people from Muslim and Arab backgrounds because their cultures are perceived to be most alien to that of white British culture. Added to this, Chakrabarti (2007) has argued, in the wake of concern about global terrorism, that the policing of Muslim groups are becoming increasingly defined by processes of Islamaphobia. In Northshire, members of the Iraqi community—and especially those seeking asylum—held an incredibly low status within rank and file culture. This was not necessarily expressed in overtly racialized tones, but many officers displayed hostility and insensitivity towards the cultural signifiers of this group; including their religion and language; family values; and seemingly indolent work ethic. A broad narrative was that Iraqi men were the main clients of prostitutes in the area and were responsible for most of the violence committed against these women. As the following episode demonstrates, this was explained by reference to Iraqi values. It was around 2am and I was accompanying two IMU officers:

Rob and Shaun were dispatched to Baker Road, a known red light area, in order to assist the Prostitution Unit with issuing a producer to a man who had been detained. An unmarked police car with two members of the

---

[8] This means that the man would be required to 'produce' his driver's licence, vehicle registration, and certificate of insurance to a police station.

unit was parked up in the bus stop. One of the unit members called me over and told me to get into the car. I got in and realised there was a man sitting in the back seat. The officer explained that the man was from Iraq and had been seen driving round the red light area and, because of this, he was suspected of looking for prostitutes. A vehicle check revealed that the man had no driving licence. The officer explained that he was probably an asylum seeker which meant he would have no insurance either. The officer sitting in the back of the car with the man said to me in a loud, exaggerated voice, 'He appears not to know the English language, so I am going to give him a warning letter in his own language.'

When we got back into the police car, Rob explained that Iraqi men went with prostitutes because it was 'inbred' in their culture to treat women disrespectfully. Shaun agreed and surmised that they were 'sly' and 'liars'. This was further demonstrated through the man's alleged dishonesty about not being able to speak English; as Shaun put it, 'I bet he would be able to say, 'How much for a blow job love'?

As I explore later, the idea that minority ethnic groups deliberately used their own language—rather than English—to dupe the police was a common discourse put forward by officers. This perception could influence the quality of service afforded to such groups.

Organizational trouble

The new onus placed on the police to provide an equitable service to minority ethnic communities resulted in a heightened anxiety about dealing with such groups. While officers were anxious about being labelled racist by colleagues, 'race' was very much at the forefront of their minds when interacting with black and minority ethnic members of the public. This culture of anxiety meant that officers were reluctant to deal with minority ethnic communities on a day to day basis. During the observations, I noted that some officers consciously avoided initiating any proactive encounters with members of minority ethnic communities for fear of being reprimanded by the organization should such an individual make a complaint against the officer. On the occasions where officers were called to incidents involving a person from a minority ethnic background, some displayed anxiety and were disinclined to attend:

11.40am

Rachael was asked to attend a house which was occupied by a female Iraqi asylum seeker. The woman reported that someone had been kicking her front door in the night before as she lay in bed. As the woman did not speak English, it had been arranged that a friend would be there to interpret for the police. On the way to the house, Rachael kept saying that she didn't like this type of job because the police are under enormous pressure to deal with potential hate crimes correctly. [. . .] Rachael took down every detail in a very careful and sympathetic manner but, once back in the car, said she was 'glad to be out of there' and hoped she didn't get called to a similar incident for a while.

As the extract demonstrates, the finely tuned awareness about the new organizational approach to minority ethnic people as victims of crime had the effect of ensuring that officers dealt with such incidents thoroughly and professionally. Yet the extent to which this reflects a genuine desire by officers to help and support such groups, as opposed to fear of reprimand, is debatable.

Within the occupational culture, minority ethnic groups represent what I would term organizational trouble. The enhanced political status afforded to people from minority ethnic backgrounds meant they were seen as a group that could cause problems for officers. For the most part, such groups have become 'disarmers'; that is, 'a member of a group who can weaken or neutralize police work as a result of their ability to invoke public sympathy' (Holdaway 1983: 77). Yet while anxiety surrounding minority ethnic populations is a new and important characteristic of police culture, it generated strong feelings of resentment towards such communities. Many officers believed themselves to be 'easy targets' for accusations of racism. They argued that minority ethnic groups deliberately used their ethnicity as a powerful instrument during interactions with the police. This point was particularly salient in a stop and search context, as the following comments demonstrate:

John: Some police I know won't stop any cars with blacks in now in case they get a complaint . . .

Derek: It's the race card, the card. I'm not harassing anyone but they say, 'It's because we're Asian, it's because we're black' . . .

Mark: It's dead easy for them to complain about you. And that's what they do. They see it as an easy way of getting at you don't they? But not because you've done anything wrong, we are easy targets; 'I'm black—I'll have your job, watch this' . . .

Howard: It gives you four hours of paperwork and three months of grief.

Sandra: You do get people who abuse the fact that we have things in place to deal with race. You can go to what may or may not be a racial incident, and you will have people threatening you before they open the door. They will talk about the Racial Equality Council before they tell you the circumstances . . .

John: [. . .] It's open to abuse. Police are frightened of their own shadows.
If they say jump, we jump.

Group discussion

The idea that people from minority ethnic backgrounds could neutralize the effects of routine policing by 'playing the race card' assumed an important place within officers' informal talk. Officers frequently relayed stories to each other about incidents where they had stopped a member of a minority ethnic group who had said; 'You only stopped me because I am black.' In responding to this, officers reported themselves as using quick-witted tactics to respond to this potentially damaging accusation:

Robert: The best one I have ever done is when they say, 'You only stopped
me because I'm black', you say, 'You only said that because I am
white.' It stops them dead in their tracks. Or you say to them, 'You
only said that because I am white, which makes you racist, and
I can lock you up for that.'

Group discussion

These narratives are an important way of managing the tensions associated with the policing of minority ethnic communities, but they also become a way for officers to buttress the idea that minority ethnic groups are problematic.

Losing the edge and mutual hostility

Police insensitivity to the language and cultural differences of minority ethnic communities has been the source of much criticism. Along with placing information about rights and entitlements in different languages across custody suites, Northshire Police has also employed several interpreters to assist with interviewing suspects, victims, and witnesses. On the ground, however, the issue of language was vehemently criticized. Officers argued that minority ethnic communities deviously used their own language, rather than English, in order to gain an advantage over officers. The effect, for the police, was that they 'lost the edge' when dealing with potential offenders:

Brendan: We struggle don't we with a lot of the jobs we go to with your
different cultures? We have an immigration department which
works 9am until 5pm, Monday to Friday. Well, what use is that
to us? That person can disappear into the asylum black hole for
some time, and that is always happening . . .

Peter: They are out there committing crime, driving around with no documents, illegal immigrants . . .

Scott: You lose the edge as well I find, with people who speak a different language. When you've got a car full of Asians, who start speaking a completely foreign language, it's a logistical nightmare. They could be saying quite openly in front of you: 'See that heroin in the back of the seat? Just chuck it out of the window for me.' And you're not going to have a clue. You completely lose the edge. Perhaps a better representation of that ethnicity would give us the edge back—or perhaps me getting off my arse and learning ten different languages, which isn't going to happen.

Group discussion

For the rank and file, the new organizational stance towards diversity challenges their need to maintain 'the edge' over their adversaries. The assumption that some minority ethnic groups deliberately concealed their ability to speak English prevented officers from making suitable arrangements to assist such groups. During several interactions, officers became irritated with people who had little—if any—understanding of English (see also Foster *et al* 2005). This could interfere with the quality of service given to those people. I recall one occasion where the officer I was accompanying was stopped in the street by a Chinese woman who had little spoken English. After a few minutes, the officer became visibly impatient and merely told her to phone the Force helpline.[9]

For the most part, officers viewed their relationship with local minority ethnic communities as one based on conflict and hostility. Consider the following comments made by a CAT officer:

Scott: You walk round Northville and you can feel the tension in the air. But you go to say Manchester or London and walk round their Asian communities, and it just doesn't feel so tense does it? But here, you walk round in your uniform and they start hissing at you and making comments. The tension is there all the time.

Group discussion

This perceived tension served to distance the police from local minority ethnic communities. Although some officers were aware of the potential for conflict when interacting with members of ethnic minority groups, others appeared unconcerned about the tension their presence could cause. On numerous occasions,

---

[9] From what I could gather, the woman was trying to follow up an inquiry about an incident she had previously reported to the police.

I noted that the relationship between the police and minority ethnic people could be strained and antagonistic, as the following episode demonstrates. It was early evening and two IMU officers responded to a call about an assault:

[. . .] Officers put the young Asian man into the back of the car with me. He had been arrested for assault, and it was thought he had used a blue bike chain to hit another male. Acting Sergeant Evans told me to get in the car with him because he wanted to go to the garage where he thought the bike chain was being hidden by the 'prisoner's' family. The garage was run and owned by a middle-aged Asian man and all of the workers in the garage were also Asian. There was a great deal of suspicion and apprehension towards the police, and Evans thought they were hiding CCTV footage of the incident. He wanted to search the garage, but the owner kept insisting that they needed a warrant. This annoyed Evans, who then stated the legal conditions under which a search could be conducted.

The owner was still arguing and saying that he wanted to see a warrant. Evans then said, 'Fine. If you want me to get all of my officers down here, I will.' He then went on the radio and said loudly so all of the shop could hear him, 'Can all available crews come over to Cross Garage. We have a serious assault and a case of police obstruction.' This seemed to scare the owner who then gave in and said, 'Fine. Look wherever you want.' About five minutes later six [all white and male] officers arrived and started to vigorously search the premises. The owner and the other Asian men just stood and watched. The whole atmosphere was very antagonistic and Evans said to me 'The Asians round here hate us—but as you can see they make our job more difficult.' Evans eventually found a bike chain near a shelf in the garage and seized it as evidence. He later told me that he didn't think it was the chain used in the incident, but that he wanted to inconvenience the Asian shop keeper; as he put it, 'While we have it, he won't be able to sell it.'

As several writers have noted, black and minority ethnic communities are inclined to perceive any police attention as 'racial' (Foster *et al* 2005; see also McLaughlin 2007*a*). From the police perspective, however, young black and minority ethnic men are unpredictable and confrontational (Foster 1989; Bowling and Phillips 2003). From my observations, it was clear that police and members of minority ethnic groups anticipated hostility from each other during interactions. This mutual hostility and suspicion could manifest in conflict. In the next extract, I was accompanying two IMU officers when the following happened:

Gareth had been driving round The Reservation Estate for half an hour. As we were leaving, a number of black and Asian young men were sitting on a wall at the entrance to the estate. Gareth pulled up and asked them what they were up to. Although this was not necessarily expressed in an accusing manner, the young men perceived it as such. One of the young men said to Gareth, 'Go away and stop harassing us, all of you lot are the same.' Gareth said sarcastically, 'I'm not harassing you. I am just doing my job, driving round this place to make sure all you lot are protected.' One of the other young men got really annoyed and said, 'Look, just fuck off and stop harassing us.' Gareth quickly jumped out of the car, walked up to him and threatened, 'Don't swear at a police officer my friend, or you'll be coming in.' The same person loomed towards Gareth but, after Mike also got out of the car, then backed off and apologized for swearing. However, he still maintained, 'I just want you lot to go away and leave us alone.'

Just then an IR came in about a 'burglary in progress'. Gareth stared at the group of young men and said, 'You've been saved by the bell', and got back into the car. As we were driving off, Gareth said to me, 'Now you see the type of shit we have to put up with. We can't do anything or we get called a racist. It's a political nightmare.'

To be disrespectful to a police officer is an infringement of an important occupational law and, in this incident, may partly explain the sudden burst of conflict between the two parties. However, in the current policing climate where issues of diversity are salient, the *ethnicity* of the young men entered the equation and shaped the nature of the interaction. Police officers are encouraged to be aware of how their actions might be interpreted by ethnic minorities. Some officers were sensitive to the occasions where their presence may have caused conflict or anxiety, but others failed to appreciate how their attitude and actions could inflame existing tensions. As Foster *et al* (2005: 67) point out, adverse experiences of policing can rapidly penetrate the 'community consciousness' and consequently undermine the progress that police organizations have already made to increase confidence in the police. We could also add that the above incident illustrates how the anticipation of hostility can result in routine peacekeeping functions shifting towards a potential law enforcement objective (Holdaway 1996).

Policing rural diversity

Most of the sentiments and practices I observed in Northville about minority ethnic communities were also evident in Southville. But, in some respects, a different set of dynamics emerged. It will be recalled that while the crime problems facing officers in

Northville was perceived as internal, the problem in Southville was considered to be external. This way of viewing the environment had significant implications for the policing of minority ethnic groups, and relates to the different geographical and social context in which officers worked.

Dominant groups in rural communities tend to make finely tuned distinctions between themselves and 'others' (Holloway 2005). Invariably, however, such distinctions are racialized (ibid; see also Tyler 2003). In the seemingly idyllic, white English village, members of minority ethnic groups are viewed as out of place; they are seen as belonging in the city and this is a space which has always been synonymous with the 'undesirable black Other' (Hall *et al* 1978; Neal 2002). The juxtaposing of the 'respectable' rural white landscape and the 'rough' multi-ethnic city found strong support in the occupational culture of officers working in Southville.

Because the area has a predominantly white populace, officers thought that organizational notions of diversity were largely irrelevant. Yet, at the same time, ideas about race and ethnicity were firmly associated with the areas main crime problems. Officers believed that young, low status, male 'outsiders' who originated from the deprived and multi-ethnic centres of Long City were responsible for the serious crimes which took place on the LPU, as one sergeant put it during an interview:

Our number one problem is cross-border criminality. We are a nice affluent area so travelling criminals come onto us from across the border to commit crime. They know we are thin on the ground so we are an easy target. [. . .] As long as we are Southville, our problem will be outsiders.

In the wake of anxieties about crime in the area, officers' feelings of 'otherness' became racialized. These themes are captured in the following exchange during a group discussion with a mixture of IMU and CAT officers:

Bethan: Going back to how your work has changed, it is often said that Britain is a multicultural and diverse society. Today, police organizations are having to respond to the challenges of policing diverse societies. Do you think that has had an impact on your job down here?

Jennifer: Not so much to be honest. It hasn't really had an impact. We do have a small pocket of ethnic minorities within the LPU, but it is not so much of an issue. We don't have a mosque or anything like that, which seems to have a major impact on how the community functions and focus. Because a lot of the time, they will have their own system before the police even become involved. Where it can be an issue, we have a lot of travelling criminals . . .

Matt: We always have to be aware that a lot of outsiders . . .

Jennifer: We have to be careful that they are not being targeted because of their race. But we balance that with the fact that we know we have a low ethnic population so, unfortunately, people of colour do look out of place . . .

Philip: It's true . . .

Jennifer: So, it's not that they are being stopped because they are black or Indian or whatever. It is just that we don't carry that population. We know that they are not local, so they are stopped to find out what they are doing in the area . . .

Matt: The same as any person for any other reason would be stopped if they are not local, and driving round Millionaire's Row at two o'clock in the morning.[10] We want to know why they are here . . .

Jennifer: But they are dealt with exactly the same—fairly and equally. [. . .] But diversity, it is not really relevant to us. It doesn't have so much of a major impact on your day to day policing because we don't really have any.

Officers did not necessarily articulate their suspicion towards 'outsiders' in overtly racialized terms, yet black and minority ethnic men held a central place within their cultural knowledge. Their main concern was to protect the patch from outsiders and they policed their rural landscape in an incessantly defensive state. The theme of incongruence has particular resonance here. Based on a notion of outsiders as perpetrators of crime, officers in Southville were routinely suspicious of people and vehicles which were 'out of place' in their white, affluent, rural surroundings. To this end, officers relied on their experience about what types of people and vehicles were potentially involved in crime. The standard from which to assess suspects was measured against what I would call a Mr and Mrs Southville background appearance. In other words, the 'background expectancies' (Sacks 1972) of the police related

---

[10] Millionaire's Row was a nickname for an area which was characterized by large and affluent houses.

to white, middle-aged, middle class, and affluent people—and cars—which officers recognized as being local. This occupational commonsense invariably set the rationale for police interactions with people seen as outsiders. The next extract records a night shift where I accompanied two seasoned IMU officers. We had just finished a coffee break and were heading back out on patrol:

3am

As we pulled out of the station, Nick and Tony saw a dilapidated dark blue Peugeot which was full of passengers driving past. Nick accelerated out of the station and said 'Fucking outsiders, I bet you', before pulling the car over. Five young men were in the car. The driver was white and the front seat passenger seemed to be of mixed heritage. The three passengers in the back were all of Black Caribbean descent. Nick told the driver that he had stopped him as part of a routine vehicle check, before asking him where they had been, and where they were going now. The driver told him that they hadn't been anywhere in particular and that they had just been for a drive to Fortson and were heading back to Long City. Nick replied sarcastically, 'I think you are a few junctions away mate—decided to take a detour through sunny Southville did you'?

Meanwhile Tony began to question the passengers about their movements. One of them said that they had been to Newtown to see his dad. Seizing on this inconsistency, Nick and Tony began to search the passengers and the car. To justify the search, Nick said that he could smell what he believed to be a 'controlled substance' [*I was later told that some officers often used this line so they can get access to a vehicle to do a search*]. Tony also ran police checks on the young men and all of them had previous convictions for drugs and other offences, including burglary.

This was enough to do a very lengthy and rigorous search of the men and the car. Tony asked me to search under the car seats, and to make sure the passengers didn't say, or pass, anything to each other while they looked in the boot and glove compartment. No drugs were found on the young men or in the car, but they came across a hammer, a rusty chair leg, a pair of gloves and a woolly hat. Nick took Tony and me to one side and said, 'They are definitely going equipped. I'm not racist, but why are black lads with records and from Long City over on us at this time of night'? They radioed through to Sergeant Peel and asked his advice. The sergeant told the officers to arrest them all for going equipped. [. . .] Sergeant Peel congratulated the officers for the 'good nick'. He thought the incident would teach outsiders a valuable lesson, and show that officers on the patch weren't a soft touch.

Suspicion towards members of black and minority ethnic communities has long been identified as a feature of police culture

(Skolnick 1966; Lambert 1970; Cain 1973), but this stereotyping can become self-reinforcing. In Southville, the practice of stopping and searching young, low status, minority ethnic men only 'confirmed' the stereotype that they are more likely to be criminal and, in broader terms, reinforced the differential treatment of this group.

In both locations, then, officers retained enduring stereotypes about the involvement of minority ethnic men in crime. However, the practical policing of such groups was contradictory and uneven. In Northville, anxiety about being labelled sometimes led to the avoidance of proactive encounters with members of minority ethnic groups. But a less ambiguous scenario was evident in Southville where minority ethnic men were invariably targeted by the police. The disparities in behaviour relate explicitly to the different social and geographical arrangements of the two policing areas. Northville is responsible for policing a notable minority ethnic community and, as a result, sits at the forefront of policing diversity policy agendas. Unlike their rural counterparts, moreover, Northville officers police a densely populated terrain and experience a higher level of supervisory oversight.

Revisions in policing ethnicity

It would be inaccurate to portray officers as culturally homogeneous in their response to minority ethnic communities. It will be recalled that overt racist language was virtually non-existent amongst officers and I noted that some even challenged the racist comments articulated by members of the public. I wrote the following fieldnote while accompanying two IMU officers in Northville on a night shift. After giving two teenage girls a lift back to their local foster home, the following conversation developed:

Sergeant Williams: You girls should be careful walking round by yourselves at this time of night. There was a nasty assault here last week on a young girl.

Girl A: Well, last week a dirty Paki tried to grab me into his car . . .

Geraint: [Shouting] Oi! What did you just say?

Girl A: Sorry—an 'Asian' tried to pull me into his car.

Sergeant Williams: That's better. Don't use that kind of language any more please.

In Southville, some officers expressed criticism towards their colleagues for being overly suspicious of members of minority ethnic
communities, as the next extract demonstrates:

Jeremy responded to an incident at the local youth club. An argument
between a black teenager and a white teenager had broken out, and each
of the teenagers' respective friends had become involved. Although there
had been no physical assault, a hammer had apparently been 'waved
around' by one of the group.

When Jeremy and I arrived, Mike and Anton were already at the scene.
The black teenager in question was the only person from a minority ethnic
background at the youth club. Anton had taken the black teenager to
one side and was vigorously searching him. [. . .] While Mike and Jeremy
walked back to their cars, they began to complain about Anton. Jeremy
asked Mike, 'I bet you Anton only searched the black lad didn't he? He
only did it because he is black. He always does it.' After getting back into
the car, Jeremy said to me, 'Unfortunately some of our officers have old-
fashioned views about black people. Not all of us are like that though.'

It is also noteworthy that officers were not alone in viewing ethnic
minorities with suspicion. It was a Wednesday afternoon and
I had spent the day with Jacqui, a CAT officer:

3.30pm
It was raining and we were nearing the end of the shift. As we approached
the station, we saw four young black men walking up the hill with their
hoods up. Jacqui laughed and said, 'I bet you we'll get a call about suspicious people from the public about those. If I asked the caller what was
suspicious about them they would say, 'Well they *are* black—Southville is
more racist than anything!' [. . .] As I was leaving the station, Jacqui ran
down and told me that a caller had rung in expressing suspicion about the
group of men; 'I told you, Beth,' she laughed.

This episode highlights the importance of the public in determining the patterning of police attention (see McConville *et al*
1991). For the most part, nevertheless, the role of local residents
in constructing minority ethnic people as suspicious only served
to intensify the stereotypical cues drawn upon by officers. On
a final point, the ethnic component of police suspicion should not
be overstated. An important aspect of their suspicion towards
minority ethnic males related to the low economic status of this
group. In their work, the police differentiate between the 'respectable' classes and the 'roughs' (Cain 1973) and minority ethnic
populations are invariably relegated to the lower end of the class

system in our society (Jefferson 1991). From my observations, when officers used their powers against minority ethnic people they were always *poor* minority ethnic people. To be sure the low visible presence of black and minority ethnic people in Southville exacerbated the situation, but social class was an underlying factor in shaping police discourse and practice towards this group. Signs of 'roughness'—particularly dilapidated vehicles and young men in shabby or dirty clothing—precipitated police suspicion and, to this end, the *white* residuum also became targeted.

Responding to the New Realities

I have in this chapter examined how the accent on diversity has shaped the way the police think about, and interact with, their socially and culturally diverse publics. Officers manage the new realities in different ways. On the one hand, aspects of the culture are being revised and unlearned. We are witnessing the beginnings of multiple policing outlooks and styles which conform with the requirements of the diversity agenda. For instance, officers have integrated the new guidelines of policing domestic violence into their daily practices. In addition to arresting perpetrators of domestic violence, officers are invariably recording key information relating to the case. In comparison with earlier works, these are important developments in policing culture. Several new dynamics have also emerged with respect to the policing of ethnicity. Particularly in Northville, many officers had begun to rethink the way they policed minority ethnic communities. Against the backdrop of a culture of anxiety, some officers avoid initiating any proactive encounters with such groups for fear of recrimination from the organization. In many ways, then, the occupational culture has accommodated aspects of the revised policing terrain.

These changes, I think, can be explained by the following factors. The British policing landscape has been transformed following official criticism of the way ethnically and socially diverse groups are policed. Policing agendas now insist that officers afford better regard and treatment to people who have previously not been equitably served by policing. The rank and file are acutely aware of the policing demands, and are alert to the fact that their behaviour is closely monitored. In other words, the police have had to change their behaviour—particularly in public. In addition to this wider context, the personal biography of the individual officer also determines how they will react to the altered policing landscape. It is well-known that officers bring their own experiences, personalities, and variations of outlook to the police role (Fielding 1988; Chan 1997) and I would add that the different ways of viewing their work interact with type of unit and shift in which they work.

Yet despite the emergence of new policing identities, various problems remain in respect to how officers perceive and treat their diverse publics. Notwithstanding the measures introduced to improve the way officers respond to social diversity, many features of the culture remain unchallenged by the reorganizations which have occurred in the local and national policing landscape. Domestic violence incidents continue to occupy a low position within police ideologies, and many responses to the women and non-normative sexualities operate within a framework of masculinity. Officers have also retained enduring stereotypes about the criminality of minority ethnic men, and many appear unconcerned with the tension and conflict that their presence can cause. Anxiety surrounding black and minority ethnic groups is a new feature of police culture, but it invariably provoked resentment towards this group. In particular, there was a pervasive discourse that minority ethnic people deliberately exploited their ethnicity in order to neutralize the effects of policing. But, in broader terms, this narrative adds force to the existing belief that minority ethnic groups are problematic.

It remains clear that the concerted accent on diversity has been incapable of fully dismantling the accepted cultural resources of the police. The reasons for this are explored in the concluding chapter. In what follows I call into question the dominance of diversity within policing discourse and practice. I argue that issues of class remain crucial in understanding police culture.

6

The Continuing Significance of Class

The incremental slide away from [class] is marked as more than an economic retreat; it is also a retreat from regarding the white poor as 'people like us'—the white moral majority population (Haylett 2001: 358).

The properties found in police culture invariably reflect the 'iso-morphic relationship' (Reiner 2000*a*: 136) between the police and wider arrangements of social disadvantage. As several commentators observe, late modern societies are increasingly characterized by widespread inequality in which a structurally marginal 'under-class' features prominently (Dahrendorf 1985; Young 1999; Crowther 2000*a*). In this new landscape, the police property grouping has become 'far larger than ever before and more fundamentally alienated' (Reiner 2000*a*: 216). Notwithstanding the widening of economic inequality, the issue of class is of declining interest in current social thought and political practice. This occlusion of class has coincided with the sharp ascendance of identity politics where previously marginalized groups, defined along axes of ethnicity, gender, and sexuality, are seeking recognition of their social differences (Fraser 1997; Ray and Sayer 1999). However, while the shift towards culture has decentred class from debates of social justice, it has also positioned the *white* poor as 'illegitimate subjects' (Haylett 2001). Gender may also be a pertinent issue for it is the white working-class male who currently constitutes the abject and who is constructed as the embodiment of disorder and distaste (McDowell 2003; see also Collins 2004; The Economist 2006; Harris 2007).

In Chapter 3 I presented the argument that the British policing terrain is characterized by a contemporary politics of 'diversity'. The vision of equality is synonymous with the policing of minority ethnic communities, and other cultural and gendered identities. The emergence of this dominant policing paradigm is clearly significant for those groups who have previously not been well served by policing. But in my view it overlooks the stubborn durability of class in policing. In addition to greater political recognition of diversity, the field of British policing is simultaneously marked by widespread *economic* exclusion and division. As I will show, the changes which have occurred in the political economy of Western capitalism have profound implications for the policing of a new residuum.

In this chapter I expose a contradiction which emerged between the police organizational emphasis on diversity and axes of class. While efforts aimed at changing police culture focused on notions of diversity, it was predominantly poor and low status white males who occupied centre stage in both the practical workload of officers and in their occupational consciousness. One prominent feature of their culture was the class contempt (Sayer 2005) displayed towards this socio-economic grouping. My central argument is that in the wake of the diversity agenda, the white residuum operates as unproblematic terrain for the police use of discretionary powers and authority.

Rethinking Police Culture

In exposing this disjuncture I wish to appeal for a rethinking of police culture which recognizes how class continues to permeate cultural knowledge and everyday practices. A recurring finding of police ethnographies is that officers deal overwhelmingly with the least powerful and marginal (Westley 1970; Ericson 1982; Young 1991). Yet while the common denominator among these perennial police targets is their social, economic, and political powerlessness, the class natured aspects of this have become obscured in recent years. Current debates about police culture have, quite rightly, been concerned with police perceptions of and treatment towards differing groups along axes of ethnicity (Chan 1997), gender (Westmarland 2001), and sexuality (Moran 2007). While there has been a great deal of public and professional debate concerning the policing of these social divisions, police perceptions of the poor—and their treatment of them—have been largely ignored. This is especially the case with the white poor.

Explicit reference to the issue of class is examined chiefly in relation to the historical emergence of the police (Storch 1975; Cohen 1979) and in the context of the spectacular and relatively rare outbreaks of industrial conflict (Scraton 1985; Green 1990).

Although the latter works acknowledge the influence of class in policing, they inevitably present these dramatic moments as somehow set apart from ordinary life. But class is not just an occasional condition; it is something that people live in and experience through their bodies and minds. In equal measure to gender, ethnicity, and sexuality, class has the potential to be a considerable source of injury (Sennett and Cobb 1972; see also Charlesworth 2000; Bourdieu *et al* 2002; Sayer 2005).

My purpose in this chapter is to foreground the importance of class in a 'low' policing context; that is, class as it was policed in the routine and mundane dimensions of police work. This focus on the ordinary has crucial significance for discussions of social justice. As Sayer (2005) reminds us, the general retreat from class in current social thought and political practice is problematic because it allows 'class contempt' and other forms of symbolic domination to persist largely unobserved and unchallenged. A defining feature of symbolic domination is its capacity to persuade a subordinate group—through ideology and everyday practices, and institutions—that certain economic, political, and cultural occurrences are the natural order of things (Bourdieu *et al* 2002). In the absence of a clear focus on class in current discussions of policing and reform, it is the ordinary and mundane dimensions of police culture in relation to the poor which needs to claim our attention.

There has been no shortage of testimony to the ubiquity in British society of contempt towards the working class (Skeggs 2004; Hayward and Yar 2006; Sayer 2005). As outlined in Chapter 2, class contempt is a potent force of othering and can be detected through facial expressions—'from the raising of the upper lip into a sneer' or 'from slightly grimaced smiles to aggressive sneers' (Sayer 2005: 164). Although primarily experienced as an emotion, class contempt does have a tangible dimension which manifests itself through a person's response to visual and moral 'markers' including appearance, accent, language, demeanour, values, actions, possessions, and lifestyle (ibid). What is important here is that such signifiers of class serve as prompts for judgements of worth—or, more to the point, worth*lessness*. Describing someone as 'rough' or 'dirty' is a code for their perceived class and carries powerful moral connotations. At this most basic level, class contempt can colour the way people are perceived and can profoundly affect their life chances (ibid). As I shall illustrate, the police make judgements based on the personal and behavioural qualities of the poor and thereby reproduce the symbolic domination of this group. Yet in the new policing discourse—the contemporary organizational and operational policing context—of respect for diversity and recognition of cultural and gendered identities, the enduring dimension of class has disappeared from view. The focus on the poor, including outright class contempt, remains simply taken for granted and unheeded in policing practice.

A Contradiction Emerges

The Northshire change programme focused on improving the working conditions of personnel inside the organization and on the delivery of an effective and equitable policing service to the various publics outside the organization—with a particular focus on ethnic minorities. A core policy focus was the explicit official interdiction of discriminatory conduct. Expressions of racism were especially deplored and a strong disciplinary line taken against racist conduct. The diversity agenda emphasized and on some instances demanded that officers afford better regard and treatment to groups who have previously not been adequately served by policing. The organization was saturated with notions of diversity and its recognition; and officers had a clear awareness of the official hard line taken against discrimination.

Yet an important contradiction emerged during the course of my research. Officers inexorably came into contact with their diverse publics, but the overwhelming focus was on sections of the local 'underclass'—of which a large proportion were young, white, men. This also finds support from statistics relating to police stop and search patterns. According to a Force Monitoring Report, Northshire officers across all LPUs stopped and searched around 1,800 people from a minority ethnic background during the period of the ethnography. They similarly subjected over 19,000 white people to the same practice. The vast majority of these were males and if the monitoring procedures further allowed for employment status, then my observations suggest that significant numbers of unemployed white males had experienced an adversarial relationship with the police for that period.[1] What is more,

---

[1] Black and minority ethnic groups may be over-represented within recorded stop and search practices, but my point is that in absolute numbers the police came into contact with white people far more than their minority ethnic counterparts.

this was also the group that occupied an overridingly prominent position in the police mind as socially defiling and in need of control. A brief reflection on the social arrangements of the two research sites is useful for understanding how and why this group came to be the enduring targets of the police.

For all its rich history in heavy industry and exportation of manufacture, Northville is now a place of severe and uniform social and economic decline, with numerous factory closures and systematic withdrawals, and relocations on the part of key employers. In Northville and its neighbouring areas over 15,000 jobs were lost between 1998 and 2001. But while factories have been closed down, little has emerged to replace them. Economically this is a zone of long-term and intergenerational unemployment; low income and wealth; and poor educational attainment and health. The dramatic deindustrialization has also left a landscape of boarded up buildings, empty factories, and derelict land with pockets of chronic poverty in large housing estates and run-down terraced streets.

The geographical and social arrangements of Southville were markedly different to Northville, but the issue of class and economic exclusion is equally pertinent. Southville lies in close proximity to the urban sprawl of Long City which, like other major centres, experiences acute levels of social and economic deprivation. It will be recalled that officers believed Southville was under constant threat from 'outsiders' who originated from the less affluent regions of Long City. To be sure, ethnicity prompted police suspicion towards 'outsiders', but an underlying factor of their suspicion was class-driven. In their search for potential criminals, officers were attuned to signs of poverty and 'roughness'. As a result, impoverished white males also fell under police suspicion because they were incongruent with the respectable surroundings. Equally, however, to focus exclusively on the police preoccupation with 'outsiders' would be to conceal the extent to which they attended to people deemed problematic *within* the LPU. Southville is certainly one of the most affluent areas in Northshire but just like other rural locations (Cloke 1997) it too has key pockets of poverty. The unemployment and under employment experienced by those living in the nearby city was replicated and even compounded in Southville.

Although local in consequence, these are symptoms of broader processes at work. Across Western liberal democracies, whole spheres of work have disappeared and have created a structurally marginal 'underclass' (Dahrendorf 1985; Young 1999). Poor young men increasingly constitute the never-employed and are propelled, in turn, to live out their daily lives in public spaces. In Northville and Southville, young men have become particularly displaced. Compelled to occupy public (and thus police) space through lack of employment, they have become the visible emblem of the post-Fordist paradigm and, for officers, stand as the direct and evident embodiment of local disorder. The high and discernible concentration of 'whiteness' in these areas also meant that officers came mainly into contact with poor, young, white men. And it would appear that their emblematic whiteness is what marked them out for denigration. As Haylett (2001: 355) observes in the current project of multiculturalism poor whites have become a source of 'offensiveness' and 'embarrassment'. Large concentrations of this group undermine traditional systems of class and race based privilege. For these systems to maintain their legitimacy, it is necessary to separate the working class along the lines of deservedness—with the 'roughs' becoming segregated from the 'respectable' working classes (ibid). The police perceive themselves as falling into the latter and, in their work, differentiate between those they do things *for* and those they do things *to* (Shearing 1981).

Despite being close in terms of ethnicity (white) and gender (male) to their adversaries, officers in Northshire were not sympathetic to this group and treated them with active disdain. One explanation for this hinges directly on class in what Taylor (1999: 17) identifies as the 'fear of falling'. In circumstances of economic insecurity, a fear of slipping in status permeates the social structure as a 'metaphorical displacement' (ibid) of a wider set of anxieties about position in the economic order. This kind of uncertainty breeds intolerance of the poor, and manifests itself in the drawing of moral boundaries between those at the bottom of the social strata and those who, for time being, are secure. For the most part, officers in Northshire came from a 'respectable' working class background and sought to distance themselves from the residuum. Of course the police have always controlled and displayed contempt towards their property. This in itself is nothing new. What is of *contemporary* significance is that this occurs against the backdrop of a policing agenda which emphasizes respect for and recognition of 'diversity'.

During the course of my fieldwork, the economically excluded were the prime targets of police concern and practice. Officers saw themselves as locked in battle with what they termed 'scrotes' who would otherwise infest their respective areas. I deal below with the etymology of this term, but it chiefly denoted poor, white, men. If policing has been described as a genus of 'dirty work' (Waddington 1999: 299) then in Northshire the police were essentially street cleaners. Their work was intimately linked to those who experienced intense disadvantage and who were stripped of personal dignity: the homeless and unemployed; drug addicts, alcoholics and prostitutes; as well as those condemned to living in poverty. In their own estimation, the police were the thin blue line protecting the moral majority from the 'social scum'. Moreover, policing the 'scrotes' became heroic—even exciting. Their vision of themselves as bold venturers into the seedier side of the world fed into their sense of solidarity and moral conservatism, and also confirmed the demarcation of a common adversary.

Classed people, classed places

As Hanley (2007) notes, the residuum primarily reside in impoverished and stigmatized neighbourhoods. From my observations, this fact was highly relevant for the cultural expressions of the police (see also Young 1991; Chambliss 1994; Choongh 1998). In tending to their patch, certain places stood out in officers' cultural knowledge about the who and where of 'trouble'; impoverished council estates, terraced streets, derelict buildings, and other areas to which the most marginalized were relegated. Officers invariably viewed lower working class areas as places to target and gather intelligence. While stable areas were viewed as appreciative and deserving of policing services, poor and decaying areas were denounced for seemingly containing anti-police populations and criminogenic families. Moreover, these were localities in which a crime control model of policing took precedence. The following fieldnote provides an illustration of these themes and describes a familiar interaction between the police and the white residuum. The extract records a night shift where I accompanied Scott and Andy, two young IMU officers with whom I had been out on a number of occasions. The radio had been quiet and, like many officers, they took the opportunity to do some proactive police work; in other words, not just random patrolling but actively seeking out places where they thought there was a chance of running across criminal activity and 'troublesome' individuals:

Scott and Andy decided it was time for some 'sneaky policing'. They drove to The Barracks Estate which was especially impoverished and known among some officers as 'Scrote City'. They didn't like the layout of the estate because it has too many roads going into and out of it—'the estate is like a rabbit warren, they can hide anywhere', Andy theorized. Switching the car lights off so we would not be seen, Andy drove slowly round and round the same run-down streets paying particular attention to public walkways and addresses of those already known to them.

After a while, they saw four young men sitting on a wall next to a street lamp, said 'Right, here's some shit', and pulled up next to them. They were local men who were white, aged between seventeen and twenty-two, and were smoking and drinking cans of beer. Andy asked them what they were doing out at this time of the night. They sheepishly murmured they were just hanging around because there was nothing else to do. After making some small talk, Scott asked the group for their names, addresses, and dates of birth and said, 'Will any of you be known to me?' The group nervously said no and consented to the questioning. None of them were 'known' and we left. Once back in the car, Scott and Andy were pleased that they had gathered some personal information from the 'scrotes' off the Barracks estate—and were particularly pleased that the young locals would go back and tell their associates about the encounter. For Scott and Andy, their presence would indicate to the rest of the 'scrotes' on the estate that the police 'were watching them'.

Northville

The Barracks Estate was branded by officers as a problem place with socially contaminating people. In reality, it was a large council estate inhabited mainly by an impoverished white populace. 'Shit', as the collective here for the young white males, is grammar that plainly captures police disdain for the estate and its inhabitants. Yet officers were not necessarily out to make arrests. In the style of policing observed by Choongh (1997) they were content to informally discipline and subordinate this section of the community—most notably, by sending out a symbolic message that they had the estate's population under surveillance.

The concerted focus on the spatial locations of the poor was also noted in Southville. Officers believed that the affluent and picturesque landscape was defiled by an impoverished housing estate called The Brickworks. Inhabited mainly by a white population, the estate was denigrated for being disorderly and distasteful:

Bethan: What about on the patch? Are there any problems within the LPU?

Jennifer: Because of targets and paperwork, we can't patrol like we should. The Brickworks Estate is a place that is left to run riot. Trying to deal with the people on there is just . . .

Matt: It's one of those estates, everywhere has got one. But to us, it's the thorn in Southville's side isn't it? . . .

Anthony: It brings the area down doesn't it?

Jennifer: It's one of those estates that constantly needs that extra presence and work to say to its residents, 'Well actually, this is *our* area and *we* are in control, not you' [her emphasis] . . .

Matt: You haven't got the time to be constantly on their backs, you know, just to remind them, 'Hey—settle it down a bit.' It's a never-ending cycle. If we could keep on top of it, it would settle.

Group discussion

In addition to experiencing material hardship, poor people living in rural areas are typically stigmatized as dysfunctional, unintelligent, and incestuous (Cloke 1997). These cultural representations of the poor found strong support within the occupational culture and, in similar fashion to their urban counterparts, officers viewed their task as one of containing the estate (see also Bittner 1967; Young 1991). When officers patrolled working class locales, they were chiefly concerned to seek out criminal activity and troublesome individuals. In targeting these areas, an interesting paradox emerges. The incongruity rule so often followed by officers was largely redundant in that they deliberately focused on those poor populations who were *expected* to be on the estates. Encouraged by external pressures to get 'results', operational police work was geared towards places where the residuum were available for the culling (see also Young 1999). We could add that the focus on the economically marginal also enabled officers to achieve an authentic policing experience as crime fighters.

During my observations, I became aware that a key function of Southville police was to protect the materially affluent classes from the residuum—whether such a threat came from urban 'outsiders' or the local 'scrotes'. The dominant crime control values underpinning the manner of patrol undertaken on The Brickworks Estate did not extend to areas considered decent and respectable. Rather, when officers attended to the latter, it was with a robust service outlook. Various fieldnote extracts would demonstrate this, but I think the following episode stands out:

At around 6.30pm, an IR came over the radio. A burglar alarm was going off at Grand House—a private residential address which was located at the other side of the LPU. Ben quickly jumped up, grabbed the car keys and ran to the car as I followed. With the full blue lights and sirens blaring, he drove over 70 miles an hour to the address. He was convinced that the house was being burgled by 'outsiders' or other 'scrotes', and appeared desperate to catch them in the act.

We arrived fifteen minutes later at a large mansion in a secluded part of the LPU. As we drove up the long driveway, Ben commented to me, 'How the other half live, hey?' He parked the car and began to look around. The house had four tennis courts, six garages, and extensive gardens. Ben conducted a thorough search of the grounds before contacting the ACR to report that there were no signs of a break-in, nor were there any suspects in the vicinity. The ACR subsequently informed him that they had located the owners of the property who were now on their way to switch off the alarm. Nevertheless, Ben suggested that to be 'on the safe side' we should sit in the car outside the property and wait for the owners to arrive.

From what I saw, I doubt whether such urgency and attention would have been given to this kind of incident if it had occurred on The Brickworks Estate. One explanation for this disparity in policing practice relates to the changes in modes of policing under conditions of late modernity. As Reiner (2000*a*) observes, policing increasingly involves patrolling a social order which is divided between the dreadful enclosures of the poor and the defensible locales of the wealthy. Moreover, the styles of policing to which these two are subjected also differ; while the police serve the populations of the stable areas, they are chiefly concerned to keep the lid on the symbolic locations of the underclass (ibid: 217).

The language of class contempt

Although the general absence of overtly racist language among officers was one of the most salient features of their culture, routine articulations of class contempt were pervasive. Officers rarely employed specific class terminology, but they drew regularly on powerful class imagery in their denigration of the poor. Consider the following set of comments made by an IMU officer in Northville:

Tom asked me, 'Has anyone told you what a scrote is yet'? After replying that nobody had, he offered me the following picture: 'scrotes' are 'the dregs of society', the 'lazy', 'unemployed scum' who reside on 'shit estates that should have walls built around them to stop them from leaving'. And, just like their council houses, 'scrotes' are 'dirty' and 'smelly'—they are 'like animals'. Tom assured me that I would meet a lot of 'scrotes' over the coming eighteen months, particularly in 'Beirut', where policing the large number of 'scrotes' in the area was like 'shovelling shit uphill'.

This fieldnote was written after the first police shift I attended and Tom's comments were made as he drove around in order to acquaint me with the patrol area. I recall being surprised at his matter of fact disparagement of the lower working class since he had otherwise presented himself as 'politically correct'—subscribing, at face value, to the language and spirit of the diversity agenda. Indeed, moments earlier Tom had shown me where 'members of our local ethnic minority community' live. A number of other important issues are raised by this fieldnote.

First, there is the term 'scrote'. A shortened version of scrotum, this was a descriptor for an identifiable section of the population.[2] Saturated with meaning, the term was used to describe members of the residuum, including drug addicts; the homeless; residents of impoverished neighbourhoods; the unemployed hanging around in public space; and individuals already known to the police. The term appears 'race' neutral, but its most universal characteristic was that it indicated the low social and economic position of the person to whom it was being applied—and in practice, for the police, scrote predominantly denoted 'young, poor, white male'. As Stinchcombe (1963) reminds us, the institution of privacy depends on the class position of a person. Thus in the current social landscape, where young white males are relegated to living their lives in street space through lack of employment, the assigning of the term 'scrote' to this group may not be wholly surprising.

---

[2] According to a number of dictionaries the meaning of 'scrote' ranges from 'a term of abuse' to a 'despicable person'. One dictionary refers to a newspaper article which features a man from West Belfast recounting his treatment by British paratroopers during the 'troubles'; he reported, 'they had a name for us—it was scrotes—they were young guys and aggressive' (*The Sunday Times* 29/01/05 cited in, *Dictionary of Contemporary Slang*, 3rd edn, London: A & C Black).

'Scrote' was a peculiarly derogatory epithet which reflected a moral judgement on the social complexion of the local poor. The term makes no explicit reference to class, but the classed component of the disparagement was clear enough. It symbolizes police disdain at the lack of material possessions and the associated lack of moral and cultural virtues of the residuum. In the police mind, scrotes are assumed to have a natural propensity to crime because they are 'too lazy to get a job' or, more simply, because 'their scrote families are the same' (see also Young 1991). As the above comments suggests, 'scrotes' stood as the omnipresent adversary of the police—reflected most notably in the remark that policing them was like 'shovelling shit uphill'. In short, 'scrote' was a convenient blanket term for a range of prejudicial meanings, and provided officers with a handy, quick-recognition shorthand for a preconceived population. Yet, as I explore in a moment, it also shaped the way officers *interacted* with the individuals so identified.

First, though, it is worth reflecting briefly on some of the issues that the currency of a term like this raises about the role of language in an occupational culture. 'Scrote' is clearly a reincarnation of the epithets used by the police to describe their property in different settings—from 'pukes' (Ericson 1982) in Canada to 'slag' (Smith and Gray 1985) in London. A detailed examination of the tacit meanings and stigmatization processes behind police labelling has been provided by Van Maanen (1978a) who recognized the importance of assigning epithets to 'assholes'. This kind of labelling serves to establish social distance from those who are routinely policed, but it also adds meaning to their role as protectors and crime fighters. For Northshire officers, scrotes represent not only their main adversaries but, also, what is wrong with the world 'out there'. Furthermore, the general currency of the idiom throughout the organization 'solidifies police organizations around at least one common function' (ibid: 235). This latter point comes out in the way officers handled photographs of suspects and persons known to the police. The official term for the mainly young, white, males whose images were pinned up around the parade room walls was 'nominals', but scrawled next to the photographs on one wall was, 'scrotes'.

Returning to the previous fieldnote, a number of further points need to be made clear. Tom's comments were made in the context of his role as a police officer. He was extremely open about his contempt for the poor, but felt no need to *manage* his talk in relation to this group. Widespread expressions of class contempt among front line officers did not attract any rebuke or moral condemnation from immediate colleagues or, in some instances, superiors. While some senior personnel may have disapproved of such overtly explicit language, officers' articulation of class contempt was unabashed and in no way atypical. Consider the following episode which I recorded in Northville:

Duncan, Scott and Chris came into the parade room where Nick, Matt, Sergeant Jones, and I were sitting. They seemed excited and were laughing as they began to recount an earlier incident involving themselves and Shaun—a 'known scrote' who, by all accounts, is homeless. The officers had initially suspected Shaun of having some drugs on him but, in the beginning, he would not let them search him. The general conversation was very animated, full of bravado and laughter, and revolved around their disgust at Shaun's poverty and lack of dignity:

Duncan:	The little scrote definitely had some on him but he was being an arsehole.
Scott:	Yeah, wouldn't let us touch him though—as if I wanted to. Honestly, if you could swap smack [heroin] for soap our job would be easier.
Nick:	You should have done a section 5 [Public Order Act] on him, brought him in and stripped searched the dirty shit.
Chris:	Fuck that—that's what he probably wanted. Dirty bastard gets a nice clean bed, cup of tea, and a roof for the night.
Sergeant Jones:	[Laughing] You wouldn't make it [tea] though! Did you take him in then?
Duncan:	No—he let us search him in the end but we found nothing, probably swallowed it.

It is of pivotal interest here that this pervasive and widely tolerated way of talking about the poor stands up in sharp contrast to the current organizational stance which takes a strong disciplinary line against expressions of racism, sexism, and homophobia. Most officers were at pains to avoid using discriminatory language, yet they were remarkably nonchalant when talking derogatorily about the white poor. Police talk has been much debated in recent years. Although its value as an indicator of police behaviour has been criticized (see Waddington 1999*b*), some argue that language is *the* primary aspect in the production and reproduction of police culture (Shearing and Ericson 1991). The classed nature of police culture was most apparent in officers' talk but, importantly, it also manifested itself in the practical policing of the residuum.

Classed bodies

Class contempt is peculiarly sensitive to indicators of appearance, and such markers extend into judgements about moral worth (Sayer 2005; see also Skeggs 2004). The poor were visible and recognizable within the occupational culture because, for the police, they exuded clear signifiers. In other words, the police could *see* scrotes 'a mile off'. The following fieldnote, which I recorded during the policing of a local football match, provides only one illustration of this:

John and I went over to stand with two of the sergeants and their officers who were located by the parking bay. The stadium gate had now been opened and a number of fans started to get out of their buses and cars and make their way towards the entrance. Those coming through the gates were predominantly young (aged around eighteen to thirty) white men with short or shaven hair. As they started to walk past us the police stopped talking amongst themselves and stared intently at the group. Although some of the men stared back, many of them dropped their eyes to the floor and continued to walk towards the stadium. As they were doing so the following conversation ensued:

Richard: [Looking them up and down with a stern frown] Look at them—they're like a bunch of animals.

Phillip: I know. Why is it you can tell a scrote a mile off? I'm telling you, if you see anyone in shell suit [tracksuit] bottoms, cheap bling [jewellery], T-shirts with a waft of stale cigarettes and shit trailing behind them—a guaranteed scrote.

Shaun: What gets me though is that they have started to wear Stone Ivory jumpers, £200 a piece, yet they can't be arsed to work and live in shit holes.

Richard: [Sniggering] They're probably nicked—they can't buy them with their giros [state benefits] can they? . . .

Phillip then approached some of the young men and told them that there was a lot of bobbies about tonight and if there was any 'agro' they would all be 'coming in' for the night. There were some murmurings from the group, but no conflict on their part.

Northville

Signs of class lifestyle are emblemized in the flesh; or as Bourdieu (1984: 190) puts it, 'the body is the most indisputable materialisation of class taste'. The above incident further confirms how sections of the white residuum were viewed within a framework of class, but it also reveals how their bodies were implicated within the occupational culture. Marking of lower working class bodies as defiling and socially deficient came to be associated with a visual register lodged within the culture (see also Young 1991) and officers readily recognized and delineated their property through associated markers. For the police, clothes, bodily comportment, and even smell—actual or imagined—all betrayed the class origins of 'scrotes'. Furthermore, the identification of the poor according to their cultural dictionary (Chan 1997: 68) invariably set the rationale for interaction. Even though this kind of recognition operated at the deeper level of cultural knowledge, it was also overtly acknowledged and used to the advantage of the organization. Officers involved in covert operations to suppress certain forms of street crime—operations inevitably aimed at those with least resources (Box 1994)—often adopted the dress, manners, and speech associated with 'scrotes' in order to pass as one of them.

The bodily appearance of the poor came to be associated not only with their perceived innate criminality but, also, their intrinsic lack of moral worth. The following extract records a shift where I attended a court session with a CAT officer who was giving evidence against two eighteen-year-old males charged with affray and criminal damage:

Jim and Dave [the defendants] were outside the courthouse having a cigarette with Jim's dad when Matthew and I arrived. [. . .] We were sitting in the witness room when Jim and Dave came back up the stairs and walked past us. Matthew scowled and said angrily to me, 'It's disgusting that people think they can turn up to court dressed like that. It makes me sick. Have they no respect for anything?' Jim and Dave were pale and thin. They were wearing T-shirts, jeans, trainers, and chunky gold jewellery. They both had skinheads with tramlines cut into the back of their hair. Matthew said that he couldn't wait to see them get 'potted' [sent to prison] as there would be 'two less scrotes to worry about' on his patch.

As Sayer (2005) argues, a person's class can significantly affect how others value and respond to him or her. The injuries of class are inflicted not only in economic disadvantage but, also, in experiences of class contempt and symbolic domination—including a withholding of recognition. It is perhaps unsurprising, therefore, that a frequent complaint made against the police is that they are impolite in their dealings with certain members of the public— with the unemployed feeling particularly disrespected (Choongh 1998). Equally, and referring back to the emotional force of class contempt, the facial expressions of the officers in the above extracts also betray their repulsion and disgust at the poor.

In both reactive and proactive encounters, the white poor occupied a prominent place in the practical daily workload of the police. Yet it is important to focus on the latter type of encounter for the choices officers make regarding the *who* and *where* of crime conveys a great deal about their priorities, values, and commitments in controlling their respective areas (Rubinstein 1973). As noted earlier, officers' rejection of the poor extended to whole areas such as public housing estates. These locales were robustly targeted and held significance in the culture as brimming with problem populations—ranging from the disorderly and criminal, to benefit scroungers (see also Choongh 1997). While the bodies of the residuum were coded in terms of dirt and filth, their homes were likewise condemned as sites of disorder and uncleanliness. This is captured in the following comments made by a group of IMU officers in Northville:

Samuel: It was a big culture shock for me joining the job because I have walked into a house in West Street . . . [all laughing: 'ahhh that one'!]

Howard: Name and shame them, I would . . .

Samuel: I walked into the house and my feet were sticking to the carpet it was that dirty. I actually couldn't breathe, the smell of piss. I had to say to the guy can you come and sit in the car . . .

Gary: [Laughing] Your shift sent you there on purpose!

Scott: [Quite aggressively] People seem to not have a grasp of how to live their life. Their idea of a life is finally getting your house off the council, and then being able get your benefits, to sit in, drink beer, smoke and watch television. And that's their life, their lifestyle.

Group discussion

Police criticism of lower working class predicaments, such as being on state benefits and relegated to living in substandard public housing, appears to be bound up with notions of cleanliness and respectability. As Young (1991) explains, the police are particularly averse to the poor because they stand in opposition to what they themselves represent as enforcers of respectability (see also Ericson 1982). We could also add that the organizational emphasis on discipline and uniformity accentuates police disdain for those regarded as falling short of such standards. Nevertheless, references to bodily waste, disease, and impurity are crucial in the exclusion of marginal groups. As Sibley (1995) reminds us, exclusionary discourses in respect of the poor have always centred on notions of filth and the attribution of animal characteristics to the impoverished. While this is apparent in a number of extracts presented here, the police emphasis on dirt and disease also manifested itself in a directly physical aspect of procedure—namely, through putting on surgical gloves before touching the poor and those dispossessed groups who were the subject of a policing operation.

Unemployment and the erosion of worth

Unemployment was an issue that loomed large throughout the research and presents a further instance of the way class pervaded the occupational culture. It had a practical dimension where the employment status of an individual needed to be established for some bureaucratic requirement (such as taking a formal statement or collating the file of a person brought into custody), but it was also clear that 'unemployed' was in itself a category saturated with meaning and signalling the moral worth of a person. Officers routinely asked their property for his (very seldom her) employment status—often in the *absence* of any bureaucratic need. The question, 'Are you working?' was a generally loaded one aimed at exposing the moral worth of that person. The following episode demonstrates how these notions of worth played out in the course of everyday interactions. Will was a young IMU officer who had been in the job for just over two years, having previously been in the army. He was extremely crime control oriented and known affectionately among his colleagues as the shift 'terrier' for his high arrest rates. Will and I had been driving around on patrol when an IR came in concerning an accident in one of the more impoverished streets in Northville:

A young boy had been hit by a car in Lower Lane—a narrow terraced and rather run-down and dilapidated street. Will and I were at the other side of the LPU and arrived just after the rest of the shift and the ambulance crew. [. . .] Residents had come out of their houses to see what was going on and were standing around and watching all of the commotion.

Will was approaching some of them and asking whether anybody had seen anything. He saw Jamie sitting on a kerb (a white male who was in his twenties). He was wearing a scruffy white vest; tracksuit bottoms with holes in them; and had a muddy face and hands. Will said, 'Come on Beth, let's go and check out this scrote while we are here.'

Will walked over, stood over the lad and said, 'I know you don't I'? Jamie uncomfortably shuffled and replied, 'Don't know.' Will then asked him, 'Are you still on the bad stuff [drugs] or the good stuff now'? Jamie said that he was being good and staying out of trouble. Finally Will asked, 'Are you working?' When Jamie answered that he wasn't, Will turned to me, rolled his eyes and gave me a knowing smirk. Walking away, Will commented that: 'If he can't be arsed getting a job he is never going to sort his shit out.'

In more private spaces, such as the police car, officers would give moral lectures to 'prisoners', in which the common catchphrase would be admonishment to 'get themselves a job'. For officers, getting a job was the surest route to respectability and staying out of trouble. In the police mind, the unemployed are the social dirt of society. Ironically, because of current structural arrangements in which generations of young men are excluded from traditional employment trajectories, officers did frequently come into contact with people who had no legitimate employment—and it was, then, just a short step for them to associate unemployment with crime and disorderliness. Males who inhabited public space during the days and times associated with work prompted a reflex of suspicion and predetermined what the police interaction would be. As the next encounter illustrates, this had particular resonance in Southville:

2.45pm
John and Martin were driving through Millionaires Row to 'fly the flag' (*engage in public reassurance policing*). A white male in his late twenties was walking in the opposite direction. He had shoulder length hair and his top was tucked into the back of his jeans exposing his pale torso. Slowing down to look more closely, John then said, 'What the hell is he doing walking round here on a Monday afternoon?' He turned the car around, pulled up next to the man and asked, 'Hey mate. Do you mind if I ask you what you are doing around these parts?' The man replied that he had stayed with some friends over the weekend in the area, and was walking to the bus stop. John asked him where his friends lived and started to ask other questions. Annoyed at the police intrusion, the man queried why he had been stopped but, after a short while, was allowed to go.

In the car I asked Martin why his suspicion had been aroused. He explained that the man was stopped because that 'type' of person looked out of place in the area. He went on to explain that burglars are aware that the people who live in the 'posh houses' are out at work during the daytime, and because 'criminals don't have jobs' it is a perfect time to steal from them.

Young unemployed males were regarded as 'trouble' because work is believed to be the main way in which males acquire discipline and their major source of identity (Box 1994). These cultural meanings of work found strong support within the occupational culture. From the police perspective, the unemployed have the idle hands needed for doing the devils work (Clarke and Critcher 1985) and are more likely to commit economic forms of crime, such as burglary and theft. It is also worth remembering that the police view themselves as the guardians of public morality. They consequently juxtapose the 'rough' unemployed classes with the 'respectable' *working* classes and support the interests of the latter in discourse and practice (Cain 1973; Shearing 1981).

Under acknowledged: victimization and the white poor

In line with approaches taken by other British police forces (Heidensohn 2003; Foster *et al* 2005; Moran 2007) the improved recording, investigation, and prosecution of crimes committed against minority groups has been placed high on the Northshire reform agenda. However, the revised organizational stance on minority victimization did not appear to be so concerted when officers responded to sections of the white residuum.

Poor and low status members of the public were nearly always viewed with suspicion, and this was heightened if the person was previously known to the police. Having a record of past criminal encounters with the police undoubtedly served as a prompt for attention (see also Smith and Gray 1985; Choongh 1997), but it could also shape their responses to *victims* of crime. As the following episode makes clear, some officers failed to display sympathy or quality of service towards people seen as 'scrotes':

12.50am

Collin and Don responded to an incident on The Westville Estate. The ACR was giving them further details as they drove there: a young couple had been lying in bed when they heard their front living room window get smashed in. The boyfriend came downstairs to find two bricks on his living room floor and the girlfriend, who was still upstairs, saw three men running away into the night. When we arrived at the house Collin said, 'I'm sure I've been here before. If it's the same guy, he's known.' We walked into a very dilapidated and run-down house, which had no carpets and hardly any furniture, to find glass shattered all over the front room—which the young woman was now brushing up. Her boyfriend came through from the kitchen and was very angry about what had happened, and he told the officers to go and find out who had done it. This irritated Don whose manner was extremely standoffish and unsympathetic. Collin was also very blasé, but told the couple that they would drive around the estate to see if they could see anyone.

However, the main solution offered was that they would send another officer around in the morning to take a proper statement. Back in the car, Collin surmised that the boyfriend was only a 'scrote' drug dealer who had probably had his window smashed by disgruntled customers or people to whom he owed money. He then did a police check *on the boyfriend*— despite him being the victim of criminal damage. He was 'known' on NPIN, but had no formal record. Officers put very little effort into the search for the perpetrators of the incident, and it seemed to me that the low status of the victim profoundly influenced their response to the situation.

Northville

People who have been found guilty of past crimes, or indeed, are merely suspected of being involved in illegal activity, are never considered entirely innocent (Choongh 1997). Yet while the combination of being poor and 'known' clearly influenced the nonchalant police response in this incident, I would also argue that the whiteness of the complainant played a tacit role. As I demonstrated in preceding chapters, when officers were called to incidents involving minority ethnic people as victims of crime, some were visibly anxious. This unease stemmed from the heightened awareness that the police are under pressure to deal with potential hate crimes effectively—and this new understanding could inform the way officers practically dealt with such incidents. However if minority ethnic groups now represent organizational trouble within police culture, members of the white residuum certainly do not. This is somewhat problematic when the poorest sections of society experience the highest levels of victimization (Mooney and Young 2000) and thereby have the greatest need for policing services. From my observations, it would appear that the white residuum fail to rouse an equivalent level of concern in officers than their socially and culturally diverse counterparts. This was particularly apparent on the following occasion in Northville. It was around 11pm and we were sitting in the parade room when the shift sergeant asked two IMU officers to respond to a report of a man who was lying seemingly unconscious down an alleyway in Cobble Street, an area known for attracting homeless people:

Paul and Nick seemed in no rush to attend, and it was over half an hour later when we arrived. It was dark, but the dimly lit streetlamps gave a clearer view of the alleyway. A middle-aged white man was curled up on the floor with his eyes closed. He was wearing a thick overcoat and looked very dishevelled. A large black dog was standing over him and began to bark and growl at the police car. Almost immediately, Paul and Nick presumed that the man was a 'homeless drunk'. Because of this assumption, they didn't get out of the police car to attend to him. Instead, they began to shout and throw sweets at the man in an attempt to wake him up. When the man looked up and began to mutter something, the officers decided he was indeed a homeless drunk and drove away.

In addition to promoting a more proactive approach to victimization, it will be recalled that the Force has also developed an Anti-Discrimination Code of Practice. This places an onus on officers to 'treat everyone with whom they come into contact with dignity and respect'. Yet as the above extract demonstrates, some officers fail to follow this tenet when dealing with poor whites. In broader terms, we could also add that this way of treating the poor is the polar opposite of the mutual respect called for by Sennett (2003).

Redundant identities

What is notable in many of the extracts presented here is the way in which the white residuum merely consents to police intrusion. Some interactions between the police and this group were clearly characterized by friction and hostility, but another salient feature of the fieldwork was the level of compliance displayed during encounters. Significant numbers of interactions were seemingly unproblematic and consensual, as demonstrated in the following extract which I wrote after an organized drugs raid in Northville:

[. . .] The sniffer dog started to bark at the sofa. Tony and Stephen cut the lining of the sofa open and found a pipe which they suspected was being used to smoke crack and heroin. Tony also found a small amount of heroin in a hole in the floor. The man who lived there was a chronic heroin addict. He was extremely thin and many of his teeth were missing. After being subjected to a strip search, he was now sitting on the uncarpeted floor in handcuffs. The man was cooperative throughout, and was even laughing and joking with the police. He seemed to know the officers, and his relationship with the police was very relaxed, friendly, and consensual. At one point, the arresting officer asked him, 'Do you want a brief [solicitor], or shall we keep this quick?' The man answered that he would rather 'get it over and done with' as he didn't want to spend the night in the cells. The officer replied, 'Yeah—no problem mate. If you don't have a brief you should be out by tonight.'

Interactions between the police and the subject of their attention may appear sociable but, as Dixon (1997: 92) reminds us, 'they are never equal exchanges'. In addition to reflecting how some officers discouraged access to a solicitor, this incident also raises the twin issues of consent and compliance. It is well-known that the police prefer to obtain the consent of those with whom they come into contact, rather than rely on legal powers (McBarnet 1981; McConville *et al* 1991; Dixon 1997). Several reasons explain why people readily submit to police intrusion, with fear of the police and a lack of knowledge about rights being particularly influential. However, to view the issue of consent as based solely on ignorance about rights is to overlook the social, economic, and political position of those who form the targets of routine policing. The study by Charlesworth (2000: 77) found that the poorest sections of the working class find themselves 'linguistically dispossessed' in describing their diminishing dignity, and sense of alienation and domination. He warned that the poor have become unreflective actors and lack the resources necessary to guard themselves against hegemony and symbolic domination. Without wishing to portray this group as cultural dopes, I think that poor, white males are increasingly unable to defend themselves against police intrusion. This was frequently borne out during the fieldwork where they merely handed themselves over to the police as passive and submissive bodies:

Warren, a seasoned CAT officer, drove up to a group comprising older teenagers and young men who were huddled around an old bike outside one of the houses on The Brickworks Estate. Pulling up to the group, he wound down his window and said, 'Simon says put your hands in the air.' Looking at each other apprehensively, the group began to put their hands in the air. Warren let out a loud laugh—much to the relief of the group—before asking them why they were not in work or college.

Most of the group muttered that they didn't have a job, but were looking for one. Warren was already acquainted with some of the young men, but asked each of them for their names, dates of birth, and addresses; as he explained, 'I want to check whether any of you are wanted for anything.' All members of the group unquestioningly provided the information— which subsequently came back clear. Warren later told me that one of the lads in the group had an older brother who had been in prison and because of this he wanted to keep an extra eye on him.

Southville

What transpired during my observations was an apparent difference between those who demonstrated a heightened awareness of their position as enduring targets of policing, and those that did not. As discussed in earlier chapters, the relationship between the police and certain members of minority ethnic communities were strained, and could be fraught with conflict. This was usually because the latter believed that their ethnicity was the basis for police attention—a factor which caused a fusion of anxiety and resentment among officers. But while minority ethnic groups increasingly possess a clear consciousness of being discriminated against (Reiner 2000a) poor whites have been unable to construct an authentic political identity in recent years (Haylett 2001).[3] It should also be remembered that a defining feature of the term 'police property' is that their control is 'supported by an apparent social consensus to "let the police handle these people"' (Lee 1981: 53). In the wake of their social, economic, and political exclusion, it would appear that poor white men operate as a reliable and safe population for the police to control without any risk of recrimination or reproach from the organization and wider public.

Throughout this book I have endeavoured to provide a more nuanced account by considering the moments where officers transcend what is usually regarded as the core values of policing culture. It is important, then, to reflect upon the differences I observed in relation to the classed nature of police dispositions and practices.

The idea that policing impacts most heavily upon the marginal has achieved academic orthodoxy. It is nevertheless worth

---

[3] Paradoxically, political engagement about the predicament of the white working class has come from the far Right—most notably through the British National Party (BNP). However, this kind of association arguably dampens the likelihood of sympathetic debate about this group.

noting that the police themselves are aware that the bulk of their work involves dealing with the poor. Class contempt towards the residuum was an entrenched feature of the culture, but some officers adopted a sympathetic attitude towards the predicament of this group. Consider the following interaction which I recorded while accompanying a female CAT officer in Southville:

Jacqui headed to The Brickworks Estate for a drive round. Many parts of the estate are extremely run-down, and it has gained a reputation amongst officers as where the local criminals come from. As we pulled into the entrance, Jacqui began to criticize her colleagues' targeting of the estate, and explained that she liked to talk to the residents to show that the police were 'human'.

Even though it was pouring with rain, a few older teenagers were hanging around on River Street, and were kicking a football against a garage wall. Jacqui pulled up in the car to talk to them. They were familiar with her, and she was asking them why they were out in the rain. The group were saying that there was nothing for them to do in the area, and that they were bored. Jacqui agreed and was encouraging them to write to their local Member of Parliament to try to get a new park, or other facilities, set up. After we drove off, Jacqui expressed a lot of sympathy for the group, and said that she could understand how young people became involved in crime, and how more should be done to 'help get them off the streets'.

Of course this response may have a gendered dimension, but it nevertheless demonstrates the varying police outlooks towards the poor.[4] Through their occupational experiences, the police become acutely aware that 'society does not bestow fair and equal chances' (Reiner 2000a: 92). Although most officers gave narrow-minded explanations for crime, some understood that it is a consequence of broader social and economic problems, as the following comments made by some CAT officers in Northville make clear:

Robert: I think with Northville because of the decline of the manufacturing industry. . .

Neil: It's a very depressed area.

Robert: There's a whole lot of people who were good, hardworking people, but have had their livelihoods just snatched away from them. And now there is nothing else for them. So it's a depressed

---

[4] As several have observed, women police tend to display a more sensitive and less confrontational approach to their work (Young 1991; Westmarland 2001b). It is also worth adding that Jacqui was a lone parent with two teenage sons, a point which may explain her sympathetic treatment of the young men in this episode.

place, and that's where a lot of crime is generated from. A lot of the people you arrest or speak to, because they are on these drugs, were once hardworking and decent people.

Ken: Or it's their families—the children of the parents who were in industry but have been made redundant. Then the family life has gone down and the children, it just splinters out into all sorts of crime. . .

Robert: There is a saying about this area; 'Nobody retires from Northville. They are made redundant' [murmurs of agreement]. For the last decade or so that is true.

Neil: There's nothing. They have a few call centres up and coming, but there's nothing in this area. If you weren't born here you wouldn't move here. There is nothing that would attract people. So being so depressed is one of our greatest problems for crime.

This extract once again reflects the police preoccupation with employment as a marker of decency, but it also signals a deeper understanding of how adverse economic restructuring can influence a person's involvement in behaviours defined as crime. It is also worth noting that the *public* initiated some of the interactions between the police and the residuum. To some extent, police contact with the poor was influenced by deployment patterns. Nevertheless, what I have tried to emphasize in this chapter is that the acquired cultural knowledge informed officers that, primarily, it was those residual working-class populations living on impoverished housing estates and occupying public spaces which were more likely to engage in crime.

The Classed Nature of Police Culture

Much as in the past, operational policing functions to control the economically marginal. Notwithstanding these clear echoes with historical patterns of policing, there are several new dynamics at work. Interactions with diverse publics formed an important part of routine policing, but the overwhelming focus of police attention was on the white residuum. Within the occupational consciousness, this group was reviled and invariably set the rationale for interaction. Class contempt pervades the daily narratives and interactions of the police. Not always operating at the surface level, the class iconography drawn upon by officers implies it was present at the deeper level. Police cultural knowledge was infused with class themes and orientated officers towards those whose bodily appearance and comportment betrayed their class origins.

In this regard, an important disjuncture emerges between the dominant organizational discourse and the realities of day to day policing; the Northshire reform agenda placed robust emphasis on the equitable policing of minority ethnic, gay, lesbian, and female members of the public, but there is no similar injunction on officers to treat the white poor with the same level of professionalism and respect. Policing culture is now characterized by a heightened awareness and anxiety when dealing with minority ethnic people, but officers are remarkably undisturbed when dealing with white 'scrotes'. To this end, the official emphasis on respect for diversity has had the unfortunate effect of delivering up powerless white males as uncontentiously legitimate terrain for the unchallenged exercise of police discretion and authority.

Several further points can be made here. The police act as an important carrier and authorizer of class contempt. At an implicit level, the value choices reflected in their cultural knowledge, along with the routine attention devoted by the police to lower working-class crime, serve to reinforce the more widely diffused disregard for the poor in society at large. Moreover, the impunity with which officers focus on and talk about poor whites also 'confirms' their status as legitimate targets for contempt. Exacerbated by the burgeoning performance culture, the result is that the focus of street policing continues to be on the poorest sections of the working class. In focusing unproblematically on the residuum, moreover, the police help to reproduce the exclusion and symbolic domination of this group (see also Manning 1994).

In taking class contempt as a relatively unexamined aspect of police culture, I have in this chapter raised some questions about the place of class, explored here through the white poor, in current 'policing diversity' debates. Notions of diversity promote a better public image of police organizations, but they can obscure the enduring realities of routine policing. The accent on diversity is undoubtedly crucial for those who have previously not been well served by the police but, as I have showed, it is also precarious because of its potential to divert attention away from the policing of the white residuum.

PART III

Conclusions

7

Police Culture in Transition?

I have in this book endeavoured to produce a revised and fully contemporary account of police culture. In particular, I have tried to document and make sense of how the occupational value systems and practices of officers have been shaped by two reconfigurations in policing: firstly, the national context of social, economic and political change and, secondly, the local context of changes made to reform the culture of what I have called Northshire Police Force. The fieldwork comprised direct observation of operational policing across two contrasting terrains and a series of group discussions and interviews with officers. The case of Northshire Police provides an invaluable context for examining the relevance of previous studies of police culture for the altered policing landscape.

In this concluding, penultimate chapter I offer an assessment of the current condition of police culture. I review the central findings I have presented in this book and discuss the implications of the research. My analysis is guided by the following questions: have the reorganizations in policing posed any significant threat to established police dispositions and practices? Which elements of police culture have been challenged? Which elements stand dominant? The argument I present here posits a tension between the transformations that have clearly occurred in the policing landscape, and the persistence of police cultural characteristics as observed by earlier scholars. There have indeed been a number of important shifts in policing, including major reforms in organizations. However, I question the degree to which developments in policing have changed the occupational culture of officers on the ground.

I want to begin the discussion by calling into question the dominance of current thinking on police culture. In recent years there has been growing consensus that police culture is in transition. There are, I think, two main conceptualizations of police culture to be found in the literature. The first is a supposition that police culture responds innovatively to change. Authors have pinpointed a range of developments which, they argue, can be expected to impact upon and transform the cultural expressions of the police. These generally include the cultural, ethnic, and gender diversification of police organizations, impact of operational changes such as community policing and the influence of official critiques of the police (Chan 1997; Paoline 2003; Marks 2005; O'Neill and Singh 2007; Sklansky 2007). These works, and others, are guided by an underlying assumption that innovations in policing have presented enough of a threat to modify the culture. The second focuses upon what I term the search for difference. Authors writing in the field have challenged traditional interpretations of police culture by critically interrogating its assumed homogeneity and universality (Fielding 1989; Hobbs 1991; Foster 2003). Adherents of this approach appeal for a more nuanced and diversified way of understanding the complexities of the police identity. For these authors, identifying common themes in police culture is unhelpful and 'results in crude generalizations . . . so as to make the results virtually meaningless' (Hobbs 1991: 606). Taken together, these two approaches have generated a discourse that orthodox characterizations of police culture no longer make any sense (see especially Sklansky 2007). The developments in policing contexts have been interpreted as contributing to the demise of an 'old' police culture and the beginnings of 'new' cultures.

I agree with many of these authors. But there are some key points at which our views on contemporary police culture diverge. In particular, I would question the *extent* to which police culture has changed in light of developments in policing. By emphasizing the novel aspects, I think that they lose sight of the remarkable continuities and inertia within police values and practices. In contradistinction with current scholarship, I think there are good reasons to retain the orthodox view of police culture. While there have been important breaks with the past, the manifest continuities with older patterns should not be overlooked. In the prevailing intellectual climate where identifying diversities and innovations in policing culture takes precedence, it is surely the enduring dimensions which needs to claim our attention. This is not just a question of theoretical preference; as the extracts presented in this book confirm, there are sound empirical grounds for retaining and continuing to think about the orthodox conception of police culture.

In order to explore this further, I return to three central themes which cut across preceding chapters. The first is the apparent survival of police ways of viewing and carrying out their role as found in the classic accounts. The second addresses how reconfigurations around questions of diversity have crystallized in the dispositions and practices of police officers. The final theme considers further the enduring, but often neglected, dimension of class.

Classic Characteristics in an Altered Landscape

The study of police culture involves examining the ways officers think about and act in the world around them. Yet recent discussions about the inner world of the police have focused almost exclusively on racism, and other forms of discrimination and intolerance (Martin 1994; Chan 1997; Westmarland 2001*b*; Miller *et al* 2003; Foster *et al* 2005). These works are undoubtedly crucial for understanding the social impact of police culture, but they nevertheless obscure other salient themes which comprise the occupational identity. They also underestimate the implications of these other themes for implementing reform. A wealth of research has identified recurring characteristics within the culture that go beyond seminal questions of ethnicity, gender, and sexuality.

An undeniable feature of my ethnography was the persistence of a substantially similar set of cultural traits to those identified almost half a century ago by earlier police research. A collection of dominant features remain within rank and file culture, and continue to exert considerable influence over the day to day functioning of operational policing. Mirroring earlier research, Northshire officers displayed a robust sense of duty towards their job and saw their role as protecting the innocent and weak from the lawless elements (Cain 1973; Reiner 1978). Invariably, this self-understanding provoked a crime fighting mindset which then interfered with what was viewed as 'proper' police work. Community policing initiatives tended to be disparaged because they failed to conform to the values of proper police work. The preoccupation with crime also meant that most officers sought out work that was considered to be exciting. Like the observational study by Smith and Gray (1985) the prospect of action commonly resulted in an overzealous police presence at incidents. In the more informal settings of the job, officers likewise relayed stories that emphasized dangerous and confrontational encounters with the public (see also Punch 1979). Yet, for the most part, these overt displays of aggression were merely bravado; a backstage aspect of the role mobilized to protect officers' occupational esteem in the absence of action and excitement (see Waddington 1999*a*).

Much as in previous works, masculinity was a theme that ran throughout the culture (Martin 1980; Heidensohn 1992; Smith and Gray 1985; Westmarland 2001*b*). It solidified the crime fighting image and influenced officers' attitudes and behaviour towards certain colleagues and sections of the public. There were some notable conflicts among officers, but the norms and values that were consistent with a predominantly male workforce created and reinforced a collective sense of togetherness with colleagues (Westley 1970; Van Maanen 1973; Reiner 1978; Graef 1989). This was exacerbated by a shared sense of isolation from the outside world, and many officers displayed the proverbial 'Us' versus 'Them' mindset. In Southville, feelings of detachment from the wider Force fostered a heightened sense of local solidarity and subsequently encouraged the covering up of widespread 'easing' behaviours (Cain 1973).

Another integral feature of the occupational culture was suspicion towards people, places, and events (Skolnick 1966; Sacks 1972; Rubinstein 1973; Brown 1981). The ability to identify potential offenders was highly valued, and police suspicion was driven by aesthetic and behavioural cues (Ericson 1982; Van Maanen 1978; Smith and Gray 1985). Police stereotyping invariably resulted in patterns of differentiation along distinctions of class, age, gender, sexuality, and ethnicity. Most officers, also possessed a cynical and pessimistic view of their surroundings which became directed towards the public, senior officers, and the criminal justice system (Neiderhoffer 1967; Reiner 1978; Graef 1989). Because officers in the deprived urban context of Northville were routinely exposed to the darker sides of society, they came to expect nothing but the worst in human behaviour. In both sites, the police were liable to adopt an outwardly detached manner during interactions. When officers perceived a challenge to their authority, they invoked a range of responses to regain control (see also Sykes and Clarke 1975). The rank and file also displayed cynicism towards their bosses. They trusted only their immediate colleagues because, as they saw it, they were the only people who understood how the world 'really' is. This omnipresent cynicism was also directed towards the law and criminal justice system. Ideas about the futile delivery of justice underpinned a robust law and order stance on crime, and officers displayed hostility towards people who challenged conventional morality. Much as in the study by Baker (1985) the authoritarian ideologies championed by officers were accompanied by a conservative political persuasion. Finally, the cultural mores exhibited by officers were communicated and reinforced through on-the-job socialization (Punch 1979; Ericson 1982).

It has not been my intention to simply duplicate the clichés of police culture. However, there unequivocally remains a range of dispositions and practices which mirror a whole history of earlier research. It is clear, in other words, that the defining elements of police culture have extended into the contemporary policing landscape. This is not to belie a more nuanced interpretation; there were indeed variations within police values and practices. In a break with most works I have provided an insight into rural policing culture. Officers in Northville and Southville displayed remarkably similar cultural traits, but there were subtle differences in how these features were enacted. For instance, although the theme of suspicion cut across both locations with striking resemblance, there were some nuances in the *who*, *when*, and *where* it was performed. Officers likewise shared a pervading sense of danger, but this was heightened among those working in Southville because of the low staffing levels and perceived threat of 'outsiders'. These finely grained distinctions between officers working in unique environments underlines the importance of accounting for contextual and localized differences in shaping policing culture. It would also be inaccurate to portray officers as culturally homogeneous. It was possible to detect fractures in the culture between different subgroups of police based on personal biography and the kind of shift on which they worked. For example, although female officers mainly espoused similar characteristics to their male counterparts, some enjoyed addressing the mundane problems of day to day policing and approached interactions in a responsive—as opposed to adversarial—manner. These differences reveal how officers can support and develop policing styles which exist in opposition to the prevailing culture (Chan 1997; Foster 2003;

Cockcroft 2007). Such instances are valuable for illustrating the complexities in the police identity, but they should not be accepted at the expense of overlooking the dominance of the key cultural features. There is little doubt that my observations show that the orthodox account of police culture possesses considerable value today.

Yet of particular interest here is how these enduring characteristics interact with the altered policing landscape. Most of these classic features remain virtually untouched by current reform initiatives, but they do nevertheless have implications for police change. One pivotal change in policing is the general shift towards community policing. Officers are encouraged to view members of the public as people with a legitimate right to and involvement in policing services—and not as a faceless mass distinct from the police (Fielding 1995; Tilley 2003). However, the endurance of the mission perspective and associated view that the whole point of policing is to lock up criminals undermines these endeavours to reinvent the police role. This is captured by Marks (2005: 27), who reminds us that 'when officers conceive themselves as the thin blue line separating chaos from order in society that is also a motivation for policing to be aggressive and action centred'. Likewise the desire for excitement and stimulation produces a reluctance to undertake less adventurous forms of police work (see also Bowling and Foster 2002). The survival of conservatism, isolation, and cynicism also shapes the way officers think about and behave towards people.

Police Culture in a Diverse Society

The British policing landscape has been steadily transformed following official criticism of the philosophies and practices of the policing of ethnically and socially diverse groups. Following the Macpherson Report (1999), police forces are under enormous pressure to understand, and indeed project, themselves as sites of diversity. In the local context of Northshire, senior officers embarked on a conscious top-down reform effort aimed primarily at improving the working conditions of personnel inside the organization, and the delivery of an effective and equitable service to the various publics with whom they were charged to serve. The question remains: has the Northshire initiative reformed the working culture?

It will be recalled that recruiting people from previously excluded backgrounds, and ensuring their career progression, was elevated as pressing concern. To some extent this process of diversification has begun to take shape. There has been a gradual rise in the number of minority ethnic, female, and gay and lesbian officers working in Northshire—some of whom have progressed to occupy supervisory positions. This has been bolstered by the establishment of internal support associations organized around ethnicity, gender, and sexuality. The institutionalization of diversity has altered the interior culture in some important, and contradictory, ways. As discussed in Chapter 3, there was a sense among some minority officers that the working environment has been transformed in the new diversity terrain. There was a perception that discrimination could now be challenged and that formal complaints would be listened to and acted upon by managers. It was specifically felt that the accent on diversity and discrimination had significantly reduced overt expressions of racism—and it should be remembered that an established feature of police culture has almost certainly been challenged and unlearned. The general absence of overtly racist language among officers is a significant and manifest demonstration of change (see also Foster *et al* 2005). The institutionalization of diversity has also produced a workplace where relations are increasingly sensitive. The police organization is an environment where new cultures are emerging to challenge old ones. These contestations have evolved primarily from minority officers, but a new generation of white, heterosexual, male officers are also confronting and questioning established sentiments. This multitude of different outlooks and identities implies that the culture which has long dominated the organizational environment is becoming eroded. Nevertheless, it would be erroneous to overstate the extent to which these new emerging cultures have displaced the hegemonic police culture. The transposition of identity politics onto the policing terrain may have begun to transform the internal culture, but its impact has not been decisive. The considerable resentment and hostility displayed by the dominant white, heterosexual, male culture towards the increasing recognition of their minority colleagues shows that the challenges made to the 'old' police culture remain partial. In furtherance, minority officers continue to feel discriminated against. Whether or not feelings of exclusion translate into real experiences is largely irrelevant; they demonstrate that minority officers believe that their social difference still poses problems for them.

Several new dynamics emerge in relation to how officers perceive and interact with those members of the public currently emphasized in the Diversity Strategy. In particular, the position of ethnic minorities has undergone transformation within policing culture. As a result of the heightened political status afforded to minority ethnic groups, officers had accusations of racism at the forefronts of their minds. This anxiety about 'race' meant that some officers revised the way they dealt with such groups. During the fieldwork some deliberately avoided initiating encounters with minority ethnic people for fear of being reprimanded by their superiors should the individual make a complaint. This finely tuned awareness also ensured that some officers adopted a non-adversarial approach in their interactions with such groups and dealt with potential hate crime incidents professionally. In an unusual twist, the contemporary emphasis on diversity appears to have redefined minority ethnic groups as 'disarmers' (Holdaway 1983: 77). There have also been important developments in the police response to domestic violence. Along with recording the relevant information into an incident form, most officers have likewise incorporated the pro-arrest policy into their routine policing practices. This runs counter to previous research which revealed that officers commonly avoided arresting the perpetrator and accordingly undermined the legal implications of what had taken place (Muir 1977; Stanko 1985; Grimshaw and Jefferson 1987).

In these respects, the culture of Northshire Police *is* in transition; in responding to the new diversity terrain there have been significant ruptures with the past. What such developments show is that aspects of police culture have been sensitive to the altered policing landscape. The changes are almost certainly the result of transformations which have occurred in the wider 'field' of policing (Chan 1997). Political sensitivity around policing has changed remarkably since the classic studies and present day officers inhabit a moment where they are expected to better serve all sections of society. The rank and file are acutely aware of these policing realities and are alert to the fact that their working practices need to change in order to meet these requirements. Officers are only too aware that their behaviour is closely monitored and has, therefore, had to change. The policing terrain has undoubtedly shifted and police culture has accommodated aspects of these changes. However, the extent to which these changes reflect a genuine desire to provide a better service to those emphasized in reform agendas is less clear.

Without doubt the salience of exclusion and othering within police culture has extended into the post-Macpherson era.

As Marks (2005) argues, meaningful police transformation must encompass not only structural and behavioural changes, but also attitudinal shifts. Although I located some changes in behaviour, these were not matched by amendments in police dispositions. Anxiety about and revision of practices in relation to ethnic minorities are clearly novel features of police culture, but officers continue to manifest a sense of antipathy towards such groups. As evidenced during the fieldwork, the heightened political status afforded to minority ethnic groups is vehemently resented within rank and file culture. Likewise, notwithstanding the altered practices in relation to domestic violence, officers still regard these incidents as marginal to their proper police work activities. The officers I accompanied were mainly concerned to 'cover their arse' rather than protect and support female victims. The predisposition to cover your arse has always been a deeply ingrained feature of police culture (Van Maanen 1978*b*), but it is clear that the current political and organizational context of policing has only intensified the desire for officers to conform to external rules and thereby avoid the scrutiny of management.

There is, then, an interesting contradiction in the Northshire attempt to change police culture; while there have been some shifts in police behaviour, old norms and assumptions have largely persisted (see also Marks 2005). In my view, the observed changes in behaviour are merely a perfunctory response to external and organizational constraints. Police managers directed officers to change their behaviour in accordance with new rules—and have had some degree of success. However, the imposition of guidelines did not fully penetrate the deeper level cultural knowledge of the police. That the Diversity Strategy was able to engender changes in police behaviour, but without impacting upon police dispositions, has at least two implications for understanding and reforming police culture. Police culture is conventionally understood as a set of values, beliefs, and assumptions which determines police behaviour. Yet, as we have seen, police practices can have a relative autonomy from attitudes. In attempting to reform policing practices through the implementation of rules for conduct, the change initiative was able to bypass and override the entrenched occupational attitudes. Police reformers tend to concentrate on the visible outcomes of their efforts—such as behaviour. This means that less prominence is placed on changing the informal values and belief systems of officers (Chan 1997; Marks 2005). As I found, the persistence of extant norms and assumptions is hugely problematic. Under certain conditions deeply ingrained attitudes come to inform police behaviour, and there were numerous occasions when officers undermined the requirements of the reform programme in both discourse *and* practice. This underlines the need to consider modes of thinking as much as behaviours and organizational structures for any lasting police change.

Meaningful cultural change at the level of dispositions is notoriously difficult. Transforming the entrenched values and perspectives requires not only a radical refashioning of the police role, but also a concerted dismantling of the image officers have of that role (Brogden and Shearing 1993; Della Porta 1998; Reiner 2000*a*; Brown 2007). At the mundane level, this might include changing the daily discourses of the police. As successions of researchers have warned, the significance of storytelling for constructing and maintaining the police identity should not be underestimated. The anecdotes told by officers reflect the sensibilities that comprise the culture; they serve as an influential source of information for the socialization of officers and provide cues for behaviour (Van Maanen 1973; Manning 1977; Punch 1979; Shearing and Ericson 1991). One way of changing extant dispositions is to accordingly *displace* the old and revered discourses with a set of alternative sensibilities.[1] These must rewrite what gets valued, redefine what aspects of the culture are acceptable, and ensure that police culture becomes committed to a different set of values. This is not an easy task, but one way of achieving this would be to rigorously break up the demographic constitution that has long dominated police organizations. If senior officers demonstrated robust commitment to truly diversifying the workforce, there is a possibility that the embedded dispositions would become drowned out by the arrival of new ways of seeing and being in the social world.

Beyond Diversity

The extension of recognition for hitherto marginalized groups is an important development in policing, but there are good reasons to move beyond the notion of diversity. In particular, police

---

[1] See also Marks' (2005: 272) notion of 'new stories'.

culture needs also to be considered in relation to key transformations in the economic landscape of late modern Britain. Despite all the attention given to diversity, class is one of the most enduring aspects of everyday policing. The police continue to direct attention towards the economically impoverished and thereby reproduce the exclusion and symbolic domination of this group. Class contempt towards the poor is an integral feature of the culture, but it goes virtually unremitted and unchallenged in present day organizations. Moreover, while reform agendas instruct officers to afford better regard and treatment to their socially and culturally diverse publics, there is no similar injunction on officers to treat the white poor in the same manner.

It is of course debateable whether class could, or should, form part of police reform agendas. As Sayer (2005) argues, class is peculiarly different from other axes of difference. Unlike ethnicity, gender, and sexuality, the poor do not seek recognition of their identity; they want to escape their class position rather than assert it. Moreover, class suffering does not result explicitly from misrecognition, as is usual in the case of racism and sexism. Rather, class difference is the product of the consequences of the pursuit of individual interests under capitalist economies; or as Sayer puts it 'the resulting inequalities generated by capitalism operate regardless of identities' (ibid: 23). Class disadvantage relates to far deeper structural inequalities and remedying it requires more than 'recognizing' the poor. It is well-documented that the people ingrained within police cultural knowledge as problematic reflect the wider social structure of power and disadvantage (Holdaway 1983; Reiner 2000a). The targets of police culture can only change, therefore, when the broader conditions of disadvantage are removed—a task increasingly unlikely in the context of mass deindustrialization and laissez faire economic policies (Taylor 1999; Young 1999; Charlesworth 2000).

Leaving aside these deeper theoretical questions, there nevertheless remains a pressing need to bring class into academic and professional discussions about policing and police culture. Drawing on insights from thinking in this area, a start would be to appreciate the moral dimensions of class inequality (Sayer 2005; see also Sennett and Cobb 1972). Future reform agendas should consider developing a holistic conceptualization of equitable policing, namely around the inclusion of class and whiteness. It would be particularly germane to explore how notions of citizenship can inform a more encompassing police reform effort. Rather than anxiously extending professionalism towards people only because they are emphasized in current diversity agendas, officers should be encouraged to extend professionalism towards people because they are citizens with rights. The diversity agenda is paramount for upholding group rights, but it should not eclipse concern with the individual rights of all citizenry.

The focus on class is also relevant for reforming the policing of other social groups. As Bradley (1996) demonstrates, class inequality intertwines complexly with other social differences. For the current discussion, part of the police treatment of ethnic minorities and women is undoubtedly class-related. Although these groups are accorded prominence in diversity agendas, it is striking that economically impoverished minority ethnic groups and females invariably continue to experience the undesirable face of operational policing (see also Hall *et al* 1978; Brogden *et al* 1988; Jefferson 1993). In other words, the occlusion of class within current debates is further problematic because economic deprivation often coexists with the adverse policing of cultural and gendered groups. In order to provide a more encompassing account of policing, therefore, the enduring dimension of class—and how it interacts with other axes of inequality—needs to be considered to a much greater extent. This would deepen understandings about the policing of all the social divisions which currently abound the social structure.

Police Culture and its Tenacity

The decline, and virtual disappearance, of some police cultural attributes is certainly important. However, these transformations pale into significance when the repeated and embedded aspects of police culture are considered. As I argued earlier, current scholarship overstates the degree of and potential for change in police culture, and accordingly overlooks the continuities and inertia in police dispositions and practice. The changes I found are without doubt far reaching, but my concern is that by failing to recognize the stubborn patterns in police culture we neglect to appreciate its resilience and tenacity. Notwithstanding the reordering of the policing landscape, the underlying world view of officers displays considerable continuity with older patterns.

Moreover, any newly identified features merely sit alongside and do not replace the classic characteristics.

While policing scholarship is right to identify the changes taking place within policing contexts, it nevertheless exaggerates them. For while there have been transformations in national and local policing environments, they are incomplete. In the case of Northshire Police aspects of the organization certainly seemed to contribute to old ways of thinking and behaving. There is now a greater presence within the Force of minority ethnic, female, and gay and lesbian personnel, but they remain outnumbered by their white, heterosexual, male counterparts. Likewise, although community policing was part of the new organizational ethos it was in the end sidelined by the overriding emphasis on attaining crime control targets. At least in Northshire, then, the view that developments in policing will inevitably transform police culture is difficult to sustain.

Of course, organizational issues are only part of the story. To understand the persistence of these ingrained characteristics we need to underline the enduring peculiarities of the police role. The occupational culture endures because the fundamentals of the police role remain unchanged. Policing has undergone cycles of reform over recent decades, but the police remain in the unique position of enforcing the law in a liberal democratic society. Officers continue to derive their self-identity from their work and the basic challenges of that work, identified by Skolnick (1966) all those years ago, persist. The durable occupational and organizational demands create and sustain the culture today. These cultural interpretations of policing are valuable for understanding the details of daily police work, but they overlook the wider contextual influences which shape police thinking and practice. In particular, the changes which have occurred in the field of policing are being undercut by a series of social, economic, and cultural upheavals. There has been no shortage of testimony that British society is characterized by deep social and economic division, where increasingly large numbers of the population are excluded from society (Dahrendorf 1985; Reiner 1992*b*; Taylor 1999; Young 1999; Toynbee 2003). The social insecurity of late modernity finds its expression in an increased preoccupation with crime and consequently results in more punitive sentiments in the politics and culture of law and order (Garland 2001; Loader 2006; Reiner 2007). In this new landscape, crime takes centre stage as a policing priority and the police are equipped with greater powers and resources to implement the crime control agenda. On the ground, the predicament of policing the symptoms of an increasingly divided world creates and exacerbates the cultural resources of the police. There are, in other words, countervailing pressures which inhibit the extent to which meaningful police change can occur; the reforms aimed at officers are undermined by the implications of greater emphasis on achieving crime control targets stemming from an ever more competitive politics of fear, insecurity, and law and order. Any radical dismantling of police culture must then go beyond reforms aimed at individual officers and the institution of successive policies. The findings discussed within this book relate primarily to one English police force, but they arguably have implications for other organizations across the national and international spectrum. Firstly, Northshire Police is not alone in reorienting its stance on equality, and police forces operating within western liberal democracies are under increasing pressure to understand themselves in terms of diversity and as providers of a fair and equitable service. Contemporary generations of police are expected to much improve the way they think about and interact with their socially and culturally diverse colleagues and publics. Secondly, although there are significant differences in the complexion of police organizations and broader society in which they function, the potential danger faced by the police, the authority they bring to bear on relations and the pressure to achieve results must surely be an integral feature of the working lives of officers working within many different contexts. It is reasonable to suggest that the cultural resources developed by officers as they adapt to these demands go beyond Northshire.

There is no doubt that there have been momentous changes in the policing landscape and organization—and these offer some possibilities for reform. Yet, without wishing to underplay the thorny beginnings of change, these modifications have not been matched by decisive transformations in rank and file culture. Emerging dispositions and practices certainly run counter to the prevailing culture, but these are invariably eclipsed. Unless there is a marked refashioning of the police role stemming from wider social change, it would seem there is little hope of achieving any meaningful reconfiguration of police culture.

8

Ethnography with the Police

An ethnographic study based primarily on direct observation of operational policing raises a number of methodological issues which require discussion. The value of such an approach in uncovering and documenting the informal norms, values, and practices of the police has been extensively debated (Van Maanen 1982; Holdaway 1983; Brewer 1991; Young 1991; Norris 1993; Punch 1993; Reiner 2000*b*; Marks 2005). Broadly speaking, ethnography is concerned with the discovery and description of the culture of social groups and is committed to the idea that the researcher must understand the symbolic world in which people live (Fielding 1993). Ethnographic approaches are particularly appropriate for studying the deeper level assumptions of police officers because such assumptions invariably operate beneath the presentational canopy of police organizations (Van Maanen 1973). By immersing themselves in their host society, the job of the police researcher is to pierce this structure and capture the informal face of the organization. This inevitably involves developing rapport with officers over a period of time in order to witness their 'backstage' performances (Goffman 1990; see also Holdaway 1980).[1] It is by these means that the researcher can unearth information about the sentiments that comprise police attitudes and guide behaviour. With its emphasis on participant observation, an ethnographic approach is undoubtedly the most appropriate method available to access the inner world of policing.

Yet the problems of access and trust, which are integral to most social science research, are peculiarly intensified in police research. As Reiner (2000*b*: 225) puts it, the methodological problems are 'primarily those of detectives and spies: how to

---

[1] Some ethnographers have, however, stressed the need for the researcher to avoid becoming over-involved with the people being studied—otherwise known as 'going native' (see Punch 1979 for a police-related discussion).

get information from people who are (often rightly) suspicious of your motives, have much to hide and much to lose from its discovery'. Researchers have long documented the challenges and issues associated with gaining access to the police for academic study (Fox and Lundman 1974; Holdaway 1983; Punch 1989; Young 1991; Marks 2004). A crucial distinction can be found in such works between being granted formal access and the accomplishment of social access on an everyday, interpersonal level. In what follows, I offer a reflexive discussion about my ethnographic experience with Northshire officers.

Gaining Access and Becoming 'Accepted'

In my case, acquiring formal access was greatly facilitated by a collaborative relationship between senior officers at Northshire Police and academics at the University I was later to attend to complete my doctoral research. Nevertheless, from the outset of the research it was necessary for me to become involved in various negotiations with other key personnel. There were no overt misgivings about the research during such discussions, but it soon became clear that some senior officers were concerned. Their worries revolved primarily around the dissemination of the findings and the logistics involved in allowing a 'civilian' to observe operational police work. With the assistance of an appropriate sponsor who worked within the Force I was, however, able to allay many of these fears. In return for gaining entry to the organization, I would be required to write reports for, and present key findings to, police audiences at appropriate points.[2]

Perhaps the most difficult encounter I experienced in securing formal access was during a meeting with the Police Federation. Representatives appeared extremely disturbed about the nature of the research, and the potential repercussions it posed for rank and file officers. They were particularly anxious that I would publicize negative research findings, and identify individual officers. Their suspicion was exacerbated by the BBC documentary *The Secret Policeman*, which had been aired two months earlier. The documentary uncovered outrageous displays of racism among new recruits at a number of police forces in the north of England and

---

[2] This is a prime example of what Becker (1970) terms the 'research bargain'. See Walters (2003) for a critical discussion of this.

North Wales, and was instrumental in propelling the problem of police racism into the public sphere once again. During the meeting with the Federation, the following question was put to me, 'What happens if an officer admits to you that they are a member of the British National Party?' I explained that while all individual officers in the study would have strict anonymity, to omit such a disclosure from any final conclusions would be to overlook a central part of the research framework; namely to examine officers' feelings towards greater social diversity in the internal and external policing environment. But I also made it clear that in the current climate where racism and its influence on policing had been the subject of intense debate, any such admission would be unlikely to occur. Although the local representatives of the Federation continued to hold reservations about the research, they finally agreed to the study. Having now been approved access by the top and middle echelons of the organization, I set about the task of gaining access to those people who would be the main participants of the research.

The initial stages of the research were characterized by widespread suspicion towards me and the study. As Ericson (1982) notes, being granted formal entry by senior officers can in fact *heighten* the suspicions of the lower ranking members of the police organization. Although I had been granted access by senior officers, accomplishing the trust of the rank and file was something I needed to negotiate on a daily basis. I was, by all accounts, an 'outsider'; a research position that can significantly impinge on the type of data that is accessed (Brown 1996; see also Reiner 2000b). In the early days of the research, officers were extremely suspicious of my presence at the station. On my first week, I recall sitting in the parade room when one officer approached me and asked, somewhat acrimoniously, 'Are you the girl who has come to see if we are all racist pigs'? Once again, this was intensified by the airing of *The Secret Policeman* and the media coverage which surrounded it. Throughout much of the early days, some officers even suggested that I was 'wearing a wire' and secretly recording their conversations and behaviour. The concerns shared by officers clearly reflect their general suspiciousness of outsiders (Young 1991), but they cannot be separated from the fact that the ethnography was undertaken in a rapidly changing organizational, social, and political context where the problem of police discrimination has come under close scrutiny.

There was also the broader problem that some officers saw me as something of a 'management spy' (see also Reiner 1978). Although it was officially agreed with senior personnel that no shift or unit within the research sites were prohibited, various informal tactics were nevertheless employed in an attempt to hinder my access to some behaviours and information. For instance, after changing to a new shift and asking the sergeant whether he would mind if I came back the next day, he looked a little anxious as he said, 'Bloody hell, it took me a week to decide who to crew you with just for today'! That day I had been paired with the only female on the shift who had been allocated the unpopular task of responding to the relatively trivial incidents that had been on the police system for a number of days. This task emphasized more of a 'customer focus' approach, and restricted the requirement to respond to any IR incidents. But if there were any further attempts made to put me with officers who could be trusted to behave appropriately, they were soon dispelled as my presence became more normal and accepted by the police.

For the most part, there was never any overt hostility or resistance towards me or the study. On the contrary, once my presence became the norm I was able to access much of the 'backstage' realities of operational police work. It is of course problematic to suggest that a researcher can gain access to all areas of police life (Punch 1979; Ericson 1982), but I feel a number of incidents demonstrated officers' willingness to accept me. That I was able to gain the confidence of at least some of the officers I observed was apparent on the many occasions where I was introduced to suspects and other members of the public as a colleague (see also Hobbs 1989), or when I assisted officers in operational police work. At the everyday level I was required to 'earn my keep' by writing down licence plate details of suspect vehicles, or keeping an eye out for those people already known to the police. With the aim of better witnessing a drug transaction between a pimp and a prostitute in a car park, I once acted as a bogus girlfriend of the plain-clothed officer I was with. In order to appear congruent to the surroundings, we walked slowly past the car with his arm around my shoulders. There were also occasions where I assisted in the searching of vehicles, houses—and even some people. There are clearly legal restrictions to how far police researchers can participate, and it should be emphasized that such instances did not reflect the norm. As Van Maanen (1982) observes, much police research has been carried out from the position of the 'fan', but with movement between other positions such as a 'spy', 'voyeur', and 'member'. Like other works the fieldwork involved many tests of allegiance and I was aware that an outright rejection of requests to assist officers may have reinforced my status as an outsider and, at worst, undone the trust and confidence I had gradually accumulated as the research progressed (Smith and Gray 1985; Norris 1993; Westmarland 2001*b*).

Several other incidents lead me to believe that I had become at least partly accepted by the police. Along with being privy to much of the gossip which circulated inside the organization, I was also invited along on many social occasions including birthdays and shift nights out. Halfway through the fieldwork in Northville, I even proved popular with some of those officers whom I had not managed to observe. This was demonstrated by frequent inquiries about when I would be going out with them, and many officers requested my presence at incidents and operations which they felt I would find helpful, interesting or exciting (see also Marks 2005). Although I was keen to emphasize my neutrality, many officers also seemed to appreciate the opportunity to air their views to someone who the 'gaffers' would listen to. In the organizational context of structural and cultural change, disgruntled constables and sergeants routinely asked me to support their grievances about ostensibly deteriorating resources, including slow cars and malfunctioning radios, excessive paperwork duties and personnel shortages.

There is, however, no way of knowing for certain how much my presence contaminated the 'natural' behaviour of those officers whom I observed and talked to. Like other researchers I believe that the police would not have behaved in ways which could have caused them embarrassment and, in some instances, reprimand from senior officers if they had not accepted me to some degree (Punch 1979; Reiner 2000*b*; Norris 1993). This can be demonstrated with reference to numerous incidents, but two themes spring to mind. Firstly, my participation in episodes of outrageous 'easing' behaviour (Cain 1973) makes me believe that I had gained a measure of acceptance. Secondly, I also recall several occasions where the officers I was accompanying used what I consider to be excessive force against some of their publics (Van Maanen 1983; Westmarland 2001*a*). There were also many instances where officers displayed blatant disregard and contempt for those they are charged with serving. It is also telling that after observing (usually) minor acts of police deviance I was regularly met with the line, 'Don't put that in your report.'

Reflexive Ethnography

It is increasingly common for researchers to reflect upon how their personal biography (age, class, ethnicity and gender) shapes the nature of relations that are formed in the field and the kind of material collected (May 1993; King and Wincup 2000). Because the police in my study were overwhelmingly male, there is some question as to how far my own gender prevented me from accessing the dominant male and sometimes highly heterosexist culture (see also Hunt 1984; Westmarland 2001*b*; Marks 2005). In furtherance, some aspects of my own culture were markedly different from that of the police. As a health-conscious vegetarian who does not drink alcohol, I did not easily blend in with officers' tales and instances of hardcore drinking or various meals bought from local takeaways. As Van Maanen (1982) reminds us, feeling disconnected from the setting is a normal part of conducting ethnographic research but, in my case, I think my 'quirkiness' actually facilitated access. In particular, my unfamiliarity with police operations and station etiquette was often a source of amusement. After arranging to accompany the Prostitution Unit I once mistakenly turned up to the station at 6.45am, only to realize that I should have been there at 6.45pm. Although this error on my part meant that I was the butt of jokes for a short while afterwards, I am confident that this episode positioned me as someone who could 'take a joke' whilst equally dispelling any prior stereotypes of me as a cold, detached researcher—I was in fact human and made mistakes.

My gender may have presented initial problems of accessing the covert aspects of police life, but being a young female researcher in a male dominated environment had its advantages. Like other female ethnographers, I too was viewed as 'naturally' trustworthy and unthreatening (Westmarland 2000*b*; Marks 2005). Officers confided in me about problems they were experiencing in their working and personal lives, and these moments were crucial for developing rapport. This is not to imply that frames of masculinity failed to be imposed on me. It has long been accepted that women in police organizations are under pressure to simultaneously prove themselves *and* demonstrate feminine virtues (Martin 1980; Heidensohn 1992). During the research I was subjected to many tests of trustworthiness and was required to display bravery through various initiation ceremonies (Smith and Gray 1985; Westmarland 2000*b*; Marks 2005). Much of this focused upon death and gore and I was frequently shown photographs of deceased bodies. After being asked if I had ever seen a 'real dead body' I was also once driven to a morgue—only to be saved by the bell when the officer I was observing was diverted to an IR incident. There were also moments where male officers made sexual advances towards me and I was often asked about my relationship status. One time a young IMU officer rubbed his hand up and down my leg while we were sitting in the back of a police car. On another occasion, an older (and married) officer attempted to hold my hand as we walked through dense woodland during the early hours. I should emphasize though that these instances were atypical and I never felt worried.

Other aspects of my personal biography helped ease access to the rank and file. My enthusiasm for long distance running afforded me much respect with some officers who were similarly in the business of keeping fit. I attended the station gymnasium with officers and was also invited along to a cross-country run. These shared interests proved critical in developing positive relations. Originating from a working class background I also did not necessarily coincide with the stereotype officers may have held of a pompous university graduate. Moreover, being 'white' and British, I fitted in with the dominant ethnicity of the organization. Indeed, I cannot help but think that my research experience and the material I obtained would have been considerably different if I was a researcher from a minority ethnic background. Without doubt my temperament was paramount in accessing the culture; as Marks (2004: 881) explains, 'the personality of the researcher is key to the stories that are told or hidden, and the exposure the researcher will be afforded'. During the fieldwork I was perceived as someone who was friendly and humorous, but also someone who was brave and eager to experience the daily grind of operational police work.

Attention should be drawn to the range of other people who formed part of the ethnography. The word 'observer' implies that I was somehow separate from the scene, but as we have seen in preceding chapters this was not always the case. Along with the officers themselves, I also came into contact with an array of other participants. These ranged from neutral members of the public to victims, suspects, and witnesses. I always tried to inform people about my role, but this was not always possible because of the sometimes erratic and unpredictable nature of operational policing. In the instances that allowed for such disclosure, I found that members of the public did not give much thought to my presence. For the most part I was mistaken for a police officer (occasionally by the police themselves) and, as it turned out, a number of other characters, including social worker, police cadet, psychologist, journalist, suspect or prisoner, prostitute, and independent police evaluator. Nevertheless, one instance offers an example of how police researchers can disrupt the scene and impact on these often silent participants of their research. After arresting a woman for prostitution, the officer I was with explained to her that I was a university student who was looking at the police before asking her if I could sit in during the police interview. Without warning she marched up to me and angrily screamed in my face, 'My life is not a fucking university project.' In the main, though, my perceived persona as a police officer enabled me to fully observe the interactions between the police and those with whom they encountered in their daily lives.

Recording and Interpreting the Field

Following Norris (1993) I distinguished two types of data as particularly salient in researching the occupational culture of the police; firstly, the way officers engaged in spontaneous *talk* with their colleagues and, secondly, descriptions of officers *doing* police work. I felt that the way officers talked about aspects of their occupation provided an important insight into their value and belief systems. I also believed that the way officers dealt with real situations could convey much about the norms and craft rules of routine policing. Once in the field, it was paramount to be able to record these events and develop a store of data. As I did not wish to disrupt the setting, fieldnotes were collected relatively inconspicuously during the shift. My decision to take notes in a discreet manner was also determined at the very beginning of the research when an IMU sergeant asked if he could examine my fieldnotes at the end of every shift; as he put it, 'in case you write down anything that we can use in court'. I do suspect, however, that he was eager to see how I had portrayed him and members of his shift in the notes. After some discussion I managed to convince him that my fieldnotes would not serve the purpose of a police pocket notebook. Suffice to say I felt it was important not to draw attention to my note taking. I subsequently made notes in private settings including toilets and empty offices. However, a full set of notes were always constructed at the end of each shift. As far as possible in all circumstances, I aimed to record people, places, events, and conversations (Lofland 1971.[3]

Of course for some, the real ethnography begins when researchers return from the field, attempt to make sense of their data and present it to their audiences (Van Maanen 1988). A mention should thus be made of how I gathered my fieldnotes. I cannot be sure if the themes identified in this book emerged from the 'objective' characteristics of the research settings, or were shaped by my own values and existing knowledge of research on police culture. This is a problem inherent to ethnographic research and cannot be solved (Hammersley and Atkinson 1995; see also Bottoms 2000). In observing and documenting contemporary police culture I was clearly influenced by the classic police ethnographies; to some extent the literature provided a constructive point of departure and comparison. However, against the backdrop of the transformations in the national and local policing context I was primarily concerned to note continuing *and* discontinuing aspects of the culture.

---

[3] While some conversations were written verbatim in fieldnotes, the majority reproduced for the purposes of this book are a précis of what was said.

Bibliography

Adonis, A. and Pollard, S. (1998) *A Class Act: The Myth of Britain's Classless Society*, London: Penguin.

Altbeker, A. (2005) *The Dirty Work of Democracy: A Year on the Streets with the SAPS*, Jeppestown: Jonathan Ball Publishers.

Bagguley, P. and Mann, K. (1992) 'Idle, thieving bastards? Scholarly representations of the "underclass"', *Work, Employment and Society*, 6 (1): 113–26.

Baker, M. (1985) *Cops: Their Lives in Their Own Words*, New York: Fawcett.

Banton, M. (1964) *The Policeman in the Community*, London: Tavistock.

Bauman, Z. (2000) 'Social issues of law and order', *British Journal of Criminology*, 40: 205–221.

—— (2001) *Liquid Modernity*, Cambridge: Polity Press.

Bayley, D.H. (1976) *Forces of Order: Police Behaviour in Japan and the United States*, Berkeley: University of California Press.

—— and Shearing, C. (1996) 'The future of policing', *Law and Society Review*, 30 (3): 586–606.

Beck, U. (1970) *Sociological Work*, London: Allen Lane.

—— (1992) *Risk Society*, London: Sage.

Billington, R., Strawbridge, S., Greensides, L. and Fitzsimons, A. (1991) *Culture and Society: A Sociology of Culture*, London: Macmillan.

Bittner, E. (1967) 'The police on skid row: a study in peacekeeping', *American Sociological Review*, 32 (5): 699–715.

—— (1970) *The Functions of Police in Modern Society*, Washington DC: National Institute of Mental Health.

Blackman, S.J. (1997) 'Destructing a giro: a critical and ethnographic study of the youth 'underclass', in MacDonald (ed.) *Youth, the 'Underclass' and Social Exclusion*, London: Routledge.

Bonnett, A. (1998) 'How the British working class became white: the symbolic (re)formation of racialised capitalism', *Journal of Historical Sociology*, 11 (3): 316–340.

Bottomley, A., Coleman, C., Dixon, D., Gill, M. and Wall, D. (1991) *The Impact of PACE: Policing in a Northern Force*, Hull: Hull University.

Bottoms, A. (2000) 'Theory and research in criminology', in King, R. and Wincup, E. (eds) *Doing Research on Crime and Justice*, Oxford: Oxford University Press.

Bowling, B. (1999) *Violent Racism: Victimisation, Policing and Social Control*, Oxford: Oxford University Press.

Bowling, B. and Foster, J. (2002) 'Policing and the police', in Maquire, M., Morgan, R. and Reiner, R. (eds) *The Oxford Handbook of Criminology* (3rd edn), Oxford: Oxford University Press.

—— and Phillips, C. (2002) *Racism, Crime and Justice*, Harlow: Longman.

—— and —— (2003) 'Policing ethnic communities', in Newburn, T. (ed.) *Handbook of Policing*, Cullompton: Willan.

Bourdieu, P. (1984) *Distinction: A Social Critique of the Judgement of Taste*, London: Routledge.

—— (1990) *In Other Words: Essay Towards a Reflexive Sociology*, Polity Press: Cambridge.

—— et al. (2002) *The Weight of the World: Social Suffering in Contemporary Society* (Reprint), Cambridge: Polity Press.

Box, S. (1983) *Crime, Power and Mystification*, London: Routledge.

—— (1987) *Recession, Crime and Unemployment*, London: Macmillan.

—— (1994) 'The criminal justice system and "problem populations"', in Lacey, N. (ed.) *A Reader on Criminal Justice*, Oxford: Oxford University Press.

Bradley, H. (1996) *Fractured Identities: Changing Patterns of Inequality*, Cambridge: Polity Press.

Brewer, J. (1991) *Inside the RUC: Routine Policing in a Divided Society*, Oxford: Clarendon Press.

Bridges, L. (1983) 'Policing the urban wasteland', *Race and Class*, 25 (2): 31–47.

Brogden, M. (1982) *The Police: Autonomy and Consent*, London: Academic Press.

—— Jefferson, T. and Walklate, S. (1988) *Introducing Policework*, London: Unwin Hyman.

—— and Shearing, C. (1993) *Policing for a New South Africa*, London: Routledge.

—— (1999) 'Community policing as cherry pie', in Mawby, R.I. (ed.) *Policing Across the World: Issues for the Twenty-first Century*, London: UCL Press.

—— and Nijhar, P. (2005) *Community Policing: National and International Models and Approaches*, Cullompton: Willan.

Brown, D. (1997), 'PACE ten years on: a review of the research', Home Office, London, Home Office Research Study: 155.

Brown, J. (1996) 'Police research: some critical issues', in Leishman, F., Loveday, B. and Savage, S. (eds) *Core Issues in Policing*, London: Longman.

—— J. (1998) 'Aspects of discriminatory treatment of women police officers in Forces in England and Wales', *British Journal of Criminology*, 38 (2): 265–82.

—— J. (2007) 'From cult of masculinity to smart macho: Gender perspectives on police occupational culture', in O'Neill, M., Marks, M.

and Singh, A. (eds) *Police Occupational Culture; New Debates and Directions*, Oxford: Elsevier.

Brown, M. (1981) *Working the Street*, New York: Russell Sage.

Burke, M.E. (1993) *Coming Out of the Blue*, London: Cassell.

Burney, E. (2005) *Making People Behave: Anti-Social Behaviour, Politics and Policy*, Cullompton: Willan.

Cain, M. (1973) *Society and the Policeman's Role*, London: Routledge.

Cashmore, E. and McLaughlin, E. (1991) *Out of Order? Policing Black People*, London: Routledge.

—— (2002) 'Behind the window dressing: minority ethnic police perspectives on cultural diversity', *Journal of Ethnic and Migration Studies*, 28 (2): 327–41.

Chakraborti, N. (2007) 'Policing Muslim communities', in Rowe, M. (ed.) *Policing Beyond Macpherson: Issues in Policing, Race and Society*, Cullompton: Willan.

Chan, J. (1996) 'Changing police culture', *British Journal of Criminology*, 36 (1): 109–34.

—— (1997) *Changing Police Culture: Policing in a Multicultural Society*, Cambridge: Cambridge University Press.

—— Devery, C. and Doran, S. (2003) *Fair Cop: Learning the Art of Policing*, Toronto: Toronto University Press.

Charlesworth, S. (2000) *A Phenomenology of Working Class Experience*, Cambridge: Cambridge University Press.

Chambliss, W.J. (1994) 'Policing the ghetto underclass: the politics of law enforcement', *Social Problems*, 41 (2): 177–97.

Choongh, S. (1997) *Policing as Social Discipline*, Oxford: Clarendon Press.

—— (1998) 'Policing the dross: a social disciplinary model of policing', *British Journal of Criminology*, 38 (4): 623–35.

—— (2002) 'Police investigative powers', in McConville, M. and Wilson, G. (eds) *The Handbook of the Criminal Justice Process*, Oxford: Oxford University Press.

Christenson, W. and Crank, J.P. (2001) 'Police work and culture in a non-urban setting: an ethnographic analysis', *Police Quarterly*, 4 (1): 69–98.

Clarke, J. and Critcher, C. (1985), *The Devil Makes Work: Leisure in Capitalist Britain*, London: Macmillan.

Cloke, P. (1997) 'Poor country: marginalisation, poverty and rurality', in Cloke, P. and Little, J. (eds) *Contested Countryside: Otherness, Marginalisation and Rurality*, London: Routledge.

Cockcroft, T. (2007) 'Police culture(s): some definitional, contextual and analytical considerations', in O'Neill, M., Singh, A. and Marks, M. (eds) *Police Occupational Culture: New Debates and Directions*, Oxford: Elsevier.

Cohen, P. (1979) 'Policing the working-class city', in Fine, B., Kinsey, R., Lea, J., Picciotto, S. and Young, J. (eds) *Capitalism and the Rule of Law*, London: Hutchinson.

Collins, M. (2004) *The Likes of Us: A Biography of the White Working Class*, London: Granta Books.

Calvert-Smith, D. (2005) *The Police Service in England and Wales*. Final Report of a Formal Investigation, Commission for Racial Equality.

Connell, R.W. (1995) *Masculinities*, Cambridge: Polity.

Craine, S. (1997) 'The "black magic roundabout": cyclical transitions, social exclusion and alternative careers', in MacDonald, R. (ed.) *Youth, the 'Underclass' and Social Exclusion*, London: Routledge.

Crank, J.P. (2004) *Understanding Police Culture* (2nd edn), Cincinnati: Anderson Publishing.

Crawford, A. (2003) 'The pattern of policing in the UK: policing beyond the police', in Newburn, T. (ed.) *The Handbook of Policing*, Cullompton: Willan.

Cray, E. (1972) *The Enemy on the Streets*, New York: Anchor.

Crompton, R. (2005) *Class and Stratification: An Introduction to Current Debates* (2nd edn), Cambridge: Polity Press.

Crowther, C. (2000*a*) *Policing Urban Poverty*, London: Macmillan.

—— (2000*b*) 'Thinking about the "underclass": towards a political economy of policing', *Theoretical Criminology*, 4 (2): 149–67.

Dahrendorf, R. (1985) *Law and Order*, London: Stevens and Sons.

Davis, N. (1998) *Dark Heart: The Shocking Truth about Hidden Britain*, London: Vintage.

Della Porta, D. (1998) 'Police knowledge and protest policing: some reflections on the Italian case', in Della Porta, D. and Reiter, H. (eds) *Policing Protest: The Control of Mass Demonstration in Western Democracies*, Minnesota: University of Minnesota Press.

Dixon, D. (1997) *Law in Policing: Legal Regulation and Police Practices*, Oxford: Clarendon Press.

—— (1999) 'Police investigative powers', in Walker, C. and Starmer, K. (eds) *Miscarriages of Justice: A Review of Justice in Error*, London: Blackstone.

—— (2003) 'Beyond zero tolerance', in Newburn, T. (ed.) *Policing: Key Readings*, Cullompton: Willan.

—— and Gadd, D. (2006) 'Getting the message? "New" Labour and the criminalisation of "hate"', *Criminology and Criminal Justice*, 6 (3): 309–29.

Dobash, R. and Dobash, R.E. (1980) *Violence Against Wives*, Shepton Mallet: Open Books.

Downs, D. and Morgan, R. (2002) 'The skeletons in the cupboard: the politics of law and order at the turn of the new millennium', in Maguire, M., Morgan, R. and Reiner, R. (eds) *The Oxford Handbook of Criminology* (3rd edn), Oxford: Oxford University Press.

The Economist (2006) 'Poor Whites: The Forgotten Underclass', *The Economist*, 381 (8501): 33–4; 26 October.

Edwards, S. (1987) 'Prostitutes: victim of law, social policing and organised crime', in Carlen, P. and Worrall, A. (eds) *Gender, Crime and Justice*, Milton Keynes: Open University Press.

—— (1989) *Policing 'Domestic' Violence: Women, the Law and the State*, London: Sage.

Emsley, C. (1996) 'The origins and development of the police', in McLaughlin, E. and Muncie, J. (eds) *Controlling Crime*, London: Sage Publications.

Ericson, R.V. (1982) *Reproducing Order: A Study of Patrol Work*, Toronto: University of Toronto Press.

—— (1993) *Making Crime: A Study of Detective Work* (2nd edn), Toronto: University of Toronto Press.

Feldman, I. (2002) 'Redistribution, recognition and the state: the irreducibly political dimension of injustice', *Political Science*, 30 (3): 410–40.

Fielding, N. (1988) *Joining Forces: Police Training, Socialisation and Occupational Competence*, London: Routledge.

—— (1989) 'Police culture and police practice', in Weatheritt (ed.) *Police Research: Some Future Prospects*, Sydney: Avebury Press.

—— (1993) 'Ethnography', in Gilbert, N. (ed.) *Researching Social Life*, London: Sage.

—— (1994) 'Cop canteen culture', in Newburn, T. and Stanko, E.A. (eds) *Just Boys Doing Business: Men, Masculinities and Crime*, London: Routledge.

—— (1995) *Community Policing*, Oxford: Oxford University Press.

Foster, J. (1989) 'Two stations: an ethnographic study of policing in the inner-city', in Downes, D. (ed.) *Crime and the City: Essays in Memory of John Barrow Mays*, London: Macmillan.

—— (2003) 'Police cultures', in Newburn, T. (ed.) *Handbook of Policing*, Cullompton: Willan.

—— Newburn, T. and Souhami, A. (2005) *Assessing the Impact of the Stephen Lawrence Inquiry*, Home Office Research Study: 294.

Fox, J.C. and Lundman, R.J. (1974) 'Problems and strategies in gaining research access in police organisations', *Criminology*, 12 (1): 52–69.

Frankenberg, R. (1993) *The Social Construction of Whiteness: White Women, Race Matters*, Minnesota: University of Minnesota Press.

Fraser, N. (1997), 'Introduction', in Fraser, N. (ed.) *Justice Interruptus: Critical Reflections on the 'Postsocialist' Condition*, London: Routledge.

Fyfe, N.R. (1991) 'The police, space and society: the geography of policing', *Progress in Human Geography*, 15 (3): 249–67.

Garland, D. (2001) *The Culture of Control*, Oxford: Oxford University Press.

Giddens, A. (1991) *Modernity and Self-Identity*, Cambridge: Polity.

Glaeser, A. (2000) *Divided in Unity: Identity, Germany and the Berlin Police*, Chicago: University of Chicago Press.

Goffman, E. (1990) *The Presentation of Self in Everyday Life* (Reprint) London: Penguin.

Goldsmith, A. (1990) 'Taking police culture seriously: police discretion and the limits of law', *Policing and Society*, (1): 91–114.

Goldstein, J. (1960) 'Police discretion not to invoke the criminal process: low-visibility decisions in the administration of justice', reprinted in Reiner, R. (1996) *Policing Volume II: Controlling the Controllers: Police Discretion and Accountability*, Aldershot: Dartmouth Publishing.

Graef, R. (1989) *Talking Blues: The Police in their Own Words*, London: Collins Harvill.

Green, P. (1990) *The Enemy Without: Policing and Class Consciousness in the Miners' Strike*, Milton Keynes: Open University Press.

Grimshaw, R. and Jefferson, T. (1987) *Interpreting Policework: Policy and Practice in Forms of Beat Policing*, London: Unwin and Hyman Ltd.

Halford, A. (1993) *No Way Up the Greasy Police*, London: Constable.

Hall, S., Critcher, C., Jefferson, T., Clarke, J. and Roberts, B. (1978) *Policing the Crises*, London: Macmillan.

Hallett, T. (2003) 'Symbolic power and organisational culture', *Sociological Theory*, 21 (2): 129–49.

Hammersley, M. and Atkinson, P. (1995) *Ethnography: Principles in Practice* (2nd edn), London: Routledge.

Hanley, L. (2007) *Estates: An Intimate History*, London: Granta Publications.

Harris, J. (2007) 'So now we've finally got our very own white trash', *The Guardian*, 6 March.

Haylett, C. (2001) '"Illegitimate subjects": abject whites, neoliberal modernisation and middle-class multiculturalism', *Environment and Planning D: Society and Space*, 19: 351–70.

Hayward, K. and Yar, M. (2006) 'The "chav" phenomenon: consumption, media and the construction of a new underclass', *Crime, Media, Culture*, 2 (1): 9–28.

Heidensohn, F. (1992) *Women in Control: The Role of Women in Law Enforcement*, Oxford: Oxford University Press.

—— (2003) 'Gender and policing', in Newburn, T. (ed.) *Handbook of Policing*, Cullompton: Willan.

Her Majesty's Inspectorate of Constabulary (2004) *Modernising the Police Service: A Thematic Inspection of Workforce Modernisation*, London: Home Office.

Herbert, S. (1998) 'Police culture reconsidered', *Criminology*, 36 (2): 343–69.

Hewitt, R. (2005) *White Backlash and the Politics of Multiculturalism*, Cambridge: Cambridge University Press.

Hobbs, D. (1989) *Doing the Business: Entrepreneurship, the Working Class and Detectives in East London*, Oxford: Oxford University Press.

—— (1991) 'A piece of business: the moral economy of detective work in the east-end of London', *The British Journal of Sociology*, 42 (4) 597–608.

Holdaway, S. (1980) 'The police station', *Urban Life*, 9 (1): 79–100.

—— (1983) *Inside the British Police: A Force at Work*, Oxford: Blackwell Publishing Ltd.

—— (1989) 'Discovering structure: studies of the British police occupational culture', in Weatheritt, M. (ed.) *Police Research: Some Future Prospects*, Aldershot: Avebury.

—— (1996) *The Racialisation of British Policing*, London: Macmillan.

—— and Barron, A.M. (1997) *Resigners: The Experience of Black and Asian Police Officers*, London: Macmillan.

—— (1997b) 'Constructing and sustaining "race" within the police workforce', *British Journal of Sociology*, 48 (1): 19–34.

—— and O'Neill, M. (2004) 'The development of black police associations: changing articulations of race within the Police', *British Journal of Criminology*, 44: 854–65.

—— and —— (2007) 'Black police associations and the Lawrence report', in Rowe, M. (ed.) *Policing Beyond Macpherson: Issues in Policing, Race and Society*, Cullompton: Willan.

Holloway, S.L. (2005) 'Articulating otherness? White rural residents talk about gypsy travellers', *Transactions of the Institute of British Geographers*, 30 (3): 351–67.

Home Office (2003) *Safety and Justice: The Government's Proposals on Domestic Violence*, CM 5847.

Horton, C. and Smith, D. (1988) *Evaluating Police Work: An Action Research Project*, London: Policy Studies Institute.

Hoyle, C. (2000) *Negotiating Domestic Violence: Police, Criminal Justice and* Victims, Oxford: Oxford University Press.

—— and Sanders, A. (2000) 'Police response to domestic violence', *British Journal of Criminology*, 40: 14–36.

Hughes, E.C. (1962) 'Good people and dirty work', *Social Problems*, 10 (1): 3–11.

Hunt, J. (1984) 'The development of rapport through the negotiation of gender in fieldwork among police', *Human Organisation*, 43 (4): 283–96.

Hutton, W. (1995) *The State We're In*, London: Jonathan Cape.

Jefferson, T. (1988) 'Race, crime and policing: empirical, theoretical and methodological issues', *International Journal of the Sociology of Law*, 16: 521–30.

Jefferson, T. (1991) 'Discrimination, disadvantage and police-work', in Cashmere, E and McLaughlin, E. (eds) *Out of Order: Policing Black People*, London, Routledge.

—— (1993) 'The racism of criminalisation: policing and the reproduction of the criminal other', in Gelsthorpe, L. (ed.) *Minority Ethnic Groups in the Criminal Justice System*, Cambridge: University of Cambridge, Institute of Criminology.

Johnston, L. (2000) *Policing Britain: Risk, Security and Governance*, Essex: Pearson.

Jones, T. and Newburn, T. (2006) 'Two strikes and you're out: exploring symbol and substance in American and British crime politics', *British Journal of Criminology*, 46: 781–802.

—— —— and Smith, D. (1994) *Democracy and Policing*, London: PSI.

Katz, M.B. (1989) *The Undeserving Poor: From the War on Poverty to the War on Welfare*, New York: Pantheon Books.

King, R. and Wincup, E. (eds) (2000) *Doing Research on Crime and Justice*, Oxford: Oxford University Press.

Klockars, C. (1985) *The Idea of the Police*, California: Sage.

Lambert, J. (1970) *Crime, Police and Race Relations*, Oxford: Oxford University Press.

Lawson, N. (2006) 'Turbo-consumerism is the driving force behind crime', *The Guardian*, 13 June.

Lee, J.A. (1981) 'Some structural aspects of police deviance in relations with minority groups', in Shearing, C. (ed.) *Organisational Police Deviance*, Toronto: Butterworth.

Leng, R. (1995) 'Pessimism or professionalism? Legal regulation of investigations after PACE (author meets critics II)', in Noaks, L., Levi, M. and Maguire, M. (eds) *Contemporary Issues in Criminology*, Cardiff: University of Wales Press.

Loader, I. (2006) 'Fall of the "platonic guardians": liberalism, criminology and political responses to crime in England and Wales', *British Journal of Criminology*, 46: 561–86.

—— and Mulcahy, A. (2003) *Policing and the Condition of England: Memory, Politics and Culture*, Oxford: Oxford University Press.

—— and Walker, N. (2007) *Civilizing Security*, Cambridge: Cambridge University Press.

Lofland, J. (1971) *Analysing Settings*, California: Wadsworth.

Long, M. (2003) 'Leadership and performance management', in Newburn, T. (ed.) *Handbook of Policing*, Cullompton: Willan.

Loveday, B. (2007), 'Re-Engineering the Police Organisation: Implementing Workforce Modernisation in England and Wales', *The Police Journal*, 80: 3–27.

MacDonald, R. (1997) 'Dangerous youth and the dangerous class', in MacDonald, R (ed.) *Youth, the 'Underclass' and Social Exclusion*, London: Routledge.

Macpherson, Sir W. (1999) *Report of the Stephen Lawrence Inquiry*, London: HMSO.

Maguire, M. (1988) 'Effects of the PACE. Provisions on detention and questioning', *British Journal of Criminology*, 28: 19–43.

——(2002) 'Regulating the police station: the case of the Police and Criminal Evidence Act', in McConville, M. and Wilson, G. (eds) *The Handbook of the Criminal Justice Process*, Oxford: Oxford University Press.

—— (2003) 'Criminal investigation and crime control', in Newburn, T. (ed.) *Handbook of Policing*, Cullompton: Willan.

Mann, R. and Fenton, S. (2009) 'The personal contexts of national sentiments', *Journal of Ethnic Migration Studies*, 35 (4): 517–34.

Manning, P.K. (1977) *Police Work: The Social Organisation of Policing*, Cambridge and London: MIT Press.

—— (1978*a*) 'The police: mandate, strategies and appearances', in Manning, P.K. and Van Maanen, J. (eds) *Policing: A View from the Street*, California: Goodyear Inc.

—— (1978*b*) 'Lying, secrecy and social control', in Manning, P.K. and Van Maanen, J. (eds) *Policing: a View from the Street*, California: Goodyear Inc.

——(1989) 'Occupational culture', in Bailey, W.G. (ed.) *The Encyclopaedia of Police Science*, London: Garland.

—— (1994) 'The police: symbolic capital, class and control', in Bridges, G. and Myers, M. (eds) *Inequality, Crime and Social Control*, Oxford: Westview Press.

—— (2007) 'A dialectic of organisational and occupational culture', in O'Neill, M., Singh, A. and Marks, M. (eds) *Police Occupational Culture: New Debates and Directions*, Oxford: Elsevier.

—— and Van Mannen, J. (1978) *Policing: A View from the Street*, California: Goodyear Inc.

Marks, M. (2004) 'Researching police transformation: the ethnographic imperative', *British Journal of Criminology*, 44: 866–88.

—— (2005) *Transforming the Robocops: Changing Police in South Africa*, Scottsville: University of KwaZulu-Natal Press.

Marlow, A. and Loveday, B. (2000) *After Macpherson: Policing after the Stephen Lawrence Inquiry*, Dorset: Russell House Publishing.

Martin, S.E. (1980) *Breaking and Entering: Policewomen on Patrol*, Berkeley, CA: University of California Press.

—— (1994) 'Outsiders within the station house: the impact of race and gender on black women police', *Social Problems*, 41 (3): 383–400.

May, T. (1993) 'Feelings matter: inverting the hidden equation', in Hobbs, D. and May, T. (eds) *Interpreting the Field: Accounts of Ethnography*, Oxford: Oxford University Press.

McBarnet, D.J. (1981) *Conviction: Law, the State and the Construction of Justice*, London: Macmillan.

McConville, M., Sander, A. and Leng, R. (1991) *The Case for the Prosecution: Police Suspects and the Construction of Criminality*, London: Routledge.

—— and Shepherd, D. (1992) *Watching Police, Watching Communities*, London: Routledge.

McDowell, L. (2003) *Redundant Masculinities: Employment Change and White Working Class Youth*, Oxford: Blackwell.

McLaughlin, E. (1996) 'Police, policing and police work', in McLaughlin, E. and Muncie, J. (eds) *Controlling Crime*, London: Sage.

—— (2007) *The New Policing*, London: Sage.

—— and Murji, K. (1999) 'After the Stephen Lawrence report', *Critical Social Policy*, 19 (3): 371–85.

—— and Neal, S. (2004) 'Misrepresenting the multicultural nation: The policy making process, news media management and the Parekh Report', *Policy Studies*, 25 (3): 155–74.

—— Muncie, J. and Hughes, G. (2001) 'The permanent revolution: new labour, new public management and the modernization of criminal justice', *Criminology and Criminal Justice*, 1 (3): 301–18.

Meltzer, B. and Musolf, G. (2002) 'Resentment and ressentiment', *Sociological Inquiry*, 72 (2): 240–55.

Miles, R. and Small, S. (1999) 'Racism and ethnicity', in Taylor, S. (ed.) *Sociology: Issues and Debates*, London: Macmillan.

Miller, S., Forest, K. and Jurik, N. (2003) 'Diversity in blue: lesbian and gay police officers in a masculine occupation', *Men and Masculinities*, (5) 4: 355–85.

Modood, T. (1992) *Not Easy Being British: Colour, Culture and Citizenship*, London: Runneymede Trust.

Mollen Report (1994) *Commission Report: Commission to Investigate Allegations of Police Corruption and the Anti-Corruption Procedures of the Police Department*, City of New York.

Mooney, J. and Young, J. (2000) 'Policing ethnic minorities: stop and search in North London', in Marlow, A. and Loveday, B. (eds) *After Macpherson: Policing after the Stephen Lawrence Inquiry*, Dorset: Russell House Publishing.

Moran, L. (2007) 'Invisible minorities: challenging community and neighbourhood models of policing', *Criminology and Criminal Justice*, 7 (4): 417–41.

Morgan, R. (1995) 'Author meets critics: *the case for prosecution* (author meets critics IV)', in Noaks, L., Levi, M. and Maguire, M. (eds) *Contemporary Issues in Criminology*, Cardiff: University of Wales Press.
—— (2000) 'The politics of criminological research', in King, R. and Wincup, E. (eds) *Doing Research on Crime and Justice*, Oxford: Oxford University Press.

Moston, S. and Stephenson, G. (2006) 'The changing face of police interrogation', *Journal of Community and Applied Social Psychology*, 3 (2): 105–15.

Muir, K.W. (1977) *Police: Streetcorner Politicians*, Chicago: Chicago University Press.

Murray, C. (1996) 'The "underclass"', in Muncie, J., McLaughlin, E. and Langan, M. (eds) *Criminological Perspectives: A Reader*, London: Sage.

Naughton, M. (2004) 'Re-orientating miscarriages of justice', in Hillyard, P., Pantazis, C., Gordon, D. and Tombs, S. (eds) *Beyond Criminology: Taking Harm Seriously*, London: Pluto Press.

Nayak, A. (2005) 'White lives', in Murji, K. and Solomos, J. (eds) *Racialisation: Studies in Theory and Practice*, Oxford: Oxford University Press.

Neal, S. (2002) 'Rural landscapes, representations and racism: examining multi-cultural citizenship and policy-making in the English countryside, *Ethnic and Racial Studies*, 25 (3): 442–61.

Neiderhoffer, A. (1967) *Behind the Shield*, New York: Doubleday.

Newburn, T. (2003) 'Policing since 1945', in Newburn, T. (ed.) *Handbook of Policing*, Cullompton: Willan.
—— (2007) *Criminology*, Cullompton: Willan.

Norris, C. (1993) 'Some ethical considerations on fieldwork with the police', in Hobbs, D. and May, T. (eds) *Interpreting the Field: Accounts of Ethnography*, Oxford: Clarendon Press.

O'Neil, M. and Singh, A.M. (2007) 'Introduction', in O'Neill, M., Singh, A. and Marks, M. (eds) *Police Occupational Culture: New Debates and Directions*, Oxford: Elsevier.

O'Reilly, G. (1994) 'England limits the right to silence and moves towards an inquisitorial system of justice', *Journal of Criminal Law and Criminology*, 85.

Packer, H. (1969) *The Limits of the Criminal Sanction*, Stanford, CA: Stanford University Press.

Page, A. (2007) 'Behind the blue line: investigating police officers' attitudes towards rape', *Journal of Police and Criminal Psychology*, 22 (1): 22–32.

Paoline, E. (2003) 'Taking stock: towards a richer understanding of police culture', *Journal of Criminal Justice*, 31: 199–214.

Parekh Report (2000) *The Future of Multi-ethnic Britain*, London: Profile Books.

Powell, C. (1996) 'Laughing on the other side of your PACE? An analysis of cartoons appearing in *Police Review* 1979–1993', in Paton, G., Powell, C. and Wagg, S. (eds) *The Social Faces of Humour: Practices and Issues*, London: Macmillan.

Prenzler, T. (1997) 'Is there a police culture?', *Australian Journal of Public Administration*, 56 (4): 47–56.

Punch, M. (1979) *Policing the Inner City*, London: Macmillan.

—— (1989) 'Researching police deviance: a personal encounter with the limitations and liabilities of field work', *British Journey of Sociology*, 40 (2): 177–204.

—— (1993) 'Observation and the police: the research experience, in Hammersely, M. (ed.) *Social Research: Philosophy, Politics and Practice*, London: Sage.

—— (2007) 'Cops with honours: university education and police culture', in O'Neill, M., Singh, A. and Marks, M. (eds) *Police Occupational Culture: New Debates and Directions*, Oxford: Elsevier.

Ray, L.J. and Sayer, A. (eds) (1999) *Culture and Economy after the Cultural Turn*, London: Sage.

Reiner, R. (1978) *The Blue-Coated Worker: A Sociological Study of Police Unionism*, Cambridge: Cambridge University Press.

—— (1991) *Chief Constables*, Oxford: Oxford University Press.

—— (1992*a*) 'Policing a postmodern society', *The Modern Law Review*, 55 (6): 761–81.

—— (1992*b*) *The Politics of the Police* (2nd edn), London: Wheatsheaf.

—— (1997) 'Policing and the police', in Maquire, M., Morgan, R. and Reiner, R. (eds) *The Oxford Handbook of Criminology* (2nd edn), Oxford: Oxford University Press.

—— (1998) 'Copping a Plea', in Holdaway, S. and Rock, P. (eds) *Thinking about Criminology*, London: UCL Press.

—— (2000*a*) *The Politics of the Police* (3rd edn), Oxford: Oxford University Press.

—— (2000*b*) 'Police research', in King, R. and Wincup, E. (eds) *Doing Research on Crime and Justice*, Oxford: Oxford University Press.

—— (2007) *Law and Order: An Honest Citizen's Guide to Crime and Control*, Cambridge: Polity Press.

Reuss-Ianni, E. and Ianni, F.A.J. (1983) 'Street cops and management cops: the two cultures of policing', in Punch, M. (ed.) *Control in the Police Organisation*, Cambridge, MA: MIT Press.

Rowe, M. (2007) 'Police diversity training: a silver bullet tarnished?', in Rowe, M. (ed.) *Policing Beyond Macpherson: Issues in Policing, Race and Society*, Cullompton: Willan.

Rubinstein, J. (1973) *City Police*, New York: Ballantine.

Sackmann, S.A. (1991) *Cultural Knowledge in Organisations: Exploring the Collective Mind*, London: Sage.

Sacks, H. (1972) 'Notes on police assessment of moral character', in Sudnow, D. (ed.) *Studies in Social Interaction*, New York: Free Press.

Sanders, A. and Young, R. (2000) *Criminal Justice* (3rd edn), Oxford: Oxford University Press.

Sapp, A. (1994) 'Sexual misconduct by police officers', in Barker, T. and Carter, D. (eds) *Police Deviance* (3rd edn), Cincinnati: Anderson Publishing.

Savage, S. (2003) 'Tackling tradition: reform and modernisation of the British police', *Contemporary Politics*, 9 (2): 172–84.

Sayer, A. (2005) *The Moral Significance of Class*, Cambridge: Cambridge University Press.

Schein, E. (1985) *Organisational Culture and Leadership*, San Francisco: Jossey-Bass.

Scheler, M. (1961) *Ressentiment*, New York: Schocken Books.

Scraton, P. (1985) *The State of the Police*, London: Pluto.

Sennett, R. (2003) *Respect: The Formation of Character in an Age of Inequality*, London: Penguin Books.

—— and Cobb, J. (1972) *The Hidden Injuries of Class*, London: W.W. Norton.

Shearing, C. (1981) 'Subterranean processes in the maintenance of power', *Canadian Review of Sociology and Anthropology*, 18 (3): 283–98.

—— and Ericson, R.V. (1991) 'Culture as figurative action', *British Journal of Sociology*, 42 (4): 481–506.

Sibley, D. (1995) *Geographies of Exclusion*, London: Routledge.

Silverman, D. (2001) *Interpreting Qualitative Data: Methods for Analysing Talk, Text and Interaction* (2nd edn), London: Sage.

Silvestri, M. (2003) *Women in Charge: Policing, Gender and Leadership*, Cullompton: Willan.

Skeggs, B. (2004) *Class, self, culture*, London: Routledge.

Sklansky, D.A. (2007) 'Seeing blue: police reform, occupational culture and cognitive burn-in', in O'Neill, M., Singh, A. and Marks, M. (eds) *Police Occupational Culture: New Debates and Directions*, Oxford: Elsevier.

Skolnick, J.H. (1966) *Justice Without Trial: Law Enforcement in Democratic Society*, New York: Macmillan.

—— and Fyfe, J. (1993) *Above the Law: Police and the Excessive Use of Force*, New York: Free Press.

Smith, D.J. and Gray, J. (1985) *Police and People in London: The PSI Report*, London: Policy Studies Institute.

Smith, G. (2002) 'Reasonable suspicion: time for a re-evaluation?', *International Journal of the Sociology of Law*, 30: 1–16.

Stanko, E. (1985) *Intimate Intrusions: Women's Experience of Male Violence*, London: Routledge and Kegan Paul.

Stinchcombe, A.L. (1963) 'Institutions of privacy in the determination of police administrative practice', reprinted in Reiner, R. (ed.) *Policing Volume II: Controlling the Controllers: Police Discretion and Accountability*, Aldershot: Dartmouth Publishing.

Storch, R. (1975) 'The plague of the blue locusts: police reform and popular resistance in Northern England 1840–57', *International Review of Social History*, 20: 61–90.

Swanton, B. (1981) 'Social isolation of the police: structural determinants and remedies', *Police Studies*, 3: 14–21.

Sykes, R. and Clark, J. (1975) 'A theory of deference exchange in police-civilian encounters', *American Journal of Sociology*, 81 (3): 584–600.

Taylor, C. (1992) *Multiculturalism and Politics of Recognition*, Princeton, NJ: Princeton University Press.

Taylor, I. (1999) *Crime in Context: A Critical Criminology of Market Societies*, Cambridge: Polity Press.

—— and Jamieson, R. (1997) '"Proper little mesters": nostalgia and protest masculinity in de-industrialised Sheffield', in Westwood, S. and William, J. (eds) *Imagining Cities: Scripts, Signs, Memory*, London: Routledge.

Tilley, N. (2003) 'Community policing, problem-oriented policing and intelligence led policing', in Newburn, T. (ed.) *Handbook of Policing*, Essex: Willan.

Toynbee, P. (2003) *Hard Work: Life in Low-Pay Britain*, London: Bloomsbury.

Tyler, K. (2003) 'The racialised and classed constitution of English village life', *Ethnos*, 68 (3): 391–412.

Van Maanen, J. (1973) 'Observations on the making of policemen', *Human Organisations*, 32 (4): 407–18.

—— (1974) 'Working the street', in Jacobs, H. (ed.) *The Potential for Reform of Criminal Justice*, California: Sage.

—— (1978a) 'The asshole', in Manning, P.K. and Van Maanen, J. (eds) *Policing: a View from the Street*, California: Goodyear.

—— (1978b) 'Kinsmen in repose: occupational perspectives of patrolmen', in Manning, P.K. and Van Maanen, J. (eds) *Policing: a View from the Street*, California: Goodyear.

—— (1982) 'Fieldwork on the beat', in Van Maanen, J., Dabbs, J. and Faulkner, R. (eds) *Varieties of Qualitative Research*, Beverley Hills, CA: Sage.

—— (1983) 'On the ethics of fieldwork', in Smith, R. (ed.) *A Handbook of Social Science Methods: An Introduction to Social Research*, Cambridge, MA: Ballinger.

—— (1988) *Tales of the Field: On Writing Ethnography*, Chicago: Chicago University Press.

Wacquant, L. (2000) 'Logics of urban polarisation: the view from below', in Crompton, R., Devine, F., Savage, M. and Scott, J. (eds) *Renewing Class Analysis*, Oxford: Blackwell.

Waddington, P.A.J. (1999*a*) 'Police (canteen) sub-culture: an appreciation', *British Journal of Criminology*, 39 (2): 287–309.

—— (1999*b*) *Policing Citizens: Authority and Rights*, London: UCL Press.

Walklate, S. (2000) 'Equal opportunities and the future of policing', in Leishman, F., Loveday, B. and Savage, S. (eds) *Core Issues in Policing* (2nd edn), Essex: Pearson Education Ltd.

Walters, R. (2003) *Deviant Knowledge: Criminology, Politics and Policy*, Cullompton: Willan.

Westley, W. (1970) *Violence and the Police: A Sociological Study of Law, Custom and Morality*, Massachusetts: MIT.

Westmarland, L. (2001*a*) 'Blowing the whistle on police violence: gender, ethnography and ethics', *British Journal of Criminology*, 41: 523–35.

—— (2001*b*) *Gender and Policing: Sex, Power and Police Culture*, Cullompton: Willan.

Wetherell, M. and Potter, J. (1992) *Mapping the Language of Racism: Discourse and the Legitimation of Exploitation*, New York: Harvest Wheatsheaf.

Williamson, H. (1997) 'Status zero and the "underclass": some considerations', in MacDonald, R. (ed.) *Youth, the Underclass and Social Exclusion*, London: Routledge.

Wilson, D., Ashton, J. and Sharp, D. (2001) *What Everyone in Britain Should Know About the Police*, London: Blackstone.

Wilson, J.Q. (1972) *The Metropolitan Enigma*, New York: Anchor Books.

Yar, M. and Penna, S. (2004) 'Between positivism and post-modernity? Critical reflections on Jock Young's the Exclusive Society', *British Journal of Criminology*, 44 (4): 533–50.

Young, J. (1971) 'The role of the police as amplifiers of deviancy, negotiators of reality and translators of fantasy: some consequences of our present system of drug control as seen in Notting Hill', in Cohen, S. (ed.) *Images of Deviance*, Middlesex: Penguin.

—— (1999) *The Exclusive Society*, London: Sage.

—— (2003) 'Merton with energy, Katz with structure: the sociology of vindictiveness and the criminology of transgression', *Theoretical Criminology*, 7 (3): 389–414.

Young, M. (1991) *An Inside Job: Policing and Police Culture in Britain*, Oxford: Oxford University Press.

—— (1993) *In the Sticks*, Oxford: Oxford University Press.

Zurn, C.F. (2005) 'Recognition, redistribution, and democracy: dilemmas of Honneth's critical social theory', *European Journal of Philosophy*, 13 (1): 89–126.

Index

addicts 115–16, 136
Adonis, A. 43
affirmative action 67–8
age 72, 116
agency of officers 16
Altbeker, A. 129
Anti-Discrimination Code of
        Practice 58, 179
antisocial behaviour 27
Arab backgrounds, people from 145–6
arrests 29, 102–3, 113, 115–16
    domestic violence 10–11, 34,
        61–2, 128, 132, 138, 194
    PACE 24, 25
'arse-covering exercise' 14, 132,
        133, 195
assaults and compensation 110
attitude test applied to public 112–13
audio-recorded interviews 23, 24
authority, symbol of 5, 6, 126

Baker, M. 15, 108, 191
Banton, M. 5, 6–7, 95, 105, 117
Bauman, Z. 26, 36, 38
Bayley, D.H. 15
Beck, U. 36
Billington, R. 3
Bittner, E. 4, 5, 8, 95, 167
black men, stereotyping of 143, 144–5
black population see minority ethnic
        groups
Bonnett, A. 45
Bottomley, A. 23, 24
Bottoms, A. 209
Bourdieu, P. 19, 36, 44, 161, 173
Bowling, B. 11, 28, 30, 31, 32, 141,
        150, 192
Box, S. 9, 40, 113, 173, 177
Bradley, H. 198
Brewer, J. 201

Bridges, L. 30
Brogden, M. 19, 31, 40–1, 60,
        196, 198
Brown, D. 23, 24, 25
Brown, J. 10, 54, 79, 196, 203
Brown, M. 12, 13, 91, 119,
        124, 190
burglary 110, 177
Burke, M.E. 11, 53, 77
Burney, E. 27

Cain, M. 5, 7–8, 15, 47, 91,
        120, 143, 155, 156, 177, 189,
        190, 205
Cashmore, E. 29, 32
CATs (Community Action Teams) 61,
        86, 93–5
Chakrabarti, N. 145
Chambliss, W.J. 165
Chan, J. 3, 11, 14, 16, 18, 19–20, 42,
        125, 133, 143, 158, 160, 173,
        188, 189, 191, 194, 196
Charlesworth, S. 42, 43, 44, 161,
        180, 197
children 15, 91
    criminalized 27
    domestic violence 134
Choongh, S. 22, 23, 24, 40, 41, 114,
        124, 165, 166, 174, 177, 178
citizenship 198
civilian support staff 69, 103–5
    Police Community Support Officers
        (PCSOs) 59–60, 61, 69, 104–5
Clarke, J. 177
class 156–7, 159–60, 197–8
    age of recognition: retreat of 42–5
    contempt 44, 160, 161–2, 168–72,
        173, 174, 182, 183, 184, 197
    continuing significance of 159–60,
        197–8

class (*cont.*)
    classed bodies 172–5
    classed people, classed
        places 165–8
    language of class
        contempt 168–72
    police awareness of socio-
        economic problems 181–3
    police focus: sections of
        'underclass' 162–5
    poor whites: no authentic political
        identity 179–81
    rethinking police culture 160–2
    unemployment and erosion of
        worth 175–7
    victimization and white
        poor 177–9
    difference 197
    'fear of falling' 164
    new social configuration 35–9
    policing new residuum 39–42
    police 7, 15, 164
    'scrote', meaning of 165, 169–70
    symbolic domination 161–2, 173,
        184
    underclass, use of term 39–40
Cloke, P. 163, 167
Cockcroft, T. 16, 192
Codes of Practice
    Anti-Discrimination 58, 179
    Police and Criminal Evidence Act
        (PACE) 1984 22–6, 27
Cohen, P. 40, 160
Collins, M. 159
Community Action Teams (CATs) 61,
    86, 93–5
community policing 20, 30, 31, 60–1,
    92–6, 99, 189, 192
    performance targets 103, 199
compensation and assaults 110
competitiveness 122
concept of police culture 187–9
    challenges to 15–18
    changing police culture 19–20
    classic themes, altered times 85–9,
        189–92
    beleaguered minority 105–6
    conservative ideologies 107–8
    dark humour 110–12

    dominance, maintaining 112–17
    enduring themes 125–6, 188–9
    isolation and loyalty 117–22
    masculine ethos 96–9
    mission perspective 90–1
    organizational realities 99–105
    patrol work 122–5, 126
    proper police work 91–6
    public as stupid, greedy,
        fallible 108–10
cultures 15–16, 71–3, 81, 125, 188,
    191–2
definition 3–4, 89–90
origins of sociological policing
    scholarship 5–8
orthodox account 8
    cynical disposition 13–14
    intolerance and prejudice 10–12
    isolation, mutual solidarity, and
        conservatism 14–15
    mission perspective 8–9
    suspicious disposition 12–13
    significance of 4–5
    tenacity of police
        culture 198–200
conflicts within police force 122
    rank and file view of senior
        officers 13–14, 93, 190–1
confrontation and excitement 9, 97–9,
    134, 189–90, 192
Connell, R.W. 40
conservatism, moral 6, 107–8,
    165, 191
    orthodox view of police
        culture 14–15
Conservative party 26, 108
consultations, police and community
    (PACC) 30, 31
consumerism 38
Contagious Diseases Act 1864 41
context of policing *see* field of policing,
    new social
controlling approach towards
    public 112–16
courts 107, 137
'cover your arse' 14, 132, 133, 195
Craine, S. 36
Crank, J.P. 9, 18, 96, 99,
    115, 123

crime control approach/model 7, 8–9,
     22, 91–6, 189–90, 192
  labelling 170
  patrol work 123, 165–8
  performance targets 103
  social insecurity: punitive
     outlook 26–8, 39, 103, 199–200
Crime and Disorder Act 1998 27
crime number, request for 110
Crompton, R. 36, 42
Crowther, C. 37, 38, 39, 103, 159
custody officers 23, 24
customers, public as 61, 92–3
  controlling approach towards
     public 112–16
  domestic violence 135
  performance targets 103
  unreliability and criminality of
     public 108–10
cynical disposition 6, 105, 190–1
  beleaguered minority 105–6
  dark humour 110–12
  futile delivery of justice 107–8
  orthodox account of police
     culture 13–14
  prostitutes 136–7
  rape 135
  unreliability and criminality of
     public 108–10

Dahrendorf, R. 36, 37, 38, 159, 164,
     199
danger, risk of physical 5–6, 117–19,
     126
Davis, N. 38
death penalty 108
definition of police culture 3–4, 89–90
Della Porta, D. 196
'dirty work' occupation 13, 165
disability 61
'disarmers' 15, 147, 194
discourse and practice 196
  disparity between police 12, 17, 69,
     98, 137, 171–2
discretionary powers 4–5, 19, 128,
     160, 184
discrimination 10–12, 31
  durable 73–80
  'old regime' 52–6

race see racism
  see also stereotypes
Dispatches: 'Undercover Copper' 33
diverse society 28–9
  beginnings 29–31
  towards policing diversity 31–5
  'white backlash' 81–2
diversity policies, impact of 51–2, 83,
     184, 192–6
  changing culture 56
     composition of workforce 58–60
     dissemination of new
        strategy 62
     service improvement 60–2
     structures and guiding
        principles 56–8
     training 60, 61
  decline and discontent, narratives
     of 63, 81, 83, 193
     demise of the job 63–7
     'dying breed' 69–71, 82
     erosion of white advantage 67–9
     moments of questioning 71–3
  durable discrimination: minority
     perspectives 73, 193
     hierarchies of difference 78–80
     new exclusions 73–6
     silent members of
        associations 77–8
     tokenism and scrutiny 76–7
  new contestations 80–1, 193
  'old regime' 52
     individualized experiences 53–4
     standing out 52–3
     'troublemakers' 55–6
  preservation of dominance 81–2
Dixon, D. 17, 22, 23, 24, 25, 27,
     180
Dobash, R. 34
domestic violence 9, 92, 157, 158, 194,
     195
  areas associated with 122
  arrest of assaulting partner 10–11,
     34, 61–2, 128, 132, 138, 194
  consultation with local groups 60
  dark humour 110–11
  Domestic Violence Liaison Officer 62
  masculine ethos 10–11, 130–2
  new direction, signs of 137–9

domestic violence (*cont.*)
　new practices, old
　　assumptions 128–35
　paperwork 101, 131–2, 194
　　DVIR 62, 134–5, 138–9
　risk assessment 62, 131–2, 138–9
dominance, maintaining 112–14,
　　116–17
　saving face 114–16
Downes, D. 26, 27
drug addicts 115–16, 136
due process model 22

'easing behaviour' 7, 120–1, 190
education 101
Edwards, S. 10, 34, 128, 130, 133,
　　135, 136
elderly 15
Emsley, C. 41
equal opportunities policy 57–8, 67
Ericson, R.V. 4, 14, 18, 41, 140, 160,
　　170, 175, 190, 191, 203, 204
ethnicity *see* minority ethnic groups
ethnography with the police 46–8,
　　85–9, 163–5, 201–2
　access and 'acceptance' 202–6
　recording and interpreting the
　　field 208–9
　reflexive ethnography 206–8
excitement and confrontation 9, 97–9,
　　134, 189–90, 192
excluded and marginal groups 14–15,
　　17–18, 35
　economic exclusion 160
　　class *see* class
　　new social configuration 36–9
　　policing new residuum 39–42
　stereotyping 12
　swearing by police 115
　targets of police culture 40, 160,
　　181–2, 197
extra-marital affairs 108

Feldman, I. 43
Female Support Association (FSA) 57,
　　69–70, 71, 77–8
field of policing, new social
　diverse society 28–9
　　beginnings 29–31

　　towards policing diversity 31–5
　　'white backlash' 81–2
　economic exclusion 35
　　new social configuration 36–9
　　policing new residuum 39–42
　　targets of police culture 40, 160,
　　　181–2, 197
　legal context of policing 21–2
　　challenges to police culture 22–6
　　punitive turn 26–8, 39, 103,
　　　199–200
　retreat of class 42–3
　　normative dimensions of
　　　class 43–5, 197
Fielding, N. 16, 54, 60, 79, 92, 95, 100,
　　101, 122, 158, 188, 192, 201
flexible working 59
Foster, J. 10, 12, 15, 16, 32, 33, 51,
　　63, 64, 65, 66, 71, 74, 79, 96,
　　99–100, 113, 125, 144, 149,
　　150, 151, 177, 188, 189,
　　192, 193
Fox, J.C. 202
Frankenberg, R. 45
Fraser, N. 28, 43, 159
free market economic policies 38
Fyfe, N.R. 122

Garland, D. 26, 199
gender 37, 159
　poor, low status white males *see*
　　class
　women *see* women
Giddens, A. 36, 38–9
Goffman, E. 201
Goldsmith, A. 19
Goldstein, J. 19
Graef, R. 13, 14, 93, 107, 119, 190
Green, P. 26, 160
Grimshaw, R. 11, 17, 130, 194

habitus and field 20
Halford, A. 10
Hall, S. 152, 198
Hallett, T. 62
Hammersley, M. 209
Hanley, L. 165
harassment, sexual 10, 54
Harris, J. 159

hate-motivated crime 34, 60, 61, 68–9,
        147, 194
Haylett, C. 45, 159, 164, 181
Hayward, K. 161
Heidensohn, F. 10, 34, 53, 62, 77, 80,
        128, 135, 177, 190, 207
Herbert, S. 17
Hewitt, R. 81
high-speed car pursuits 99
Hobbs, D. 16, 188, 204
Holdaway, S. 4, 5, 8, 9, 11, 12, 15,
        18, 31, 34, 73, 74, 75, 77, 78,
        98, 105, 107, 119, 122, 123,
        128, 141, 147, 151, 152, 194,
        197, 201, 202
homophobic hate crimes 34, 61, 141
homosexual officers
    diversity policies, impact of 51, 59,
        80–1, 141
        durable discrimination 73–6,
            77–80
        new approach to victimization 61
        structures and guiding
            principles 57–8
    intolerance and prejudice 11, 31
    'old regime' 52, 53–4, 55
    visibility and scrutiny 52–3, 77
homosexuality
    casual sexual relationships,
        policing of 80, 122–3, 139–40
    negative view of 140
Hoyle, C. 34, 128
Hughes, E.C. 13
humour
    dark 110–12
    as resource 14
Hunt, J. 206
Hutton, W. 37, 38

Incident Management Units
        (IMUs) 61, 86, 93–4
inequality 36–8, 42–3, 159, 197, 198,
        199–200
    crime and economic 26, 182–3
internal support organizations 57,
        69–72, 77–8, 82, 193
interpreters 61, 148
interviews 25

audio-recorded 23, 24
    delayed 115–16
intimate searches 116
Iraqi community 145–6
Islamaphobia 145
isolation, social 6, 7, 117, 190
    orthodox account of police
        culture 14
    shift solidarity 119–22
    stigmatized identity 117–19

Jefferson, T. 12, 41, 136, 157, 198
Johnston, L. 27
Jones, T. 135

Katz, M.B. 39
King, R. 206
Klockars, C. 4

labelling 4–5, 170
Labour government 26–7, 42
Lambert, J. 11, 28, 141, 155
language
    class contempt 168–72
    information in custody suites 61, 148
    minority ethnic groups 143, 146,
        148–9
    overt racist language, absence
        of 63–4, 79, 155, 193
    role in police culture 73
    sexualized 79–80
    swearing 114–15, 151
law and order, politics of 26–8, 103
Lawrence, Stephen 12, 66
    see also Macpherson Report (1999)
lawyers 15, 107, 180
lay visitors 30, 31
Lee, J.A. 14, 35, 40, 103, 181
legal context of policing 21–2
    challenges to police culture 22–6
    punitive turn 26–8, 39, 103,
        199–200
legal representation: delay 25
Leng, R. 23
Lesbian and Gay Police Group
        (LGPG) 57, 69–70, 71–2, 77–8
Loader, I. 26, 27, 81, 126, 199
Lofland, J. 209

Long, M. 34
loyalty, group *see* solidarity, internal

McBarnet, D.J. 17, 180
McConville, M. 4, 18, 24, 25, 100,
    156, 180
MacDonald, R. 37, 40
McDowell, L. 37, 40, 42, 159
McLaughlin, E. 6, 7, 21, 29, 30, 31,
    32–3, 34, 66, 74, 81–2, 83, 101,
    109, 150
Macpherson Report (**1999**) 12,
    31–4, 51, 56, 60, 61, 66–7,
    81, 141, 192
Maguire, M. 22, 23, 24
Mann, R. 82
Manning, P.K. 3, 4, 8, 9, 13, 16, 89–90,
    109, 121, 184, 196
Marks, M. 9, 19, 133, 188, 192, 195,
    196, 201, 202, 205, 206, 207
Marlow, A. 32
Martin, S.E. 10, 11, 53, 80, 96, 189,
    190, 207
masculine ethos 10–11, 96–9, 190
    domestic violence 10–11, 130–2
May, T. 206
Meltzer, B. 82
methodology 47–8
    research context 46–7, 85–9, 163–5
    see also ethnography with the police
Metropolitan Police officers 81
middle management 16, 133
Miles, R. 76
Miller, S. 11, 53, 140, 189
minority ethnic groups 28–9, 124–5
    class 156–7, 163, 198
    crime control approach 95
    'disarmers' 194
    diversity policies, impact of 63–7,
        141–3, 157–8, 194, 195
        classic stereotypes 143–6
        mutual hostility 149–51, 181
        neutralizing effects on policing 66,
            147, 148–9
        organizational trouble 146–8, 178
        revisions in policing 155–7
        rural policing 151–5
        service improvement aim 60–1

intolerance and prejudice
    towards 11–12
Macpherson Report (1999) 12,
    31–4, 51, 56, 60, 61, 66–7,
    81, 141, 192
Multicultural Police Network
    (MPN) 57, 69–71, 77–8, 82
Scarman Report (1981) 29–30, 31
towards policing diversity 31–5
victims of crime 11–12,
    29, 146–7
    hate crimes 61, 68–9, 194
    see also racism
minority ethnic groups, officers
    from 11, 30, 31, 32, 33
    diversity policies, impact of 51,
        67–8, 80–1
    composition of workforce 58–9,
        60, 193
    durable discrimination 73–7, 78–9
    structures and guiding
        principles 56–8
    training 60
    gender 54
    'old regime' 53, 54, 55
    standing out 52
    visibility and scrutiny 52–3, 77
misogynistic sentiments 10, 136, 139
mission perspective 90–1
    orthodox account of police
        culture 8–9
Modood, T. 145
Mollen Report 14
Mooney, J. 178
moral conservatism 6, 14–15, 107–8,
    165, 191
Moran, L. 140, 160, 177
Morgan, R. 25, 26
Moston, S. 23
Muir, K.W. 8, 114, 194
Multicultural Police Network (MPN)
    57, 69–71, 77–8, 82
Muslim groups 145

narratives, significance of 196
Naughton, M. 22
Nayak, A. 73
Neal, S. 152
Neiderhoffer, A. 13, 190

neighbour disputes 92, 94–5
New Poor Law 1834 41
Newburn, T. 23, 28, 31, 103
Norris, C. 201, 205, 208

O'Neill, M. 188
O'Reilly, G. 28
'others'/'otherness' 39, 44, 83, 152–3, 161, 195
'outsiders' 118–19, 152–4, 163, 191
  crime control approach 95

PACE (Police and Criminal Evidence Act) 1984 22–6, 27
Page, A. 135
Paoline, E. 5, 188
paperwork 99–101
  domestic violence 62, 101, 131–2, 134–5, 138–9, 194
Parekh Report 28
patriarchal sentiments 10, 54, 136
patrol work 122–3, 126, 165–8
  art of suspicion 123–5
  domestic violence 129
peace keepers 7, 95, 151
performance targets 101–3, 138, 167, 184
police and community consultations (PACC) 30, 31
Police Community Support Officers (PCSOs) 59–60, 61, 69, 104–5
Police and Criminal Evidence Act (PACE) 1984 22–6, 27
Police Federation 71, 78
  access for research and 202–3
'police property' groups 14–15, 40, 159, 170, 173, 181
  performance targets 103
politics of law and order 26–8, 103
positive discrimination 67–8
poverty, relative 36
  see also class
Powell, C. 14, 112
powers, police 26, 27, 28
  beleaguered minority discourse 106
pranks on fellow officers 111–12
Prenzler, T. 4, 19
prisoners

controlling tactics by police 115–16
'producer' 145
promotion
  Community Action Team and 94
  minority groups 58–9, 67, 68, 76–7, 193
prostitution 40, 124, 136–7
public goods 38
public order 134
  public order law 41
  Public Order Act 1986, section 5 113
public space 17–18, 40, 164, 176–7, 183
Public Service Desk (PSD) 104
Punch, M. 5, 8, 9, 20, 96, 190, 191, 196, 201, 202, 204, 205

Race Relations (Amendment) Act 2000 32, 57
racism 11–12, 52, 54, 55, 78–9, 162
  bad apple theory 65
  defensiveness over charges of 65–7, 79, 146
  disciplinary offence 32
  durable discrimination 73–6
    tokenism and scrutiny 76–7
  hate crimes 61, 68–9, 194
  institutional 12, 30, 32, 33, 34, 65–6
  Macpherson Report (1999) 12, 31–4, 51, 56, 60, 61, 66–7, 81, 141, 192
  overt racist language, absence of 63–4, 79, 155, 193
  Scarman Report (1981) 29–30, 31
  society generally 12, 76
  see also minority ethnic groups
rape 61, 135–6
Ray, L.J. 43, 159
records
  paper 99–101
    domestic violence 62, 101, 131–2, 134–5, 138–9, 194
  taped interviews 23, 24
recruitment 15, 20
  from minority groups 30, 32, 33, 58–60, 67–8, 141, 193
  Macpherson Report (1999) 32
  Scarman Report (1981) 30

Reiner, R. 3, 4, 5, 7, 8, 9, 12, 13, 14, 16, 17, 18, 24, 26, 27, 28, 31, 32, 33, 34, 35, 36, 37, 38, 39, 40, 41–2, 45, 90, 91, 94, 95, 96, 105, 106, 107, 109, 116, 117, 126, 159, 168, 181, 182, 189, 190, 196, 197, 199, 201, 203, 204, 205
religion
  hate crimes 61
  Muslim groups 145
research context 46–7, 85–9, 163–5
  see also ethnography with the police
resources 27, 28
  beleaguered minority discourse 106
  rural policing and 'outsiders' 118–19
ressentiment 82
Reuss-Ianni, E. 14, 15–16, 93
risk assessments
  domestic violence 62, 131–2, 138–9
risk of physical danger 5–6, 117–19, 126
Rowe, M. 32
Rubinstein, J. 5, 8, 12, 109, 122, 124, 174, 190
rural policing 7–8, 15, 47, 166–8, 191
  cynicism and pessimism 106
  diversity 151–5
  insecurity and isolation 118–19
  perception of role 125
  research context 85, 87–9, 163, 164

Sackmann, S.A. 19
Sacks, H. 123, 153, 190
Sanders, A. 25
Sapp, A. 10
Savage, S. 19
saving face 114–15
Sayer, A. 28, 39, 42, 43, 44, 160, 161, 172, 173, 197
Scarman Report (1981) 29–30, 31
Schein, E. 19
Scheler, M. 82
Scraton, P. 160
'scrote', meaning of 165, 169–70
searches 103, 150
  intimate 116
  powers 23, 24
  stop and search see stop and search

strip 145, 180
Secret Policeman, The 33, 60, 66, 202–3
senior officers
  rank and file view of 13–14, 93, 190–1
  subcultures 16
Sennett, R. 44, 161, 179, 197
sexual assault 61
sexual crime and the despised gender 135–7
sexual harassment 10, 54
Shearing, C. 9, 14, 41, 73, 164, 172, 177, 196
Sibley, D. 175
silence, right to 23, 28
Silverman, D. 62
Silvestri, M. 10
Skeggs, B. 161, 172
Sklansky, D.A. 125, 188
Skolnick, J.H. 5–6, 9, 11, 12, 13, 14, 108, 117, 119, 120, 123, 126, 155, 190, 199
Smith, D.J. 5, 8, 9, 10, 11–12, 13, 14, 41, 63, 79, 91, 96, 98, 102, 115, 128–9, 133, 143, 145, 170, 177, 189, 190, 205, 207
Smith, G. 24
social class see class
social insecurity
  risk consciousness and fear of crime: punitive outlook 26–8, 38–9, 103, 199–200
socialization of new recruits
  neighbour disputes 94–5
  paperwork 101
  violence, discourses of 97
societal context see field of policing, new social
socio-economic groupings see class
solidarity, internal 6, 117, 165, 190
  civilianization 69
  deviant practices covered up 120–1
  front-line officers 104–5
  humour 112
  orthodox account of police culture 14
  rank and file 13–14, 105
  shift solidarity 119–22

spatial location of crime 41–2, 122–3,
        165–8, 174, 183
Stanko, E. 34, 128, 130, 133, 194
stereotypes 12, 24, 75, 124–5, 143–6,
        154–5, 156, 190
    domestic violence 130, 132
    gender 10
Stinchcombe, A.L. 169
stop and search 29, 32, 72, 147
    art of suspicion 124
    ethnic monitoring processes 61
    PACE 23, 24, 25
    stereotyping 24, 144–5, 154–5
    white people 162
Storch, R. 40, 160
storytelling, significance of 196
strip searches 145, 180
subcultures/cultures within police
        force 15–16, 71–3, 81, 125,
        188, 191–2
support organizations, internal 57,
        69–72, 77–8, 82, 193
suspects 110
    Customer Focus initiative 92–3
    rights of 23–4, 25, 26
suspicious disposition 6, 109–10,
        190, 191
    art of suspicion 123–5
    orthodox account of police
        culture 12–13
Swanton, B. 12
swearing 114–15, 151
Sykes, R. 13, 190

Taylor, C. 28
Taylor, I. 36–7, 38, 40, 164,
        197, 199
theft 110, 177
Tilley, N. 60, 93, 192
tokenism 76–7
Toynbee, P. 36, 199
training
    diversity 33, 60, 67, 75
    female victimization 61
    Macpherson Report (1999) 32
    PACE 25
    Scarman Report (1981) 30
transphobic hate crimes 34, 61, 141
Tyler, K. 152

underclass see class
unemployment 37–8, 39, 40
    crime and 182–3
    disrespect 174
    erosion of worth 175–7
    research context 86, 163–4
urban policing 7, 15, 28
    perception of role 125
    research context 85–7, 89, 163, 164

vagrancy legislation 41
Van Maanen, J. 4, 8, 9, 13, 14, 95, 99,
        105, 109, 117, 170, 190, 195,
        201, 204–5, 206, 209
victims of crime
    hate-motivated crime 34, 60, 61,
        68–9, 147, 194
    minority ethnic groups 11–12, 29,
        146–7
        hate crimes 61, 68–9, 194
    police cynicism 110
    white poor 177–9
    women 10–11, 34, 54
    diversity policies: service
        improvement 58, 60, 61–2
    domestic violence see domestic
        violence
    prostitutes 136
    rape 61, 135–6
violence, discourses of 96–7
visibility, heightened 52–3, 77

Wacquant, L. 36, 37, 38
Waddington, P.A.J. 10, 13, 14, 16–17,
        18, 19, 25, 69, 83, 98, 111, 114,
        132, 165, 172, 190
Walklate, S. 34
Walters, R. 61
Westley, W. 5, 6, 14, 91, 111, 120, 160,
        190
Westmarland, L. 10, 96, 134, 138, 160,
        189, 190, 205, 206, 207
Wetherell, M. 73
'white backlash' 81–2
white poor see class
white space 64, 74
Williamson, H. 36
Wilson, D. 24
Wilson, J.Q. 16, 95, 122

women
class 198
misogynistic elements of police
culture 10, 136, 139
paperwork 101
prostitution 40, 124, 136–7
victims of crime 10–11, 34, 54
diversity policies: service
improvement 58, 60, 61–2
domestic violence *see* domestic
violence
prostitutes 136
rape 61, 135–6
women: officers 10, 31
Dispatches: 'Undercover Copper' 33
diversity policies, impact of 51,
67–8, 80–1
composition of workforce 58–60
durable discrimination 73–6,
77–80

structures and guiding
principles 57–8
domestic violence 138
'old regime' 54, 55
standing out 52–3
prevailing culture, adoption of 80
service-oriented approach 96, 191
visibility and scrutiny 52–3, 77

Yar, M. 38
Young, J. 36, 37, 38, 39, 159, 164, 167,
197, 199
Young, M. 5, 8, 9, 10, 12, 13,
14, 15, 16, 24, 47, 53, 69, 80,
101, 128, 140, 143, 160, 165,
167, 170, 173, 174–5, 201,
202, 203

Zurn, C.F. 28, 43